Dragons of

Fantasy

Acknowledgments

First off, a toast from the golden cup of the dragon's hoard to my editor and publisher, Jonathan Stein, for letting me indulge my lifelong passion for dragons. With a patient and steady hand on the tiller, Jon has guided this longship of a book through calm and choppy waters, always on the lookout for dark shapes under the surface and making sure I more or less stuck to the map without sailing off the edge of the world.

Thanks also to my stalwart copyeditors, Laura Young and Lynn Holschuh, who provided the necessary shieldwall against the marauding dragons of error and inconsistency.

And finally, a laurel and hardy handshake to my husband Bill, whose sense of humor (admittedly grim, at times) kept us both afloat during the crafting of this book, what with the late-night lumberings of too many scaly consultants in and out of the study. At least they didn't flame the cats.

Dragons of

Fantasy

∽

Anne C. Petty

COLD SPRING PRESS

Cold Spring Press

P.O. Box 284, Cold Spring Harbor, NY 11724
E-mail: Jopenroad@aol.com

For Lynn,
Who loves dragons as much as I do. Well, almost.

Contents

Introduction

❦

YEARS AGO, a childhood ritual introduced me to a creature that made a nest for itself in my imagination and never vacated the premises. When I was a preschooler, my sister – older by seven years and much more experienced in the lands of fantasy – would sit on the edge of my bed at night and tell me stories until I fell asleep. One in particular was partly an invention of her own involving a hero named Prince Cherry, a desperate quest, a beautiful princess, and an embodiment of all that is terrifying and fascinating to a five-year-old mind: a great and powerful dragon. The mental image of that fellow has stuck with me through school, marriage, and career, and he continues to beckon with an index claw through the rift in reality where the lands of Faërie lie.

The first time I read J.R.R. Tolkien's essay "On Fairy-Stories" and discovered his admissions regarding fantasy and what it meant to him both as a scholar and an ordinary person, I knew I'd found a personal hero. I gratefully joined the long line forming behind him of like-minded souls who "desired dragons with a great desire." A glance up and down the line revealed dragon fanciers of every stripe: academicians, historians, visual artists, cultural anthropologists, fiction writers, filmmakers, philologists, fans, mythologists, and true believers.

Today, more than thirty years beyond Tolkien's death, that line stretches over the hills and out of sight, and maybe even follows Tolkien's Straight Road into the West where Valinor and other marvelous lands remain hidden from ordinary eyes. Like all those others in line, I've been reading and thinking about dragons most of my life. When the opportunity presented itself for me to write about my favorite fictional dragons from both a scholar's and a fan's viewpoint, I leaped at the chance faster than a Pernese fighting dragon.

All of which leads me to Dragonology 101. Basically, you'll find that dragonologists sort themselves out into two main groups: virtual and actual. Virtual encompasses gamers and dragon lovers who immerse themselves in the realms of the dragon created by artists (in all media) and fans. Actual includes mythologists, researchers, literary analysts, and scholars of that ilk. The two divisions blur into each other, mostly among artists who use the search for dragon bones in the distant past of the world's cultures as part of their imaginative process. As a writer, you must be able to think like a dragon and inhabit its skin in order to write about it convincingly. In other words, the author must be both researcher and fan.

Although I include several chapters on background myths and legends as well as Dragonology resources that provide the basic palette used by many writers, my major focus is on fantasy authors themselves. I'm less interested in how many authors have written about dragons than how the ones who do it really well actually pull it off. For example, Terry Goodkind's muscular, graphic prose and Jane Yolen's gentle irony are worlds apart, yet both authors create memorable, three-dimensional dragon characters. This is not a book on how to write fiction about dragons. But if that's the information you're after, examining the dragon bones of successful fantasy fiction – the skeletons, if you will, on which the stories are built – might just give you the pointers you're looking for.

The range of formats employed by these writers includes everything from multi-volume series based primarily around dragons, such as McCaffrey's Dragonriders of Pern series, to novels, novelettes, and short stories. In pieces such as Le Guin's short story "Dragonfly" and Tolkien's novel *The Hobbit*, the dragon appears as a major character. In other cases, such as Tolkien's novelette *Roverandom* or Goodkind's lengthy novel *Wizard's First Rule*, the dragon is a minor but strikingly etched character. In yet other works, it's the treatment of dragons as a group that's memorable, as in Pratchett's illustrated novelette *The Last Hero*.

There are several ways you can read this book. Although the two sections are labeled Parts I and II, you don't necessarily have to read them in that order. If you want to begin with a general chapter on how to write about dragons in fantasy literature, followed by chapters on specific authors who have excelled at the task, and only then delve into the sources for dragon mythology and lore, just start at Chapter 1 and head on through to the end. For those who are fascinated with dragonlore and would like to know where imagery and inspiration comes from, before you read how your favorite authors have applied this knowledge, there's no harm in beginning with Part II, and then going back to Part I. You could even dip in and out of the Dragonology chapters as you read through the author chapters.

So join me now on a quest for the dragons of fantasy, by which I mean both the characters on the page and the skilled writers who created them. I hope you'll enjoy this in-depth look at a nest of scaly friends and foes including, among others, Tolkien's Glaurung, McCaffrey's Ramoth, Le Guin's Orm Embar, Yolen's Heart's Blood, Pratchett's Errol, Goodkind's Scarlet, and Rowling's Norbert.

Happy dragon hunting.

Anne Petty
Tallahassee, Florida
April 2004

Part One:

FOREGROUND

Chapter 1

Creating Dragons
The Writer's Craft

GELPHAR BRUSHED the top of the rec-orb with precision born of long years' practice. Amber light fractured across its surface, then went dark. Slowly, a picture formed in the haze at its center. He strained to see, his aged-dimmed eyes watering with the effort. Figures were emerging from the murk, a landscape, then wings upon wings flowing over the rec-orb's curved surface. Gelphar blinked. History was a slippery thing, he'd argued, even in well-preserved records such as these. "Just find me the damned reason they migrated!" Drll had practically shouted at him, as if his hearing too had faded. Gelphar frowned and shut off the orb. He stretched a bit, arching the stiffness from his back, feeling the bones brittle under his skin. His ridge-scales rustled like dried leaves as he got to his feet. He felt twitchy. He was old, old. With yellowed talons he carefully lifted the rec-orb from its hollow of sand and placed it back among the rows in the rock wall behind him. Eyeshine glinted in the corridor beyond.

"Come into the light, Semaj," he said softly. "What are you lurking for?"

"Apologies, Loremaster," said the acolyte, folding his wings tightly against his thin body. "The Outland messenger has arrived early." "(*Starlight Plasmodium*, 7)"

One of the most important skills a writer of fiction must have is the ability to create characters. Obviously, without characters, there is very little story. When your characters are dragons, the ante has been upped and your imagination put on full alert. How do you create dragons that really fly off the page? Both imagination and skill are required, as well as an internal ear for dialogue and the natural rhythms of speech. Writing about what you know may be hard to demand here, unless you've done your dragon research, but you can certainly write about what you imagine. For both dragon and human characters, the same wordsmithing skills apply. For example, the passage that begins this chapter employs techniques and devices such as limited third-person point of view, internal dialogue, small but data-packed actions, embedded exposition, specific imagery chosen to create atmosphere and character profile, an unexpected discovery, brief yet revealing dialogue, and an unexpected visitation.

The snapshot scene begins with the statement of the character's name, then widens to include a mysterious object and a task the character must perform. Immediacy is created when we know the character's thoughts about himself, his task at hand, and what others think of him in regard to this task. And we are given the added surprise of discovery, when in one phrase of description we learn that the character is not a human, but a dragon. Readers become intrigued from the first sentence, wondering what this character's powers are, what his status among his peers may be (it seems questionable), and just how old he really is. We wonder what his task is and why some seem to view him with disrespect while others, such as the acolyte, clearly defer to him. We wonder why he has an acolyte and what kind of order they might be part of. And most intriguing, who is the mysterious messenger and what news does he or she carry that impacts our character? Is the messenger welcome, or dreaded?

All these questions are packed into one short paragraph and two lines of dialogue. The carefully controlled style and use of storytelling techniques create a highly suspenseful, immediately engaging opening to a fantasy novel. The main character, a learned old dragon named Gelphar, and the events in which he becomes entangled are set in motion with the first sentence. Sparse but vivid imagery establishes the great age of the character as well as the surrounding atmosphere of his den – cozy, made of sand and rock, with mysterious corridors beyond it. This type of questioning that arises in the mind as we read is what keeps readers turning pages and establishing emotional connections to characters. In this book, I've applied this same kind of analysis to the fiction of dragon-friendly authors from J.R.R. Tolkien to J. K. Rowling to see how some of the most memorable dragons in fantasy literature have been created.

As I've mentioned before, Dragonology can be separated into two main branches: actual (scholarly) and virtual (popular). Actual dragon research includes the work of mythologists, linguists, anthropologists, literary analysts, and cultural historians, while the virtual world of loremasters is largely inhabited by gamers, graphic artists, writers in all media, animators, and dragon lovers who immerse themselves in the realms created by such visionaries. Obviously the two divisions merge into each other along the border where the artists themselves reside.

Creating character, imagining what it must be like to be that person or creature, may require accessing areas of the author's psyche that normally remain buried – sometimes with good reason. The Freudian and Jungian archetypes lurking beneath our surface veneer of civilized personality can help create an alien creature full of power, wisdom, and motivations that are not human. Convincing writers of dragon fiction have met Smaug, Fáfnir, Typhon, or Tiamat, and know them well. They've also managed to wrestle them onto the page, and that's what interests me most – how, from the big picture down to the sentence level, they have accomplished such magic.

The Story's the Thing

In this study of fantasy writers, I'll be covering novels from a wide range of authors, from so-called young adult (YA) titles to strictly adult fare. But transcending such book-marketing categories, here's the bottom line for any good story: is it a ripping good yarn with great characters? More to the point, no matter how well crafted and intricate the plot, it must have characters you care about if it's to lift off and soar. That's also where the line between YA and adult fiction tends to blur in writers such as J.K. Rowling, Ursula Le Guin, and T. H. White, not to mention books by Robert Asprin, Patricia

McKillip, Barbara Hambly, Peter S. Beagle, Patricia Wrede, Andre Norton, Margaret Weis and Tracy Hickman. Writers who write for the sheer love of storytelling with little concern over which market they should conform to or what the demographics of their potential readers might be fall into this cross-over category – their appeal is universal. Sometimes the best character inventions are to be found there.

In studying and teaching creative writing, I've acquired some favorite guidebooks along the way, and they have served me well during this investigation of literary dragons. In particular, I'll be referring time and again to the advice and insights of Orson Scott Card, Jerome Stern, Ursula Le Guin, Wayne C. Booth, Constance Hale, Karen Elizabeth Gordon, and Philip Martin. You'll find their works listed in the bibliography at the end of this volume. The organization of this book has, to some extent, grown out of the categories with which writing technique is analyzed. Is this a history-of-dragons book, advice on how to write compelling fantasy fiction, or a book of literary analysis? My answer is, yes.

How does one invest a dragon with personality and determine its role among the cast of characters? The generic idea of "dragon" is drenched with symbolic meaning: from earliest myth to modern psychology, its image represents the menacing unknown, crawling with unnamed threats and obstacles to be overcome. Slaying the dragon is a fairly universal metaphor for conquering inner fears and doubts. Such handy symbology can be used when assigning a hierarchy of traits to dragons in fiction.

By this I mean attributes such as color that can symbolically define power levels, magical abilities, or hierarchy among clans. Dragons of highest rank on McCaffrey's Pern are gold and bronze; blood-red scales indicate the bravest and most formidable fighters among Yolen's pit dragons; the jet-black Hungarian Horntail breed in Harry Potter's world is the most vicious. Motivations, aspirations, and personality traits will often rely on this language of metaphor and symbol. How this personal profile data bank is woven into the story will depend on the author's style and depth of knowledge. Wide reading in many areas creates a larger data bank from which to draw when it's time to put fingers to keyboard.

What's My Motivation?

Creating engaging characters, human or otherwise, doesn't happen just by accident. Like actors, characters in novels perform deeds and recite dialogue, display personality traits and affect the course of the plot, engage our emotions and make us cheer for them or hope they meet a fitting end. An adept scriptwriter or novelist is a keen observer of human (and by extension, alien) nature, translating what he or she has experienced and assimilated in life onto the printed page. Also required is a good ear; creating convincing and individual speech patterns for each personality and deciding how to display that speech in print is often what makes or breaks the reader's belief in the character.

The writers I've included here have very different approaches to these skills of the craft, yet each has successfully created memorable dragons that exist alongside their humans. In selected works of each author, I've focused on the following points:

· The dragon's first appearance – what is the reader's first impression of the creature?

· What others say – how are readers' expectations built up about the character?

· Dragonspeech – what does it sound like and how is it rendered in print?

· Alien thought patterns – when narration is from the dragon's point of view, how does the creature think and what's going on in its mind?

· Physical description – how traditional or unusual is the mental image created by the description; how specific are the details? Is the imagery literal or poetic?

· Attributes – what powers and abilities are given to the various dragons?

· Personality – how do they act and behave; do they go through changes over the course of the story?

· Plot significance – at what level do the dragon characters affect the storyline; what is their power to act?

· Interaction with humans – are they allies or foes?

· Use of humor – do the dragons provide comic relief? If so, what type of humor is used and how is it deployed in the story?

EXPOSITION. The way in which an author introduces his or her dragons sets both the tone and expectations for the character – what's the first impression thrust on the reader? Some writers give you the dragon first and then fill in the details. For example, in Anne McCaffrey's first book about the dragonriders of Pern, dragons just pop out of mid-air with no previous explanation or setup, and we develop an understanding of them as we go along. Exposition can be journalistic and straightforward, or leaked into the narrative little by little – the first approach creates distance; the second places the reader inside the story.

Asprin's *Another Fine Myth* gives us a humorous example of introducing the dragon with no previous buildup. Skeeve the apprentice magician acquires his companion dragon Gleep by accident in an otherworld market-place where he doesn't speak the language. The dragon character that will accompany Skeeve throughout the story is introduced by the noise it makes, which becomes by default its name:

> "I decided it was about time for me to go.
> 'Gleep!'
> There was a tug at my sleeve.
> I looked around. There, behind me, was a small dragon!
> …My sleeve! The beast was eating a piece of my sleeve!" (AFM, 138)

Skeeve knows only as much about dragons as he's been able to figure out for the few minutes it takes the dragon to nibble on his sleeve like a goat, become attached (impressed, like a duckling) to him, and sold in the blink of an eye by the unscrupulous dragon dealer. Skeeve is forced to learn about dragons as he goes along, with much bewilderment and opportunity for hilarity.

Other dragons, such as Tolkien's Smaug, are talked about in terms that build readers' expectations long before the beast make its physical appearance on the scene. The fun, or fear, comes about when expectations and reality clash. Tolkien creates an amusing twist on this idea in "Farmer Giles of Ham," where we meet Farmer Giles and the dragon Chrysophylax separately, as each hears rumors about the other (the dragon hears of a "knight of high lineage" while the farmer hears of a fearless "hot dragon" against whom shields and ring-mail are no protection). The fun comes as their separate paths, with increasing buildup of rumor on both sides, draw ever closer until they intersect literally at an intersection in the road. What each finds is not the creature he expected.

One of the most important truths about fantasy writing is that archetypes can be used in fresh ways. In the Dragonology chapters of this book you'll find a number of archetypes (the evil Western dragon that embodies the devil, the benevolent Eastern rain-god dragon, the primitive chaos dragon, and so on). Fiction authors have mined them in interesting and unique ways, some setting precedents of their own that further enrich the lore available to future fantasy writers. Tolkien's Glaurung owes much to Norse Fáfnir; Ramoth, the bioengineered golden queen of Pern, is mostly McCaffrey's own invention.

DESCRIPTION. Effective character description begins with imagery. By this I mean clear visual images that are so compelling or intriguing that the reader isn't going to skip over them (which you may have felt the urge to do when confronted with lengthy exposition). In fact, describing dragons is about the best fun you can have as a fantasy writer because here your imagination can truly run wild. Authors who are widely knowledgeable of dragons in history, art, early literature, and the fantasy genre itself command an arsenal of facts and details that can give depth and authenticity to their writing. The complexity of creatures such as Glaurung and Smaug attest to Tolkien's knowledge of Anglo-Saxon poetry, Northern medieval sagas, and Germanic folktales. As characters, both dragons are individuals who perfectly serve the stories in which they appear.

Imagery that appeals to specific senses can add depth to the description, giving more than just a visual picture of size and shape. An example from Ursula Le Guin's Earthsea novels is the physical presence of the great dragon Kalessin: the fiery core that sustains its massive body and causes tendrils of smoke to leak from its nostrils becomes a more tangible fact when we learn that its armor plating of scales is hot to the touch and scorches the wizard who rides on its back. A vivid sound image from Gene Wolf's *The Knight* characterizes the dragon Grengarm's voice: "Grengarm's mouth gaped, and a voice like a hundred deep drums filled the whole grotto. 'You come with spears. With swords.'"

Character depiction must be conveyed by actions, words, and thoughts, as well as by vivid external description. By using these elements to show the changing facets of a character's personality, the more that character – or dragon – begins to take on life; it's the difference between flat and rounded characters, between mere story props and three-dimensional individuals. Even in farce and parody, characters need a certain amount of depth or the reader's disbelief isn't suspended – in other words, we don't care about them. Terry Pratchett is a master at making us care about his farcical dragons such as Errol, the runt of the litter who becomes the hero. Minor characters should be vivid enough to add to the tapestry of the fictional world being created, so that they linger with you even though their onstage time may be short. For authors like Terry Goodkind or George R. R. Martin, even the minor characters have substance.

DIALOGUE. We get to know characters through their voices, and each author has his or her own personal methods for indicating dragon speech. Some specific choices must be made regarding dragons as characters that communicate with both their own kind and other species (usually humans). Will their speech be heard as words that humans can understand, or is their vocal apparatus not designed to make human sounds? If they don't speak aloud to others, how is their communication handled? Must a completely non-human language be invented and then translated? What about the problem of weird, hard-to-read spellings, or even arcane alphabets? Authors approach this challenge in various ways, depending on the type of dragons they have envisioned and the kind of humans with whom they interact, be they psychic mages or illiterate stable boys.

There are two basic tracks you can take regarding dragon speech: auditory and mental. Characters either hear the dragon's voice out loud or in their heads through some form of telepathy. Either choice can be highly effective and open to a wide range of voice timbres and speech patterns, depending on the personality and attributes of the dragon. Combination of the two is also possible, with as many variations on the theme as clever authors can come up with.

Following the auditory track, the easiest solution is simply to assume that, as a creature of magic, a dragon speaks grammatical English as well as the humans with whom it parlays – no explanation is necessary for how its lips, tongue, and vocal cords can do this. Its dialogue looks no different in print than anyone else's. Tolkien's dragons are example of this type, as are the dragons of the long-running Dragonlance Chronicles, Terry Goodkind's Scarlet, and Patricia Wrede's dragons in the Enchanted Forest Chronicles, among numerous others.

With his sharp ear for speech patterns and dialects, Tolkien is a great example to use for demonstrating how personality and status can be conveyed through dragonspeech. If you compare examples from each of his dragons who talk, you have a full range of voices from high fantasy diction to clever and devious to colloquial and chatty:

(1) "Hail, Nienor, daughter of Húrin. We meet again ere the end. I give thee joy that thou hast found thy brother at last." (Glaurung, *The Silmarillion*)

(2) "Bless me! Had you never thought of the catch? A fourteenth share, I suppose, or something like it, those were the terms, eh? But what about delivery? What about cartage? What about armed guards and tolls?" (Smaug, *The Hobbit*)

(3) "Good people, don't kill me! I am very rich, I will pay for all the damage I have done… I will give you each a really good present, if you will only let me go home and fetch it." (Chrysophylax, *Farmer Giles of Ham*)

When dragons are not capable making human speech out loud, but can communicate intelligently (they aren't just beasts), the exchange takes place mind to mind. Most often this is styled as italics, usually with only the dragon's thoughts given that way and the human spoken responses in regular type (as in Barbara Hambly's *Dragonsbane* exchange between Jenny Waynest and the dying Black Dragon). In other cases, entire mental conversations may take place between dragon and human in italics, which Anne McCaffrey frequently does in her Pern novels.

In cases where the mental communication is in language rather than pictures, the syntax patterns and level of diction particular to each dragon can deliver information about the character. Orm Embar and Kalessin of Earthsea use high diction ("*I need thee: follow in haste*") which is fitting to their elevated status of elemental spirits. Glaurung does the same, which gives him the *gravitas* of Norse sagas and lost ancient cultures. Barbara Hambly's Black Dragon doesn't speak with epic fantasy diction, but its vocabulary and syntax has an elegance that lifts it above the speech of the humans in the story. It is nowhere more eloquent than in its dying words to the sorceress Jenny Waynest:

> "*Have you come seeking medicines, wizard woman? Or is that weapon you carry simply what you have deluded yourself into thinking sufficient to finish what your poisons do too slowly for your convenience?*" (DB, 197)

In other cases the exchange is more visual, with color patterns and pictures forming instead of words. Jane Yolen does this well in her Pit Dragon series. The boy Jakkin's mental and emotional link with his dragon Heart's Blood results in highly visual "sendings" of swirling colors with signature patterns and fluid images that resemble surrealist paintings or exquisitely beautiful drug-induced hallucinations. Some authors have also combined the two approaches, where words and pictures intermingle, as occurs when Jenny first encounters the dying dragon: "…in her mind the singing flowed and intensified its colors into the vortex of a white core. In that core words formed." Another variation is that in which the human sends words and concepts telepathically and the dragon answers with pictures, as occurs when the Sunrunner witch Sioned asks the dragon Elisel for her identity in Melanie Rawn's *The Star Scroll*:

This time images came back, and so powerfully that Sioned winced a little. A mountain aerie, richly green with summer foliage, elk and deer easy pickings; the gentler heights of the Catha Hills in winter, storms flashing across a dark sky viewed from the snug safety of caverns. Within each picture was a myriad of colors and subsidiary images: rivers, fish, wild deer and elk, other dragons, trees, birds, flowers, flight patterns to and from each location, surrounding country-side with human settlements hazed over in dark warning colors – too much information for Sioned to take in.

Elisel! Please! Slower – you're hurting me!

The images abruptly terminated. (SS, 579)

Sometimes the dragon's speech includes sounds or syntax that suggest the alien nature of the dragon. The most common effect is a hissing sibilance added to ordinary words. In *The Knight*, Gene Wolfe's dragonlike Khimaira demonstrates how this looks and sounds: "With those big black wings open it looked as big as a house. 'You musst fight usss.' Its voice was mostly hiss, but you could understand. 'Ssee? I have sswordss for uss both.'" The same effect works when the dragon's voice is telepathic, as Jane Yolen demon-strates in *A Sending of Dragons* where young dragonets commune with their human partners telepathically in halting sibilant syntax: "'*Sssargon stays. Sssargon needs scratching. Sssargon hungers. Sssargon wants*' – 'Sssargon shuts up!' Jakkin hissed at him…'"

There may also be occasions where the dragon speaks aloud, but in a language humans can't understand. This is the case with the Earthsea dragons who use the Old Speech of magic, understood by wizards but no one else. In these situations, the narrator tells us that the dragon spoke, and "the mage answered briefly, and again the dragon spoke, poised above him on slight-shifting wings," but the actual words are not given. McCaffrey uses this technique as well; the effect is that the dragon's telepathic communica-tion is given second-hand by the narrator: "Mnementh informed F'lar that he, a fully matured bronze dragon, was no relation to any scrawny, crawling, chained, and wing-clipped watch-wher."

The passage above leads us to the issue of point of view (POV). What goes on in a dragon's mind? Interior monologue can be revealing but rarely occurs with alien creatures in fiction because the main POV character is usually a human. In cases where the dragon is the main POV character, as in the sequence that opened this chapter, the author is challenged to think in non-human ways and yet to incorporate human sensibilities to which readers can relate. In that passage, Gelphar's thoughts about himself and how others treat him reveal his alien state (annoyance at his great age, awareness of a body that's distinctly non-human, and control of a magical device). At the same time we see his very human resentment at not being given proper respect and irritated interaction with the nervous acolyte.

You are more likely to find dragon POV tales in short story collections. A clever manipulation of point of view occurs in the story "Thoughts of a Drought Dragon," by British author Geraldine McCaughrean.[1] A framework dragon constructed by villagers to bring rain during a drought comes to life after they decide to burn it when no rain comes. A boy who danced under the dragon as it was held aloft on poles falls asleep inside the wickerwork head, and the story then alternates between the dragon ("Aha! thought the Drought Dragon with its wicked wicker brain.") and the young boy trapped inside its basket-like head ("Listen! I am the voice of your conscience!"). Their contest of wills as the dragon struggles to understand what it is and the boy tries to save his village from its flames leads to a clever fable-like turnaround at the end. Another good example of dragon POV can be found in Jane Yolen's short story, "Great-Grandfather Dragon's Tale," discussed in Chapter 6, where the tale of St. George and the dragon is told from the dragon's POV.

Even though the main POV character is usually human, point of view can be shifted between characters, as in the scene where Bilbo encounters Smaug in his lair. As the main POV focus, it's through Bilbo's eyes that we see the red glow at the end of the tunnel and the terrifying sight of the great red-gold dragon lying on the hoard. But Tolkien includes enlightening glimpses into Smaug's cagey, calculating thoughts as well. Readers shift back and forth between the two characters as their verbal sparring reveals what they are really thinking. Interweaving POV thoughts and action can build momentum toward a climax, like peeling away layers of an onion – what's at the center? In this way the writer can allow the POV character to arrive at a realization or revelation, whether positive or negative, that can affect the plot in interesting ways.

A good example of this occurs in McCaffrey's description of the dragon Golanth and his rider F'lessan as they recover from a near-fatal lion attack in *The Skies of Pern*. Each hovers near death, unable to move or communicate. We feel the loss and pain each suffers separately, then are shown how once their minds connect, F'lessan makes the first slow painful act of recovery – leaving his bed to go where he can touch the dragon and be reassured of its will to live. McCaffrey cuts back and forth between them as each contemplates the emptiness of life without the other; in this way we see how they both gradually take physical and emotional steps toward rehabilitation until they can fly together again.

ACTION. Action reveals character as well as description and dialogue do, and dragons are all about action. In reading shelves of fantasy books over the years, I've discovered that most writers involved with dragons will have at least a couple of scenes where their writing is moved to greatness worthy of the magnificent beast itself. I call these scenes iconic because they are emblematic, symbolic even, of the vast scope of the book in one fell swoop. They could be over the top in lesser hands, but under the control of a skilled writer they are showstoppers. Even humorous scenes have iconic qualities, as I've discussed in the chapters on Terry Pratchett and J. K. Rowling, but the best iconic scenes occur in novels of epic scope. Take, for example, this scene that ends *A Game of Thrones*, the first novel of George R. R. Martin's Song of Ice and Fire series:

> And there came a second crack, loud and sharp as thunder, and the smoke stirred and whirled around her and the pyre shifted, the logs exploding as the fire touched their secret hearts. She heard the screams of frightened horses, and the voices of the Dothraki raised in shouts of fear and terror, and Ser Jorah calling her name and cursing. No, she wanted to shout to him, no, my good knight, do not fear for me. The fire is mine, I am Daenerys Stormborn, daughter of dragons,

bride of dragons, mother of dragons, don't you see? Don't you SEE? With a belch of flame and smoke that reached thirty feet into the sky, the pyre collapsed and came down around her. Unafraid, Dany stepped forward into the firestorm, calling to her children." (GT, 806)

Now *that*, friends, is an iconic scene of the first magnitude. Iconic scenes of this type are sprinkled throughout Terry Goodkind's novels and usually mark the emotional crest of the main characters' various difficulties. He prefers to create drama through trauma – that is, how characters react under physical and mental stress. The encounter of the dragon Scarlet with his main character Richard provides an iconic moment brimming with fear and grim humor.

Iconic scenes focus on a single episode that reveals what and who someone is – a momentary showcase with flashbulbs going off. Such scenes can sometimes make the difference between flat and rounded characters, giving them dramatic action that highlights qualities and traits that define who they are.

Style and Individualism

It's impossible, of course, to have a complete discussion of character creation divorced from the issue of style. An author's style is his or her wordsmithing fingerprint. Some styles are quite easy to recognize (and, because of that, to parody), while others are less visible or identifiable. Nonetheless, a unique style can often create great characters.

Style involves word choice and syntax as well as overall organization and approach. Level of diction (which can go from archaism to modern slang), shifting tone of voice, and avoidance (or use) of cliché are all elements of style. Genre fiction often requires cliché because it is a kind of shorthand that readers of fantasy immediately recognize and interpret; the challenge is to discover fresh ways to use certain appropriate clichés. Even single words can be clichés. It's nearly impossible to completely avoid clichés of both wording and imagery when working in genre subject matter, but the best writers consistently manage to rise above such wordsmithing traps.

As Jerome Stern points out in his wonderful writer's guide, *Making Shapely Fiction*, "traditional symbols can seem like clichés," but can be given fresh meaning and potentiality as they "gather meaning" through the course of the narrative. The uniqueness of the author's voice and vision is what allows this to happen, turning ideas into characters and events – "the word made flesh." Red dragons are a dime a dozen in fantasy, but can be made freshly significant within the context of the story, good examples being Scarlet in Goodkind's *Wizard's First Rule* and Heart's Blood in Yolen's Pit Dragon series.

Much of an author's style has to do with syntax, the relation between words and how they are strung together. You can think of a paragraph as a prose poem where the musicality of language is orchestrated. Some flow with singing effortlessness while others march along with the orderliness of a military anthem, while others jerk along in fits and starts. Some syntax produces sentences like long rolling swells that seem to go on and on, finally breaking on the shore at the end of a thought. In lengthy sentences, transitions are of the utmost importance; the author must be able to hear or feel where the words should crest and fall, and when the string is just too tangled to make any sense. In contrast, short sentences with few clauses and parenthetical expressions can have a completely different impact.

Hand in hand with syntax is diction, which simply means word choice. We've all read fiction where we suspect the writer kept an open thesaurus propped against the keyboard. Finding the right word is important, especially where character description or dialogue is concerned, but if those right words aren't appropriate to the tone of the narration or speaker, they can sound forced instead of natural. Overly florid diction draws attention to the writer, pulling readers out of the story and dissolving their ability to become completely immersed in the fictional world of the book. Dragons require that willing suspension of disbelief, which certainly won't happen if the writing is overly self-conscious. Word choice controls tone, creating distance or in-your-face familiarity, a sense of tension or a rush of beauty.

Writers with gifted control of the language are called stylists, and many can be found working in the fantasy genre. Let me show you what I mean with two widely differing examples. The first excerpt is a plain yet highly stylized, unadorned, reporter's approach that many readers will recognize as belonging to Jack Vance, author of the 1962 Hugo Award-winning novel, *The Dragon Masters*. In this paragraph where alien invaders (Heavy Troopers) meet a desperate assault of humans riding various breeds of dragons there are no similes or metaphors, no symbolic imagery to convey the sense of desperate conflict, yet the passage pulses with energy:

> "The Heavy Troopers were doomed. Striding Murderers hewed from above, Long-horned Murderers thrust from below, Blue Horrors pinched, clipped, dismembered. The battle was done, but Joaz, with men and Termagants, had already charged up the ramp. From within came the hum and throb of power, and also human sounds – cries, shouts of fury." (DM, 123)

Compare that passage with the work of Barbara Hambly, whose lyrical style creates atmosphere and tone through metaphor and simile ("dragons hung in the air, bright chips of color, like butterflies in the glory of morning"). A simile makes the connection of meaning that says something is *like* something else ("the dragon folded its wings like a thunderclap"), whereas metaphor states that a thing *is* something else ("the dragon was a thunderbolt shot from the clouds"). For an ornate style using these literary conventions to be effective, it can't be forced. When it's inspired, the imagery creates layers of meaning and associations that add immeasurably to the character or scene being described. Here is a passage from *Dragonsbane* that demonstrates an ornamented yet carefully controlled description:

> "A dragon isn't vermin. And this one was truly beautiful. …The patterns of the scales on its sides were like the beadwork on a pair of slippers, like woven irises, all shades of purple and blue, its head was like a flower, too; its eyes and maw were surrounded with scales like colored ribbons, with purple horns and tufts of white and black fur, and with antennae like a crayfish's tipped with bobs of gems. It was butcher's work to slay it." (DB, 15)

The passage begins and ends with two terse, declarative statements that essentially serve as bookends for the lyrical material in between. The contrast between subject matter (beast/dragon) and imagery (flowers, ribbons, jewels, colors) creates interest and tension while the syntax of the paragraph flows like poetry, then stops in its tracks at the word *butcher*, which creates a "whoa" moment for the reader. I love when that happens.

The Power of Comedy

A final word about style. You might be more likely to think of serious writing when discussing style, but the need for skillful wordsmithing applies equally to successful comic fantasy or fantasy humor. Whatever you call it, being funny on paper demands absolute control of style with an instinct for audience reaction. It's not so much what you say, as how. As any standup comic would tell you, a poor delivery will kill a joke no matter how funny its content. To achieve comedy at the level of Terry Pratchett, one must be a master stylist, which he is. The elements that make Pratchett's fantasy humor so dead-on hilarious are discussed briefly below and at length in the chapter on Pratchett.

If you try thinking of famous writers of humor, you'll find you are listing master stylists with immediately recognizable voices. From classics to popular fiction, great humorists include Horace, Juvenal, Chaucer, Swift, Fielding, Dickens, Wodehouse, Twain, Vonnegut, Robbins, Hiassen – the list goes on. Jerome Stern's comments on the comic voice explain that it must come through "a firm control of diction, image, and the rhythms of language" as well as subject matter of substance: engaging villains and heroes as well as "penetrating social observations and … insights into human foibles. The richer the social texture and the truer the insights, the greater the success." In most comedy, a basically simple story is twisted through many convolutions; in comic fantasy, the possibilities are even greater if dragons are involved.

Parody, according to Stern, involves "imitation of a literary work or style that exaggerates and caricatures the features of the original." It can mock affectations or pretensions, especially as a mock epic – a silly subject treated as if it were great and heroic, or a serious subject turned inside out as a burlesque. Parody requires writing skill, otherwise it falls flat or is just too obvious to be funny – a mechanical one-to-one correspondence simply becomes boring. The more distinctive the style or genre being made fun of, the easier the parody, but once readers get the joke, the parody then has to sustain itself – it can't be a one-joke routine. The writer must become the equivalent of a comic impressionist on paper. To give you a prime example, Terry Pratchett's parody of McCaffrey's Dragonriders of Pern series is priceless, but still funny even if you don't know the Pern stories for reference.

Irony is "discrepancy between appearance and reality, surface and depth, ignorance and knowledge." The discrepancy between what is said and what is meant can be very subtle or can bludgeon you with its absurdity. An example from the Harry Potter books that gives J. K. Rowling a lot of humor mileage is Hagrid's obsession with dragons and other dangerous magical beasts; he continually sees them as harmless and adorable while they are chewing his ankles and threatening his house with incineration. Inversion of expectations, where characters don't do or say what is expected, is another technique of irony: instead of the ordinary or expected, something else occurs, which may lead things in an entirely different direction. A great example is the dragon Chrysophylax, who turns out to be a bit of a coward all the while he's eating villagers and admiring his hoard. The bargain he strikes with the King's champion (who also isn't what the dragon expects) is the most unexpected turnaround of all. This is Tolkien's favorite brand of humor.

Satire is humor that exposes human foolishness or wrongness; it often aims criticism at large-scale institutions such as governments or religions. It can range from playful to vicious, but is at its best when it makes people laugh at themselves and the world around them. The best satirists find a balance between the criticism and the comedy. For example, the Dragon of Ankh-Morpork's scathing put-down of Discworld society in Pratchett's *Guards! Guards!* is almost too true to be funny while at the same time providing slapstick antics from the city police and subtle irony from the deposed Patrician.

Satire is a " wry humor wreathed with barbed insights," to use Stern's terms. The barbs can be painful or gentle, but they must strike home to elicit humor, even in dragon tales. To demonstrate the range that's possible within the fantasy genre, Michael Swanwick's nihilistic tale, *The Iron Dragon's*

Daughter, includes satire that's more scathing than funny, although a grim humor is apparent if your mind works that way. Swanwick manages to satirize both fantasy and cyberpunk in the same story, in which an abused orphan, drug-dealing elves, and a mechanical dragon bent on the destruction of all existence habit a Dickensian world that's part Faërie and part ghetto.

On the other end of the scale is the gentle satire of books like Kenneth Grahame's *The Reluctant Dragon* in which the common motif of the vicious, maiden-devouring evil dragon is inverted into a comic peace-loving or even cowardly creature who'd rather befriend the humans than eat them. Another example is E. Nesbit's story "The Last of the Dragons," where a modern sacrificial princess, a totally civilized tame dragon, and a rescuing prince find a way to buck convention and live in harmony.

Whimsical satire of archetypes abounds in the dragon novels of Patricia Wrede, which have been described as everything from "zany" to "madcap" to "hilarious." The dragon Kazul's decision to take in a volunteer princess fuels the humor of the story – most princesses just get abducted or eaten on the spot; they certainly don't volunteer for "princess duty" with a group of dragons. But Kazul rises to the occasion: "'You start right away,' said Kazul. 'I'll want dinner at seven. In the meantime you can begin sorting the treasure ...The rest of your job I'll explain as we go along. You don't object to learning a little magic, do you?'" You get the idea.

One of the best non-fiction dragon satires I've come across is Pamela Wharton Blanpied's hilarious sendup of overly-academic dragon research, *Dragons: The Modern Infestation.* The tongue-in-cheekiness of this tome is so subtle and her mock scholarship so convincing that a surprising number of readers have failed to realize it is satire. They take it as a straight research project by someone trying to convince others that dragons are real. As one reviewer put it, "Once you see the joke, it is merciless in tooth and claw."

Farce involves outrageous coincidences and deus ex machina inventions. Farce, according to Stern, "allows exaggerations, improbabilities, slapstick, old jokes, bad puns, and caricatures," all found in huge doses in any given Asprin or Pratchett novel. To create farce, the writer needs an uninhibited imagination but also the ability to know when to reign things in before readers start to lose belief in the author's fictional world. Characters have to retain some shred of reality to which readers can relate even in the most ridiculous of circumstances. The scenes between Hagrid and Norbert the baby dragon in *Harry Potter and the Sorcerer's Stone* provide some good examples of farce.

Picaresque is the story of a *picaro*, a rogue or anti-hero who gets into trouble through a series of adventures, and in spite of himself solves the mystery or fulfills the hero's role, often with liberal dashes of farce and satire. Human (or dragon) folly is revealed through the adventures of a disreputable central character who is appealing in spite of his vices. In Tolkien's novella, *Farmer Giles of Ham*, you could make a case for both the human Giles and the dragon Chrysophylax as having a touch of the *picaro*.

Imagination, the Final Requisite

When an author is a bestseller, most likely his or her style is quite recognizable. For some readers, it's a liability, for others a delight. In Tolkien's case, a half-century of reactions to his fiction show that most readers (including critics) either love him or hate him – rarely is someone neutral about his very identifiable writing style. However, even if someone complains about the "high-fantasy" mode of his language, very few fault the depth of his imagination. The world he created in all its rich detail has the feel of authenticity, of realness, of believability. Even when such in-jokes as the philological source of Smaug's name are too arcane to grasp, the world of Middle-earth in which Smaug terrorizes lake-men and eats dwarf ponies is wholly believable.

In fact, all of this could be said of most of the writers covered in this volume. Readers either love or hate the way they write, yet the breadth and range of their imaginations – infusing the worlds they build with detail and memorable characters and creatures – can't be denied. Some readers find the level of detail in Terry Goodkind's *Sword of Truth* style too graphic and sadistic for their taste (if you've survived the Mord-Sith chapters you know what I mean), while for others this makes the reading experience more gripping and intense. Prolific writer Anne McCaffrey's Dragonriders of

Pern books also demonstrate the love-her/hate-her situation, in which her writing style is perceived by some as ham-fisted and continually overstating the obvious, yet is experienced by others as clear, straightforward, and highly engaging. But few would fault the unique and inventive creations that are her Pernese dragons.

As creatures of the imagination, literary dragons owe their lives to authors who see into other worlds, or into our own world from a unique, skewed perspective. These worlds – sub-creations, to use Tolkien's term – beckon the unsuspecting passerby, and those who are of like mind are swept away on journeys so intense and real that emotions are laid bare and lives are changed. If you don't believe me, read the Internet fan forums that swirl around the works of each of the authors in Part I of this book. A great deal of that adoration and admiration is fueled on the backs of dragons. Tolkien puts this idea into words better than anyone, so I'll let him have the final say, from his essay, *Beowulf: The Monsters and the Critics*: "A dragon is no idle fancy. Whatever may be his origins, in fact or invention, the dragon in legend is a potent creation of men's imagination, richer in significance than his barrow is in gold."

Notes

AFM – *Another Fine Myth*, Asprin
DB – *Dragonsbane*, Hambly
DM – *The Dragon Masters*, Vance
GT – *A Game of Thrones*, Martin
SS – *The Star Scroll*, Rawn

1. Geraldine McCaughrean's story can be found in the collection *Fire and Wings, Dragon Tales from East and West*. Other collections worth dipping into are *The Ultimate Dragon*, edited by Tanith Lee, and Jane Yolen's *Here There Be Dragons*.

Chapter 2

J. R. R. Tolkien
A Treacherous Twosome

"DRAGONS ALWAYS attracted me as a mythological element. They seemed to be able to comprise human malice and bestiality together so extraordinarily well, and also a sort of malicious wisdom and shrewdness – terrifying creatures!"

So said Tolkien in a now-famous BBC interview from 1965. From his earliest dragons to his later, more developed versions, he took great pains to show this contrast of physical ferocity and mental cunning. His writing style of omniscient narration was well suited to giving readers a glimpse inside the alien minds of these beasts, as well as presenting them from the reference point of the humans and elves who encounter them.

There are no active dragons in *The Lord of the Rings* (although Scatha the Worm gets a passing mention in an appendix). Tolkien's homage to the great beast that fascinated him from his childhood onward lies in *The Hobbit*, *The Silmarillion*, a novella (*Farmer Giles of Ham*), and a couple of essays and poems. The dragons we're after in this chapter are Glaurung from *The Silmarillion* and Smaug from *The Hobbit*.

Tolkien's literary sources for his dragons have been well documented,[1] so I'll only mention the main sources here and we'll move on to his abilities as a fiction writer. For Tolkien, writing about what you know meant the body of Anglo-Saxon, Icelandic, and northern European medieval literature and language, of which he was a master. Lurking in those ancient tales you'll find Fáfnir in the tale of Sigurd, Norse mythology's World Serpent Jormungand, and the unnamed dragon who bested Old English hero Beowulf, as well as the various worms connected with St. George, Arthur Pendragon, and other heroes of medieval romance.

These are the archetypal Western dragons, whose modus operandi comes with some well-known standards: wicked and devious, fire-breathing, bat-winged, hoard guarding, and poison spitting lizard-like beasts, with the ability to ensnare the unwary through their voice and gaze. Tolkien used those models, plus the general plot device of the dragonslayer, but with some interesting twists of his own. One familiar technique is to delay entry of the dragon into the story in order to build up its reputation before we actually meet it in the fiery flesh. This works in interesting ways in the stories of Glaurung in *The Silmarillion* and Smaug in *The Hobbit*.

In the Footsteps of Fafnir

First we take up the trail of Glaurung, a typically evil Western dragon – a "worm," which is a wingless, smelly, slug-type dragon found in Northern tales and legends (you'll find more on the origin of the term in Chapter 10). The classic worm is completely malicious and vile, as opposed to other types of dragons that may occasionally show some redeeming features.

A thorough character study of Glaurung, one of Tolkien's earliest dragons, is an interesting challenge. Glaurung dominates the tragic tale of Túrin Turambar in *The Silmarillion*, but a fuller treatment of Glaurung and his human adversary appears in "The Tale of the Children of Húrin," in *Unfinished Tales of Númenor and Middle-earth*, edited by Christopher Tolkien after his father's death. The question is whether to look at only what's in *The Silmarillion*, published in 1977, or to cast a wider net for the character by reading alternate, somewhat differing versions of the Glaurung and Túrin story available from Tolkien's notes and unfinished chapters.

The Glaurung/Túrin story as given in *The Silmarillion* is a compact summary, consisting of 28 pages of mostly third-person narration that gives us vital information about the wicked worm from the narrator's POV, yet this type of storytelling creates emotional distance for the reader. The other version of the tale (nearly three times as long, with extended passages of dialogue and more descriptive detail) gives us a much more personal experience of Glaurung through actual dialogue and omniscient narration that enters his thoughts. To effectively discuss Glaurung – Tolkien's Middle-earth version of the saga dragon model – we'll need to work back and forth between *The Silmarillion* and the *Unfinished Tales*.

Besides the two versions of this story, two important historical sources must be added to the mix. They provide the models with which he was most familiar: Fáfnir from the tale of Sigurd the Dragonslayer (recounted in the *Poetic Edda*, the *Prose Edda*, the *Völsunga Saga*, the *Nibelungenlied*, and eventually Andrew Lang's *Red Fairy Book*) and the unnamed dragon that ends the life of the hero Beowulf. Both Glaurung and Smaug owe some debt to these two paragons of draconic evil, so I'll be pointing out the borrowings as we go along.

Since we have two versions of Glaurung's story (both important), your initial impression of him depends on which version you read first. In *Unfinished Tales*, the very first reference to the beast is an oblique one found in the tale "Of Tuor and His Coming to Gondolin," where only the beast's track leading down into a poisoned stream can be seen. Glaurung isn't mentioned by name, but by epithet, "Great Worm of Angband." As readers we receive the impression that this dragon is evil and highly dangerous, with the ability to taint pure waters with its mere presence, and that it is associated with the chief villain of Middle-earth, Morgoth. We are set up to accept Glaurung as completely wicked and terrifying.

In *Unfinished Tales,* Glaurung is first presented as an icon, a symbolic image that crowns the Helm of Hador. Made for the dwarf lord Azaghâl who wounded the mature Glaurung during the Battle of Unnumbered Tears, the famous helmet featured on its crest an image of the great dragon's head sculpted in gold. The sheer audacity of putting one's mortal enemy on a helmet designed for ultimate protection represents the highest defiance of that enemy's power. It's thumbing your nose at the biggest bully on the block. The importance of this introduction is that it establishes Glaurung as a formidable foe with an almost mythic history of battles against men and elves, and also assures us that he's loathed and despised. We know that when we meet him in the scaly flesh, he will be a terrible foe. We have also been given a hint about his color: gold.

With his love of words and especially their subtleties of meaning, Tolkien regarded naming and labeling as one of the most important (and enjoyable) aspects of storycrafting. Names of objects as well as characters often reveal aspects of their nature and many contain ironic references or puns. We have already encountered one of Glaurung's aliases, Worm of Angband. Adding to the lore, Tolkien creates others that emphasize the worm's association with Morgoth and his standing among the foes of elves and men. Among Glaurung's aliases we find Father of Dragons, the Great Worm, Worm of Morgoth, First of the Urulóki, gold-worm, and Glaurung the Golden. The name Glaurung itself suggests (from Tolkien's Elvish language derivations) something like "golden fog or cloud." As we'll find out later, the fog reference is directly related to one of Glaurung's most evil deeds.

Tolkien's basic form for Glaurung is that of a wingless serpent of vast bulk, long in the body and slimy on his belly like a slug – a Fáfnir-type worm. Tolkien creates a category for him, the Urulóki or fire-serpents (a worm that can breath flames), engineered by Morgoth in Angband. When enraged, this dragon radiates heat, with glimmers of fire around his golden scales, and can charge in a flash. But once he has expended his flames, he is sluggish and slow, with his color drained to a dull grey. This is an important point, for in Tolkien's universe, there is always a price to pay for power used with evil intent.

Like many Western dragons, including Fáfnir, Glaurung's breath and blood are venomous, and his reserves of internal fire are powerful enough to burn forests, scorch stone, and reduce puny men to cinders. His senses of sight, smell, and hearing are much sharper than that of humans or even elves. He has the gaze of a basilisk and uses it to cast the dragonspell over his victims. Under the dragon's gaze, both Túrin and his sister Nienor are paralyzed and must answer as commanded when questioned by the dragon.

In this state, Glaurung has the power to wipe their memories and plant false information. The dragonspell removes all conscious will and self-awareness, tainting the victim's perceptions of his or her surroundings, as happened to Nienor: "...all became dim about her; and slowly a great darkness drew down on her and in that darkness there was emptiness; she knew nothing, and heard nothing, and remembered nothing." (UT, 119)

The dragonspell is cast through both gaze and voice. Dragon speech in Tolkien's stories is handled in print like all other dialogue. Tolkien doesn't make use of typographical features such as italics or offset text to indicate the dragon's thoughts or speech. As in Fáfnir's dialogue with Sigurd, it is assumed that the dragon has the power to utter human speech normally and have it understood by his audience. Tolkien creates a speech pattern for the dragon that distinguishes it from the human characters by elevating the diction. Glaurung's speech is formal in syntax and grammar, with mock courtesy. For example, he torments Túrin in this fashion (boldface added): "**Hail**, son of Húrin. Well met!" and further, "As thralls **thy** mother and **thy** sister live in Dor-lómin, in misery and want. **Thou art** arrayed as a prince, but they go in rags; and for **thee** they yearn, but **thou carest** not for that."

Glaurung is also a typical treasure hoarder, making his lair on the heaped wealth of the sacked elven fortress of Nargothrond, once inhabited by the renowned Finrod Felagund. Felagund's ruined domain is Glaurung's reward for leading the assault, and the worm takes great pleasure in blasting and scorching the remains of the great hall before massing its stores of treasure into a dragon bed. So greedy is he that he even denies the orcs who fought beside him in the battle any piece of the treasure.

The reader's first encounter with Glaurung in *The Silmarillion* occurs as the narrator's second-hand description of the dragon's premature assault on the elves of Fingon. Here the impetuous dragon is still young and untested. We learn that Glaurung is a new creation of Morgoth and that Fingon's archers are able to send him scurrying back to Angband because his armor of scales was immature. Of even more interest, however, is the almost casual observation that "Morgoth was ill-pleased that Glaurung had disclosed himself over-soon," letting us know that Glaurung is not his own master and must act according to the dark will of someone else. Tolkien's dragons are typical Western dragons in that they are truly evil and cunning, but as demonstrated here, they are not Satan himself or even an incarnation of him, as medieval dragons were often portrayed.

This fact is emphasized numerous times in both versions of the story – Glaurung is not a free agent and, in fact, may be possessed by Morgoth on occasion. Only after he does his master's bidding can he then turn to his own wicked devices. In the *Unfinished Tales* version, when Nienor first looks into the dragon's eyes, we experience from her POV how terrible they appear, "filled with the fell spirit of Morgoth, his master." In this same scene, Tolkien shows us Glaurung's heightened senses that can detect the elf warrior Mablung hiding by the river bank; the dragon speaks to him in Morgoth's voice: "…there came from him the laughter of Morgoth, dim but horrible, as an echo of malice out of the black depths far away." Glaurung also serves as the eyes of Morgoth, who senses what the dragon knows, as when the narrator tells us that "it was well known to Glaurung and to his Master that in Brethil there abode still a remnant of free men." In *The Silmarillion*, when gloating over the sack of Nargothrond, Glaurung acknowledges satisfaction that "he had accomplished the errand of his Master."

The evil nature of Glaurung, which he draws directly from his maker Morgoth, is relentlessly presented through vivid imagery of fire, darkness, and stench. Tolkien is a master of the use of imagery to set atmosphere, describe setting and character, and carry themes. Regarding Glaurung, the nouns, verbs, and adjectives that appeal directly to the senses do the heavy lifting to give us a first-hand experience of the dragon's physical presence. Let's sample some of Tolkien's diction that brings this Great Worm to life through imagery and viewpoint. In the passage that follows, Tolkien creates suspense with imagery of sight and hearing through the wary POV of the elf Mablung as he approaches the entrance to Nargothrond not long after its destruction. The air is tense with the hidden presence of the dragon (bold added):

"But he could **hear** no sound, and he could **see** no sign of any foe, nor any token of the Dragon, save the burning about the Doors that he had wrought in the day of the sack. All lay **quiet** under a pale sun." (UT, 117)

From the omniscient narrator's descriptions in both story versions, we encounter repeatedly the nouns *fire, flame, smoke, blast, rage, terror, armor, strength, power, malice, darkness, shadow, stench, serpent,* and *worm.* Among the most recurrent adjectives are *foul, evil, baleful, vast, lithe, heavy, chill, grey, dark,* and *stealthy.* Repeated verbs include *defiled, withered, swept, crawled, taunted, burned, blinded, stank,* and *screamed.* You'll also notice a distinct absence of adverbs in Tolkien's high-romance style, except for a few such as *moveless* and *straightway* that contribute to the formality of the diction. The effect is both stark and immediate. Tom Shippey points out that Tolkien tended to substitute adjectives for adverbs, which also elevates the diction and creates a sense of archaism.

In addition to the narrator's imagery, Tolkien reveals Glaurung's mental and physical attributes both directly and indirectly. The worm in action appears in three peak scenes: (1) the confrontation with Túrin at the bridge of ruined Nargothrond, (2) the entrancement of Nienor, and (3) the final duel with Túrin at "Deer's Leap" (Cabed-en-Aras), the deep gorge of the river Teiglin. Tolkien also presents the dragon indirectly; we can glean a great deal about Glaurung from what others say and speculate about him. These scenes also reveal Tolkien's subtle use of POV to slip us in and out of the dragon's mind without breaking the flow of the omniscient narration. The passage quoted below demonstrates the total control and skill with which Tolkien crafted his tale-telling; he knew exactly what he was doing as a wordsmith. In just a few sentences of Glaurung's dialogue, we are shown how he weaves the dragonspell over Túrin, using his own wicked imagery to instill guilt, fear, and self-loathing in his captive. The great irony is that the words he uses to do this also truly describe his own nature.

> "Evil have been all thy ways, son of Húrin. Thankless fosterling, outlaw, slayer of thy friend, thief of love, usurper of Nargothrond, captain foolhardy, and deserter of thy kin....' And Túrin... saw himself as in a mirror misshapen by malice, and loathed that which he saw." (SIL, 214)

Tolkien gives us access to Glaurung's thoughts with similar skill. In fantasy fiction, if narration is from a dragon's POV or the omniscient narrator dips into a character's mind, the writer must deal with alien thought patterns – how does the creature think and what's going on in its mind? Is there anything we can relate to as human readers? We enter Glaurung's head and look out through his eyes only a few times, but those moments are quite enough to convey a consummate sense of evil, cunning, and utter disdain for humans and elves as species. For example, the approach to sacked Nargothrond from the safety of the hillside and then down to the river and its rocky shore are all described from Mablung's POV. This viewpoint is briefly interrupted by one short paragraph that shifts our mental image from looking toward the entrance to Nargothrond to looking *out* of it. We are suddenly shown that the intruders have been watched all along. The use of the word *spies* conveys the dragon's attitude toward them:

> "But Glaurung lay there, just within the shadow of the great passage that led inward from the ruined Doors, and he had long been aware of the spies ... indeed he knew also that some remained behind and sat upon the bare top of Amon Ethir." (UT, 117)

The blast of fire that hits the river when Glaurung emerges creates a huge cloud of steam and fog reminiscent of both the *Beowulf* dragon and the White Dragon in Tolkien's novelette *Roverandom*. While most of this scene is narrated from the terrified and confused viewpoint of the people on the hilltop who flounder around in the mist as if blind, one telling sentence brings us back into Glaurung's head: "The neighing of the horses and the cries of the riders came to the ears of Glaurung; and he was well pleased." This final phrase shows us an important aspect of the worm's character: he enjoys the misery of others and has a strong sense of self-satisfaction. Glaurung's obvious sense of invincibility and disdain for his victims will be brought into play by Tolkien as an element that contributes to the dragon's death at the hand of a mere mortal.

Another way we learn about Glaurung is from what others say – in this way readers' expectations are built up about the creature. A good example occurs in the discussion of what to do about the dragon's continued marauding after the battle of Nargothrond, with many speculations offered.

Those few who actually spot the worm describe his progress toward the river Teiglin in terror-stricken terms, especially "the stench of him" and the "foul swatch" stretching out behind him. Glaurung is described as "a deadly peril" from whom the woodsmen should flee rather than attempt to repel with force. Foreshadowing the dragon's demise, Tolkien has Túrin note that although the dragon has grown craftier and more evil over the years, it may be possible to outwit him.

This passage also confirms Glaurung as a tool of Morgoth, with the logical conclusion that this is really the source of his power rather than his brute strength. Thus the fact that he must slither like a snake on his unprotected belly, since he has no wings, is revealed to be the worm's weak spot. We are also given an instructive bit of history, namely the story of the battle of Unnumbered Tears in which the dwarf lord Azaghâl stabbed Glaurung in his soft underside, causing him to retreat to his master. This scene is strongly reminiscent of Beowulf's discussion with his kinsmen about their own marauding dragon, which ends in Beowulf's declaration of his intention to slay the dragon on his own terms; as we know, only his kinsman Wiglaf has enough courage to stand by his side at the moment of assault. This idea was used by Tolkien as well. Because of what other characters have said about Glaurung ("the tale of the scouts that had seen him had gone about and grown in the telling"), Túrin is able to recruit only two companions for the quest to kill Glaurung. What others say about the dragon can sway the course of the plot as well as give added character information.

The plot points involving Glaurung indicate the level at which the dragon affects the storyline, i.e., his power to act. He is not just a piece of the scenery; he is a character crucial to the climax of the story. As a receptacle for Morgoth's evil spirit, Glaurung reflects his master's hatred of both the races of Middle-earth (men and elves), which adds unique evil to his naturally cunning, malicious reptilian personality. Twice the dragon uses his spellbinding powers of deception to tamper with the minds of the human characters, with disastrous effects.

Particularly chillingly written is the scene in which Glaurung deliciously toys with the spellbound hero, holding him paralyzed while orcs herd the captives past him, including his lover Finduilas, who calls out to him in vain. The dragon's spell allows him to hear her cries, but not move a muscle to help her. Glaurung only releases Túrin from his paralysis after the captives are long gone down the road to their deaths, knowing that the miserable hero could not "stop his ears against that voice that haunted him after." Glaurung has total mastery of the situation, adding to his sense of invulnerability.

Tolkien's dialogue between Glaurung and Túrin in this same scene displays the hero's anguish and the dragon's wicked enjoyment of each twist of their duel of wills. Once the human has looked the dragon in the eyes, he is no match for the mind games Glaurung can play with him. In fact, the dragon makes him believe that his mother and sister are in peril and that he must abandon Finduilas to her fate in order to find and rescue his family. The dragon's wiliness and deceptive ways are demonstrated when he feigns pity and generosity, while the narrator slyly informs us that the dragon is incapable of feeling. Glaurung offers Túrin his freedom because it's the honorable thing to do – "At least thou art valiant; beyond all whom I have met. And they lie who say that we of our part do not honour the valour of foes." But this assertion is itself a lie, because he has sent Túrin on a fool's errand to seek his mother and sister in the land where they no longer live. The dragon is also a consummate liar.

The death of Glaurung is based on the Fáfnir model, with Tolkien's own unique additions. For demonstration purposes, I'll use the Sigurd tale as it appears in the Norse *Völsunga Saga*.[2] When the need to slay the dragon Fáfnir is presented to Sigurd, he repeats information he has heard from others, which is then countered by his foster brother Regin (very like the scene mentioned earlier in which Túrin and the woodsmen discuss what to do about Glaurung):

> "Sigurd answered: 'Although I am young, I know the nature of this serpent, and I have heard that no one dare go against him because of his size and ferocity.' Regin replied: 'That is not true. His size is no different from that of other grass snakes and more is made of it than it deserves.'" (*Völsunga Saga*, 57)

Once Sigurd begins the hunt for Fáfnir, he realizes the shape-shifting dragon is more than he expected and that Regin has given him false information. In fact, the dragon is so huge "the earth quaked mightily" under his feet, and the only way to pierce his unprotected belly is to come up under him from a deep ditch when he heads for the river. The ruse works, and Sigurd's magical sword buries itself to the hilt in the beast's heart.

Likewise, when mighty Glaurung tries to cross over the chasm of the Teiglin, he never dreams that underneath him is Túrin, clinging to the cliffside, sword in hand. Here Tolkien has taken the elements of the Fáfnir story and expanded them to mythic proportions, creating much more peril for the dragonslayer who is not cowering in a ditch, but about to fall off a cliff into the rocky gorge far below. In language that emulates the Sigurd/ Fáfnir combat, the omniscient narrator puts us on the ledge with Túrin, looking up, so that we see from his viewpoint how the Black Sword slashes "into the belly even to its hilts." In vivid detail, we experience with the hero how Glaurung in his death throes "writhed, screaming, lashing and coiling himself in his agony, until he had broken a great space all about him." This echoes the fate of Fáfnir as told in the *Völsunga Saga*: "And when the huge worm felt his mortal wound he thrashed his head and his tail, destroying everything that got in his way."

Let's take stock of Glaurung's personality, his "dragon-ness," so far. His evil nature is well-documented, both by impressions given about him and by his actual deeds that we observe. Even with his dying breath he cements the curse he initiated between brother and sister, saying "Hail, Nienor, daughter of Húrin. We meet again ere the end. I give thee joy that thou hast found thy brother at last… and now thou shalt know him, Túrin son of Húrin!" The mocking tone of this speech emphasizes yet again the depth of his depravity, knowing that his dying words will ensure the death of two more characters.

Because the dragon's death dissipates the memory block placed on Nienor, she now has full knowledge that she has committed incest through the dragon's manipulations. In this tragic tale, Glaurung represents the height of Morgoth's evil at work in Middle-earth during the First Age. Not only does the creature carry out the most devastating crimes against the human characters, he relishes the job with no hint of remorse. Through Tolkien's powers of description, dialogue, and viewpoint, we the readers feel proper revulsion for this wicked worm.

We also know that Glaurung is clever and cunning in a truly non-human way; he consistently torments the human characters in a manner that delivers the greatest mental and emotional anguish to his victims. The method with which he tricks Nienor into revealing her identity when he first encounters her is a case in point and demonstrates the facility with which Tolkien moves us between the minds of the two enemies. Trapped in the dragon's gaze, Nienor is told that her brother has fled like a coward, leaving his comrades to the flames. We feel her fury at this insult to her family and don't realize that she has fallen into a trap when she retorts that Húrin's offspring would never do such a thing, saying, "We fear you not." Slipping back into the dragon's mind, Tolkien allows us to discover what the wicked worm has just accomplished: "Then Glaurung laughed, for so was Húrin's daughter revealed to him."

Glaurung is more than a one-dimensional dragon – Tolkien develops him by letting the reader experience the beast's alien thought processes and pride in his might, which also allows us to see the flaws in his seemingly invincible bravado. For example, twice Tolkien allows him to show cowardice, as well as strength. Glaurung flees the bowmen of the elf lord Fingon when as a youngster he has gone marauding without his master's blessing. Even as a more mature dragon, he flees again when ringed by armed dwarves at the end of the Battle of Unnumbered Tears, one of whom stabs him (non-fatally). These glimpses not only add character depth, they also foreshadow that his armor of scales has a fatal flaw, which will be the means by which he can be killed.

Before we leave Glaurung, I want to mention the symbolic aspect of dragons as barriers and obstacles to be overcome. To demonstrate this, Tolkien uses the image of the bridge. Nargothrond falls easily because of Túrin's refusal to dismantle the great bridge over the river Narog; it gives Glaurung (who is flightless) and his hosts easy access to the elf kingdom. After the battle, Glaurung's stealthy appearance behind Túrin, barring access to the bridge (a means of escape to safety) repeats the symbol of the dragon as obstacle; you can find a similar image when Chrysophylax blocks the road in *Farmer Giles of Ham*. In *The Hobbit*, Tolkien shows us the opposite of Túrin's ill-fated decision. Bard the bowman commands that the causeway be broken down to prevent Smaug from crossing it on foot, thereby putting the winged worm in the position of having to fly out over the water, exposing his belly to arrows. Having mentioned Thorin's bane, let's move now to the Lonely Mountain, where Smaug, the Chiefest and Greatest of Calamities, awaits.

The Burglar and Bowman

I'll be honest – Smaug has always been my favorite character in *The Hobbit*. Certainly I've enjoyed and admired the characters of the reluctant hobbit burglar Bilbo, the inscrutable but kindly wizard Gandalf, the self-important yet ultimately noble dwarf lord Thorin Oakenshield, and the menacing, mysterious shape-shifter Beorn. But when I met Smaug the Tremendous, it was love at first sight.

The Hobbit is arguably Tolkien's more popular book, since many fans come to it first before *The Lord of the Rings*, and many have read it or had it read to them in childhood. The red-gold dragon Smaug is certainly one of Tolkien's most memorable creations. The creature was clearly a favorite of Tolkien's as well, for he finely etched the character with such affection and humor (regardless of the worm's thoroughly wicked inclinations) that readers love Smaug even though they should hate him. He's frightening, but surprisingly knowable. You get the feeling that Tolkien identified with certain aspects of Smaug's personality; "I am as susceptible as a dragon to flattery," he wrote in answer to a fan letter asking for information. He even compared himself to Smaug for behaving foolishly by feeling a twinge of pride over *The Hobbit* and its immense popularity.

Ask people what they remember about *The Hobbit* and many will respond "Smaug!" His image permeates the visual arts in paintings, posters, picture books, T-shirts, and computer graphics (Tolkien himself illustrated the dragon several times). Pretty impressive for a character who only appears in a couple of scenes near the end of the novel. Some of us believe he steals the show.

Tolkien pulls this off through ingenious use of source material as well as carefully crafted dialogue and exposition. His narrator's foreground presence (which he regretted, but most readers seem to be fond of) allows for ironic description, supported by a buildup of rumor and Middle-earth dragonlore. Long before the legendary creature's physical presence is confirmed, we feel that we know quite a bit about Smaug. The dwarf ballad sung by firelight in Bilbo's hobbit hole tells us we are dealing with a treasure-usurping fire-breathing dragon that delights in incinerating towns and villagers alike – and that's only a few pages into the first chapter.

Tolkien scholar Michael Drout believes this holding back of information and its gradual release through point-of-view characters is what makes Tolkien such a great storyteller and what allows the tales of Middle-earth to feel fresh with repeated readings. The POV characters often don't know any more than the readers do; in this way, suspense is kept taut. Readers find out little by little along with the characters – we know, for example, that Smaug might be waiting down at the end of the tunnel inside the Lonely Mountain, but we experience Bilbo's terror of discovery as it becomes gradually evident the wicked worm really is there asleep on the hoard.

Whereas Glaurung's tale closely fits the traditional dragonslayer model, and Glaurung's character is wholly cold and evil, Smaug's role in *The Hobbit* is more original and ultimately more accessible. True, he is eventually slain by a traditional hero, but not by the protagonist of the tale, the hobbit Bilbo Baggins. Smaug is a more complex character than the usual treasure-hoarding worm of medieval legend, and Tolkien is more adept in *The Hobbit* at revealing him to us. Here Tolkien's fiction writing skills appear more flexible, reaching beyond those stylized conversations of Glaurung and Túrin, so that more layers of personality come through in the dragon's interactions this time around. We know that Smaug is not just a piece of furniture on the set; he's a pivotal character around whom two important themes coalesce: greed and courage.

Although humans and dragons are worlds apart, they are brought down to the same level through their common vice of avarice, which helps build a frame of reference for readers. The dragon is alien, otherwordly, but his greed is a very real human trait. The gold-sickness (also called the dragon-sickness) causes the particularly susceptible dwarves to lose their wits. It doesn't work quite as strongly on the elves, men, or hobbits, but they can't avoid being caught up in the events spawned by the very presence of the treasure. Tolkien's vivid imagery describing the sight of it ("red-stained in the ruddy light") evokes images of the blood that dearly bought the treasure.

An eye-opener, as Sam Gamgee would say, to understanding the larger context of Smaug as a symbol for greed is Tolkien's poem "The Hoard," published in the *Oxford Magazine* the same year as *The Hobbit*. If you plunder through that amazing treasure-trove that is Michael Drout's edition of *Beowulf and the Critics*, you'll find the poem with Tolkien's comment that it perhaps sheds more light on dragons, hoards, and heroes than much literary criticism has done. It equates the hoarding instinct with greed itself – which stops the ears from hearing its warnings and kills the joy of life.

A good example is from the third stanza, which describes the dragon who as a youngster stole the hoard from its dwarf owner:

> "There was an old dragon under grey stone;
> his red eyes blinked as he lay alone.
> His joy was dead and his youth spent,
> he was knobbed and wrinkled, and his limbs bent
> in the long years to his gold chained;
> in his heart's furnace the fire waned." ("The Hoard," lines 33-38)

In successive stanzas, elves, dwarves, dragons, and men wither under the treasure's influence, and, ironically, the hoard ends up forgotten by future generations, covered once again by green grass and life. Smaug spent 171 years on the dwarf hoard before Bilbo disturbed him. If not for Thorin's expedition, who knows how long Smaug might have slept on the pile, perhaps dying there of withered old age.

Shippey points out a revealing language tie of "The Hoard" to the Beowulf dragon, and thus to all treasure-hoarding dragons. The poem's original title, "Iúmonna Gold Galdre Bewunden," is line 3052 of *Beowulf*, which is translated in context as "For all that heritage huge, that **gold of bygone men, was bound by a spell**, so the treasure-hall could be touched by none of human kind." The implication is that greed itself is the actual curse instilled by the hoarded treasure. The gold-lust can turn young heroes into old misers – all who fall under the spell wither and decline. It's the rumor of amassed wealth that draws Smaug to Erebor and the Lonely Mountain and keeps him there for such a long time that the jewels on the pile encrust his belly like a plate of armor. The dwarves begin to show signs of the dragon-sickness as soon as they enter the tunnel to the worm's lair. Even Bilbo feels momentarily overcome by it when he first steps into the dragon's lair.

The theme of courage, which Tolkien has developed all along the trail toward the Lonely Mountain, comes under the floodlights once the expedition reaches Lake-town and the prospect of encountering Smaug looms large. The warrior's code of heroic loyalty even in the face of death is easily sung about in the relative safety of the town ("Thorin looked and walked as if his kingdom was already regained and Smaug chopped up into little pieces."), but once in the mountain tunnel leading to the worm's lair, all boasting and cheering evaporates. An interesting reversal occurs here: it's the unimposing hobbit who displays the most courage, egged on by less-than-heroic dwarves. The presence of Smaug brings out the best and worst in the expedition members.

Tolkien brings Bilbo's courage to the forefront when the hobbit realizes that the rumbling noise in the tunnel is actually the dragon snoring. Tolkien puts the readers in Bilbo's head, so that we shiver with him as he conquers his fear alone in the dark. When the narrator tells us that "[g]oing on from there was the bravest thing he ever did," we believe it. We are also convinced that Bilbo is not your typical dragonslayer who routinely faces imminent death without fear or hesitation. According to Shippey, inner self-confidence lies at the core of a theory of courage in medieval Northern literature. The poems and sagas are full of motifs about conquering one's fear, including the true hero's fierce denial of it. Tolkien's treatment of Bilbo and the dwarves in the immediate presence of Smaug is a mocking reversal of this so-called northern courage.

Put in mythic terms, Bilbo's entry into the dragon's cave is equivalent to the hero's descent into the underworld, where the confrontation with the masculine god-figure (in this case, the greatest dragon alive at that time in Middle-earth) must be accomplished. Bilbo's natural caution is still strongly in play during his initial trip to the dragon's central lair, but by the second trip to confront the beast, he's grown in confidence and bravery. Randal Helms says of this scene that Bilbo's trial by fire is "an initiation...into the perilous world of Faërie," where the dragons turn out to be real.

Because the plot of *The Hobbit* is episodic, the story has numerous villains (trolls, goblins, wargs) that delay the progress of the expedition, but we never lose sight of the chief villain waiting at what Thorin and company assume will be the quest's end. The main POV character is Bilbo Baggins, who can be deemed the protagonist, but he isn't the actual hero who kills the dragon. Although he's the one who first confronts the beast in the scaly flesh, Bilbo isn't a dragonslayer at all. Instead, Bilbo tries common-sense negotiation with both the creature and the various other species who want to divvy up its treasure. In this sense, Tolkien has stood the dragonslayer archetype on its head.

Dragon expert Jonathan Evans believes that Tolkien's presentation of the death of Smaug is "a masterpiece of dramatic narrative." But it didn't start out quite that well-conceived. In Humphrey Carpenter's biography of Tolkien you'll find an intriguing entry that reveals from early notes on *The Hobbit* that Bilbo was cast as the dragonslayer, stabbing Smaug with his magical knife Sting while inside the lair. The dragon's ensuing death-throes smash the tunnel and its entrance. However, Tolkien wisely decided this end was both too predictable and not noble enough for the terrible Smaug, who was, after all, the greatest dragon remaining in Middle-earth in the Third Age, according to the entry "Durin's Folk" in Appendix A of *The Return of the King*. Instead, he staged a proper heroic death at the hands of someone of ancient lineage making use of an heirloom weapon (Bard's black arrow). The great villain meets a fitting end at the hands of an approved saga-style hero out in the open for everyone to see and marvel at.

Why do people respond to Smaug so readily even though he's the villain? I'd like to suggest that it's because basically he's the one controlling the situation for much of the plot, whether it's anticipation of him or reaction to his very real presence. He has the power and freedom to act; that is, others are reacting to him and their actions are constrained by him. He is also mysterious (non-human) and therefore intriguing – he's exotic in ways the hobbits, dwarves, elves, and men are not. As writer Orson Scott

Card says, "The audience is drawn to the strange, the powerful, the inexplicable." Tolkien was quite aware of this fact as he crafted his dragon tale. In early versions of his *Beowulf* lecture, he affirmed that "a dragon is not an idle or a silly tale," but rather it is "one of the most moving creations of the imagination, richer in meaning than his barrow is in golden treasure." The earlier discussion of the intertwined themes of greed and courage bears this out.

The way in which Tolkien incorporated the essence of his favorite Northern dragons into a wonderful witch's brew of his own is part of what makes them so fearsome. His use of the tools of the writer's craft – dialogue, exposition, point of view, and imagery – reveals a careful and sophisticated creator of fiction.

An inventory of Smaug's physical details shows that Tolkien was using the established dragon mold found in Western medieval heroic and romantic literature for his most fully realized dragon character.

- His color is red-gold.
- He is of immense size (too big for the 5-foot high secret entrance even as a young dragon), heavy in the body with a long powerful tail.
- He has a long snout full of sharp teeth.
- He has long talons or claws that are used as weapons.
- He breathes fire, and his internal furnace hasn't dimmed with the years (flickers of flame show around his eyes even when he's dozing).
- He has great batlike wings and can perform aerial acrobatic maneuvers, in spite of his weight and girth.
- Smaug himself confirms his majestic appearance: "My armour is like tenfold shields, my teeth are swords, my claws spears, the shock of my tail a thunderbolt, my wings a hurricane, and my breath death!"

Physically, Smaug is a very typical dragon that any St. George or saga hero might expect to have to slay. But looks can be misleading, and the further we investigate Smaug, the more we'll discover that he is his own dragon, so to speak. His personality is more interesting and unusual than his physical shape would indicate.

Even though the dragonslayer tales from *Beowulf* and the *Völsunga Saga* are clearly part of Tolkien's background for Smaug, his own original genius is what breathes life into the dragon. As Card points out in his book on writing fantasy, "Writers of mythic stories don't use 'formulas'; they just tell the stories they believe in and care about." The archetypes may be under the surface, but readers aren't overtly aware of them or distracted by them when the narrative is gripping.

If we look at tale types and motif indexes, it's clear that Tolkien's dragons follow the treasure-hoarding types, set in situations where an established civilized order must be protected or revenge and honor must be upheld. The archetypal elements of the *Beowulf* story that are recognizable in Smaug's situation include the dragon who guards a treasure hoard of great wealth and age, the theft of a gold cup, the dragon's explosion of rage over the missing item, its fiery retribution on the nearby town, the dragon's vulnerability through an unprotected part of its underside, and its death at the hands of a noble hero wielding an heirloom weapon. Also, the person who steals the cup is not the hero who kills the dragon.

The tale of Sigurd the dragonslayer offers more parallels, and Tolkien preferred it for its hero/dragon dialogue, unique to the body of ancient Northern literature. "Fáfnir in the late Norse versions of the Sigurd-story is better," he said in his letters, "and Smaug and his conversation obviously is in debt there." Fáfnir is also a treasure hoarder with an unprotected underside who is killed by a noble hero wielding an inherited weapon. Where Fáfnir's death departs from the *Beowulf* model is that the dragon is brought down by cunning (a plan suggested to Sigurd by Fáfnir's brother Regin) rather than the head-on brute strength employed by Beowulf and his companion Wiglaf.

Other elements from the Sigurd tale recognizable in *The Hobbit* include the dragon's ability, with cold reptilian logic, to sow seeds of doubt regarding the loyalty of accomplices and the logistics of carting all the treasure away. Another point of similarity is the curse applied to most hoards. Sigurd is wary of incurring the curse of Fáfnir's treasure and withholds his identity at first. Bilbo, likewise, is reluctant to reveal his identity to the hoard-sitting dragon. He knows enough dragonlore to be on his guard.

Those are the similarities, but there are some significant Tolkien-style departures from both sources. In *Beowulf* as well as the myth of Thor vs. the Midgard Serpent found in the Eddas, brute force alone is used to bring down the dragon, and both heroes die in the process. In contrast, Sigurd's use of a clever plan gives him better protection plus the advantage of surprise. Tolkien's choice of demise for Smaug takes a little from each approach and pulls all the secondary plot strands together into a grand climax. The element of an old thrush hearing the detail of Smaug's bare spot is now used to enable Bard the bowman, a Númenórean descendant who understands bird speech, to turn defeat to victory. It takes both wits and physical skill at arms to vanquish Smaug.

Bard's weapons, a great yew bow and a black arrow of his forefathers, tie into the thread of the usurped kingdom under the mountain – Tolkien implies that the arrow was made by the dwarf artisans living there before the dragon's arrival, thus it flies true at Bard's command, seeking its own revenge ("If ever you came from the forges of the true king under the Mountain, go now and speed well!"). In fact, it's really the Everyman protagonist Bilbo, with his personal courage and common sense approach to outrageous events, who propels this high-drama, saga-style windup of the dragon's final assault on his enemies. This is an idea worth pursuing further.

What brings Smaug to life (and death) so vividly is this contrast between ancient and modern, strange and familiar. The way in which these opposite sensibilities constantly rub shoulders in *The Hobbit* not only gives readers a great frame of reference for getting to know the characters, it also provides continual possibilities for drama as well as humor and parody. Shippey gives a great explanation of how this works: Tolkien repeatedly juggles anachronisms alongside modernisms, creates "oscillations between animal and intelligent behaviour," and juxtaposes parody of civilized, overly proper politeness with Smaug's pure animal enjoyment of the kill. One is tempted to imagine the vicious venom-spitting Midgard Serpent being offered a napkin by Thor before he smacks it on the head with Mjollnir the hammer.

Part of this is due to Tolkien's narrative style and wry sense of humor. He just can't seem to resist making philological jokes and puns or parodying his colleagues in the language business. Deirdre Greene describes Tolkien's writing style as a lexicographer's approach to language (Tolkien worked on the *Oxford English Dictionary* (OED) project as a young man). What she meant was exhaustive, overly detailed scholarship vs. plain definitions grounded in the real world (what a word *is* vs. all the things it could mean.).

Here's an example of what I'm talking about. Gandalf's explanation of why Smaug isn't likely to be using the secret entrance into the Lonely Mountain is that "Smaug could not creep into a hole that size, not even when he was a young dragon." Knowing that Smaug's name is, according to Tolkien, "the past tense of the primitive Germanic verb *Smugan*, to squeeze through a hole" adds ironic humor to the reader's mental image of Smaug. According to Shippey, the name can be linked also to Old English *Sméagan* (to inquire into; to be subtle or crafty), which is also fitting, considering the dragon's intelligence.

Tolkien's concern for styles of language in *The Hobbit* – variations in syntax, grammar, and vocabulary that fit the character's origins as well as the hidden meanings implied in names – goes a long way toward defining character. OED definitions do this as well, "identifying typical usages according to geographical occurrence, register, or style," according to Deirdre Greene.[3] Tolkien certainly would have honed these skills during the time he worked on the great dictionary project, and there is plenty of evidence for that writing style throughout his fiction.

As Green says, "Writing, like speech, betrays the author's character and context more clearly with every word." The tone of *The Hobbit* began with a good number of amused, know-it-all asides such as "Now you know enough to go on with," but Tolkien cut many of them out upon subsequent edits of the manuscript. "Some of the details of tone and treatment are, I now think, even on that basis, mistaken," he wrote to publisher Milton Waldman. "I think that *The Hobbit* can be seen to begin in what might be called a more 'whimsy' mode, and in places even more facetious, and move steadily to a more serious or significant, and more consistent and historical" mode. Even so, the tone of amused irony permeates *The Hobbit* and is one of the elements readers find most endearing. Narrator's asides such as the following, which every fan of the book will recognize – "Yes, I am afraid trolls do behave like that, even those with only one head each" – cannot fail to produce a smirky grin.

Let's turn our attention now to Smaug's "overwhelming personality," an opinion injected by the narrator that is certainly shared by Bilbo as he experiences the effects of dragon-talk. Smaug's personality is established through two main tools available to the fiction writer: exposition (including POV) and dialogue.

Tolkien's approach to exposition was to invent a background of Middle-earth folklore on dragons, so that Smaug's prehistory could be included as material that was common knowledge. In this way, we discover that Smaug is a rare holdover from earlier ages when dragons were plentiful.[4] Thorin's history of the dwarf kingdom under the Lonely Mountain gives us a baseline assessment of Smaug from which to build a working mental image: "There was a most specially greedy, strong and wicked worm called Smaug." We also know at this point (from the dwarves' song and Gandalf's explanation of Thror's map) that the dragon is huge and powerful (his wings create a "noise like a hurricane"), capable of formulating devious strategies, and fond of raiding settlements, burning buildings to the ground, and eating villagers, "especially maidens" (a somewhat snarky attitude from the narrator lurking in Thorin's dialogue, which perfectly illustrates Tolkien's semi-mocking tone toward the conventions of high saga literature in general).

If the description of Smaug were left at that, we'd have a villain much like Glaurung, who doesn't invoke our sympathy. But Smaug *is* a sympathetic character with many readers, despite his villainy. How does Tolkien accomplish this? He lets us know that, in a sense, Smaug is the last of his line (traditional "hot" dragons of great power and presence, possibly descended from the original line in Angband). While there may be lesser dragons in Middle-earth beyond the time of our story, majestic beasts such as Smaug are no more and we hate to see him go.

Anticipation of Smaug is built up through pieces of dragonlore such as proverbs, maxims, epigrams, and adages ("Every worm has his weak spot"), and old ballads shared by Gandalf, dwarves, and even Bilbo. Reference is made to this body of lore when Bilbo at last stands in the dragon's presence and finds his knowledge of dragon-hoards and their guardians doesn't begin to prepare him for the stunning reality. Tolkien also uses the folklore device to foreshadow events. For example, Gandalf uses the catch-phrase "as fierce as a dragon in a pinch" to describe Bilbo's suitability for the expedition, but it also foreshadows the scene where Bilbo actually finds himself in a pinch confronting a real dragon. The hero Bard (and indirectly Smaug's demise) are foreshadowed by Gandalf's statement that he tried to find a "mighty Warrior, even a Hero" to help them enter the Front Gates once they reach the Mountain, but unfortunately such were in short supply. In fact, Gandalf implies, heroes seem to be as legendary as dragons; in the end, however, both will turn out to be real.

Further evidence of Tolkien's careful preparation for Smaug lies in many more such foreshadowings, some obvious and some subtle, along the way. The dwarves' song performed in Beorn's longhouse about dragon smoke hanging over the mountain's bare, burned peak prepares us for Smaug's assault on the mountain once the intruders have been discovered.

The talk of the raft-men on the river adds more ominous overtones to the personality of Smaug as they idly speculate that maybe the dragon is the cause of earthquakes felt recently. Clearly the dragon may be gone from their daily lives, but he's not forgotten. The dragon's roaring approach when he eventually sweeps down upon Lake-town is anticipated in Tolkien's description of the calm length of Long Lake, where all that disturbs the quiet of the evening is the sound of the lake's high waterfall "like a distant roar." Smaug's final rampage is further foreshadowed in the way news of the King under the Mountain "spread from the doors of the hall like fire through all the town."

You will remember the sense of silent watchfulness Tolkien created as Mablung approached the front gates of Nargothrond, stumbling over the broken battle site, expecting the dragon at any moment. Anticipation of Smaug increases in a very similar scene wherein Thorin's company passes through the Desolation of the Dragon. They find plenty of evidence for the dragon's presence all about them, especially the smoke and steam trickling from the Front Gate. It's tantalizing evidence that the mountain still houses a live dragon and moves us from the realm of legend and hearsay into current physical reality. If the dwarves and hobbit had hoped to find the lair abandoned, their worst fears about the adventure must now be confronted. Again, the ongoing theme of courage surfaces.

In a very clever use of POV, Tolkien brings anticipation of Smaug to a climax by delaying the actual physical encounter with the sleeping dragon through an abrupt viewpoint shift right before the moment of contact. This is extremely effective, both in intensifying the suspense and in expanding the reader's mental picture of what is happening. We come down the tunnel in Bilbo's POV, feeling the heat and his trickling sweat, hearing the dragon's rumblings, and seeing the growing red light getting steadily closer.

Then abruptly, Tolkien stops the scene. Bilbo halts just short of the entrance to the dragon's lair, where neither he nor the reader can see what lies in wait. Once his terror is under control, he steps forward and Tolkien immediately shifts to the omniscient narrator's POV looking externally at Bilbo and telling the reader what to imagine. The narration also shifts from the "invisible" past-tense style to present tense ("you can picture him coming to the end of the tunnel ... through it peeps the hobbit's little head"). As soon as Bilbo's eyes adjust to the dark of the lair, Tolkien shifts to a cinematic POV that shows us the vast panorama of Smaug atop his treasure pile, surrounded by the massed wealth in the dim recesses behind him. Bilbo's breath is taken away by the scene, and so is ours.

It's generally agreed that Tolkien was a master of the high, formal style in narration and dialogue, but in *The Hobbit* he demonstrates a wonderful ear for other types of dialect and speech patterns as well. In Bilbo's second trip to the hoard, we are given the famous dialogue-with-the-dragon episode. In developing this famous scene between Smaug and Bilbo, Tolkien took his model, Fáfnir's deathbed discussions with Sigurd, much further. This scene is about the most fun you can have with a dragon without losing your skin (actually, Bilbo did get scorched on his head and heels as a result of becoming too cheeky with the beast).

Bilbo and Smaug are both clever, but in different ways, and they both manage to trick the other into revealing important information. They also both succumb to overconfidence, with potentially disastrous results. Tolkien deliciously unfolds the confrontation of the cold, wily, superhuman intelligence of the reptile mind with the timid, not-so-worldly thought processes of a once-sedentary bucolic hobbit. You wouldn't expect Bilbo to be much of a match for Smaug, who appears to have control of the situation for most of the exchange, but as Gandalf cautioned the dwarves, one should not underestimate hobbits in general and Bilbo in particular.

Practically every literary critic who has discussed Smaug has pointed out the varying levels of tone and diction that characterize Smaug's spoken interaction with the hobbit. Shippey describes it as reflecting both the "aggressive politeness of the British upper class" and the dragon's base animal nature. Gloriana St. Clair labeled it "worldly but wicked" with an urbanity complemented by a wide emotional range. In fact, you could say that Smaug's dialogue with Bilbo is the single most important vehicle for revealing Smaug's character.

Bilbo's verbal duel with Smaug shows the hobbit phrasing his speech to match his idea of how one should speak to a dragon, based on the dragon folklore he's learned through story and song. The result is a rather comical mixture of grandiose epithets and elevated syntax, laced with obsequious flattery. We've already seen him do this with Thorin, both to express his exasperation and to mock the egotistical dwarf's self-importance ("O Thorin Thrain's son Oakenshield, may your beard grow ever longer,' he said crossly"). The inflated phrases and epithets are not normal to Bilbo's speech pattern, which is actually quite mundane, so a great deal of humor is injected into the situation by hearing the normally plain-spoken hobbit utter such phrases. In the above example, awkwardly placing "Thrain's son" between the two parts of Thorin's name instead of at the end sounds comical, but also suggests he does it deliberately to show his displeasure.

By contrast, Smaug's initial repartee is peppered with contractions and colloquialisms such as "skulking," "Don't talk to me!" and "or I'm a lizard," which is not all high and mighty sounding. In fact, it's so natural and chatty that it lulls Bilbo into a false security that nearly gets him crisped. The menace lurking behind every turn of phrase uttered by Smaug keeps Bilbo slightly off balance, as he attempts to engage in seemingly casual conversation. Adding to the wry sense of fun, when Smaug says "O Barrel-rider!" he's actually mocking Bilbo's use of inflated diction. You can almost see them keeping tally as each maneuvers the dialogue in order to score points and gain advantage.

Bilbo gets carried away with his riddling talk and accidentally reveals that he's not alone ("Ha! Ha! You admit the 'us'," laughed Smaug). Smaug scores more points by undermining Bilbo's confidence in his companions, and he does it using Bilbo's practical, accountant's diction: "But what about delivery? What about cartage? What about armed guard and tolls?" If the reader remembers Bilbo's objections at the beginning of the expedition, this exchange is very funny. Tolkien even says that Smaug laughs out loud at his own joke. But Bilbo wins the bout in the end because his clever flattery causes Smaug to display his entire underside where Bilbo notices an unprotected spot over the left breast. This knowledge, communicated to Bard, the hero waiting in the wings, will bring down the dragon.

I should also mention that Smaug's terrible temper contributes to his undoing. His blind rage incited by the hoard-lust causes him to become reckless and heedless of his own safety. Tolkien seems to have tried out this idea in another, earlier story, *Roverandom,* written to console his five-year-old son Michael for the loss of a toy dog on the beach. The White Dragon, disturbed by Roverandom, prefigures Smaug's explosion from his den and pursuit of his enemies in a complete blind rage. The White Dragon is "enormously bad" and often "in a tantrum," spouting "real red and green flames" (when Smaug perches on the mountaintop he also spouts green and red flames). Smaug's rampage over Lake-town, diving and swooping in repeated passes over the town, flaming as he flies ever lower, recalls the White Dragon's swooping, relentless pursuit of Roverandom, whose "tail was singed by the dragon's breath."

The White Dragon's roar of rage is also a vivid precursor of Smaug's death scream. The narrator describes the force of the White Dragon's bellow, from which "mountains rocked and echoed... avalanches tumbled down, and waterfalls stood still"; similarly, Smaug's death-roar "deafened men, felled trees and split stone."

Smaug's spectacular death scene also shows his descent into total primal bestiality, a terrifying sight. As the blood-lust takes over, he sheds all traces of his former clever urbanity with which he entranced the hobbit. The closer he circles to his death, the more bestial he becomes. It's not difficult to see this as a metaphor for the devastating way in which the hoard curse takes over, robbing its owner of his senses and ultimately his life.

The imagery and similes associated with Smaug provide a wonderfully rich dimension to his character. Some depend on sound allusions: his snoring sounds like "a large pot galloping on the fire" or a "gigantic tom-cat purring." The sound of his great wings beating is more than once likened to the "noise like a roaring wind." Other similes are visual. On the hoard, his wings are folded around his body like "an immeasurable bat." He awakens like "an old volcano," and his speeding approach toward Lake-town appears in the sky "as a spark of fire." As mentioned before, Smaug's death scene is drama on a grand scale, and Tolkien's gift for vivid description is at its best in action scenes such as this.

In Conclusion

If you look over the roster in Tolkien's stable of dragons, you won't find anything but scaly villains. Some, such as Ancalagon the Black and Scatha the Worm, are mere sketches of Middle-earth menace, but they hold true to the evil worm archetype established in medieval Western literature. The two dragons having no connection to Middle-earth, the White Dragon and Chrysophylax from *Farmer Giles of Ham*, make a few interesting departures from the classic mold. The White Dragon is a draconic magician who occasionally paints the moon red instead of guarding a treasure, and Chrysophylax, who does have a hoard, is a reluctant fighter who would rather snack on an occasional parson and snooze peacefully in his lair. In his comical interactions with humans, he's a parody of the archetype that might easily be found lurking in a Terry Pratchett novel. But both are still wicked worms with testy tempers.

Glaurung and Smaug are by far Tolkien's two best characterizations of the Western dragon archetype – as evil as they come, with chilling intelligence and terrifying beastly inclinations. Through vivid imagery, imaginative dialogue, and skillful handing of point of view, Tolkien successfully created two of the most memorable dragon villains in early fantasy fiction.

Many fictional dragons have followed them, but you'd be hard put to find any worm better than Tolkien's Smaug.

Notes

UT – Unfinished Tales
SIL – The Silmarillion

1. Documentation of Tolkien's dragon sources is to be found in the works of scholars such as Jonathan Evans (especially his essays in *Tolkien's Literary Resonances* and the *Journal of the Fantastic in the Arts*), Tom Shippey (start with the "sources" chapter in *The Road to Middle-earth*), Michael Drout (*Beowulf and the Critics*), and Douglas Anderson (*Tales Before Tolkien*).

2. I'm using the Penguin Classics translation by Jesse L. Byock. This is a highly readable translation that doesn't lose the flavor of the epic style.

3. It's common knowledge that early in his career Tolkien worked on the *Oxford English Dictionary* (OED), researching and writing entries. It had never occurred to me that this might have been influential on his style (or perhaps merely brought his natural style more into flower) until I read Green's article, "Tolkien's Dictionary Poetics: The Influence of the OED's Defining Style on Tolkien's Fiction" in the 1992 *Proceedings of the J.R.R. Tolkien Centenary Conference*. Great food for thought!

4. A fascinating look at Gandalf's larger motivation for arranging the expedition to the Lonely Mountain can be found in *Unfinished Tales*, edited by Christopher Tolkien. In the tale of "The Quest of Erebor," Gandalf reveals that it's the very great danger Smaug poses if used by the Necromancer in Dol Guldur that really concerns him, not Thorin's desire to recover Thrór's lost kingdom and treasure. Gandalf says that of most importance is to find some way to neutralize Smaug. Gandalf states what Smaug repeats – the dragon has never smelled hobbits before. Thus Bilbo might not alert him to danger the way a pack of dwarves would. Clearly then, Gandalf adopts Sigurd's and Túrin's method when he asserts, "My plan is one of stealth. *Stealth*."

Chapter 3

Anne McCaffrey
The Pern Phenomenon

"RATHER WONDERFUL to have an intelligent partner that loves you unconditionally. Who wouldn't like a forty-foot telepathic dragon as their best friend?"

Anne McCaffrey's rhetorical interview question is easily answered by anyone who reads and enjoys speculative fiction. And as her comment implies, her dragons aren't anything like the reptilian villains of Tolkien's Middle-earth. They are about as far away from that model as you can get.

I refer to McCaffrey's work as speculative fiction rather than specifically fantasy or science fiction for several reasons. Although her Pernese dragons are clearly science-based (biogenetically engineered by colonists from Earth to combat a planet-wide menace known as Thread), they closely resemble the fire-breathing creature known to every reader who ever cracked open a fantasy novel. Further, although they are not magical and cast no spells on unsuspecting victims, they do have what humans regard as paranormal abilities: telepathy, teleportation, and telekinesis. The result is a unique blend of the fantastic and the scientific. Recognizing this, the *New York Times Book Review* has said of McCaffrey, "Few are better at mixing elements of high fantasy and hard science fiction in a narrative that disarms skepticism by its open embrace of the joys of wish fulfillment."

According to McCaffrey herself in a *Writers Review* interview, "...it's having a 40-foot fire-breathing telepathic teleporting dragon for your best friend that provides the indefinable thing called 'magic'." Writer Philip Martin, whose definition of speculative fiction encompasses both fantasy and science fiction, observes that fantasy "easily gives birth to dragons." In McCaffrey's world, so does science.

The setting on Pern also blurs the lines between fantasy and science fiction. Although the full-size dragons encountered in all the novels have been developed through highly specialized scientific techniques, the devolved civilization in which we first encounter Pern's dragons is medieval and agrarian in look and feel. The Pern that hatches Ramoth, Mnementh, Canth, Ruth, Orlith, Golanth, and many more contains minimal technologies and no modern science until the Artificial Intelligence Voice Address System (AIVAS) computer is discovered several millennia after colonization. In order to develop adequately the emotional and physical partnership between dragons and their human partners, McCaffrey decided "a planet with very little technology suited my needs."

Thus, although the dragons are the product of modern science, their riders are distinctly drawn from the adventure fantasy mold. Philip Martin's *Writer's Guide to Fantasy Literature* describes adventure fantasy as having "quick-thinking, fairly violent, sometimes amoral, adventurous heroes" who follow a moral code while keeping "the endless forces of chaos at bay." While clearly fitting the requirements of science fiction, the Pern dragonrider tales retain the shimmer of adventure fantasy about them as well.

Creating a New Model

A unique aspect of McCaffrey's dragons is that they are gentle giants whose frightening, fire-breathing exterior houses a very placid, loving personality that would rather eat, sleep, and make love instead of war. In this respect, she turns the Western dragon model inside out. This was a very deliberate decision, as she has explained in many interviews: dragons have "always been regarded as evil creatures in Western cultures and I felt that they'd received a rather bad press. So I thought of using dragons on my planet, coupled with human partners. Then I thought how wonderful it would be if a person was never alone, if they had a 'partner' for life, who loved them unconditionally."[1]

Not just props in the scenery, McCaffrey's dragons are very complex "critters" (her term of endearment). She puts this realization into the mouth of Masterharper Robinton, who wonders in the opening of *Dragonquest*, "And how did a man signify the dragons of Pern? No theme was grand enough for those huge, winged beasts, as gentle as they were great ... to link, mind to mind in an unbreakable bond that transcended speech! What was that really like?" Like her top geneticist, the oriental Kitti Ping, McCaffrey creates her dragons from a blend of Eastern emotional benevolence and Western physiognomy in order to have creatures powerful enough to endure the rigors of fighting Thread yet zen enough to serve as the equivalent of soul mates for their imprinted humans. She puts this concept into the mouths of several different characters from *Dragonsdawn*. Colony zoologist Pol Nietro's musings on the anatomy of newly discovered fire-lizards reveal the author's thinking about general dragon design:

> "The really strange coincidence is that our storytellers so often invented a four-legged, two-winged creature in fantasy, although none ever existed on Earth. Here they are hundreds of light-years away from the people who only imagined them... And not as badly designed as the ancient Chinese dragons." (DD, 102)

In the initial proposal for genetically altering the fire-lizards, it's McCaffrey's oriental scientist Kit Ping Yung who states the unusual Eastern/Western prototype that she intends to produce: "Yes, size, strength, and considerable intelligence would be required... And dedication, which is easy to instill in some creatures, impossible in others. The dragonets already possess the traits you wish to enhance and magnify." It's her unhurried Buddha-like approach to creating the critical genetic alterations that results in success ("One does not irresponsibly change the nature and purpose of any creature. As it was said, the person of intellect is careful in the differentiation of things, so that each finds its place.").

ANNE McCAFFREY

The three most important enhancements of dragonet traits were (1) empathic abilities strengthened by the drug metasynth, which ensured instant impression and telepathic rapport with a suitably matched human (unfortunately, this modification greatly reduced the dragon's memory to very short-term); (2) in addition to size, body modifications that would allow them to launch easily carrying a rider, which meant large-muscled back legs and tail, larger shoulder muscles where their wings connected to the back, and shorter front legs that were closer to arms with hand-shaped taloned paws; and (3) sturdiness and stamina to teleport safely through the freezing cold of *between* to distant places and times. Over the two thousand years of Pern's dragon evolution, these signature traits turned out to be the crucial enhancements that allowed dragons, teamed with the Earth colonists' computer, to save their world.

It's clear that Kitti Ping's calm and thoughtful nature is reflected in the personalities of the dragons she eventually creates. For example, in *Dragonflight*, bronze Mnementh dissuades his angry rider F'lar from taking a hasty and probably ill-advised action by laying out the situation and its consequences logically. To his credit, the human gives in to the dragon's advice, realizing that "Mnementh's judgment was more reliable than his at the moment."

Although McCaffrey's dragons illustrate her knowledge of the Western and Eastern models, her early inspirations came from more humble origins than the sagas of the Icelanders or the teachings of Lao-Tzu. Of more importance to her development of Pern and the dragons that define it was (1) the popular fiction to which she was exposed as a voracious young reader and (2) her love of animals, especially cats and horses.

As a child, her parents read Kipling's *Just So Stories* and the poetry of Kipling and Longfellow to her; also available to her were popular fantasy-adventure novels of the 1930s, '40s, and '50s, which included material such as A. Tappan Wright's mammoth novel *Islandia* and the prolific work of A. Merritt (in particular, *The Ship of Ishtar*), Edgar Rice Burroughs, as well as short "what if" fiction in magazines such as *Science Fiction Plus, Amazing Stories, Galaxy Science Fiction Magazine, Astounding Science Fiction* (now *Analog*), and *Science Fiction Stories*. Publication of her novella "Weyr Search" in the

1967 volume of *Analog* launched Pern's dragons on their long trajectory toward best-selling status.

An animal lover who grew up with various family cats and dogs (she describes herself as "good with animals"), McCaffrey added horses to her list of must-haves as a result of riding lessons taken during her pre-teens; the experience cemented her desire to own a horse. As an adult, the first horse she purchased was Mr. Ed, a dapple-gray hunter, and the first step toward Dragonhold Stables, now a thriving business connected to her estate in Ireland, was irrevocably taken.

Although McCaffrey has been quick to emphasize that dragons are not horses, some equine trace elements have made their way into her basic dragon model. As she explained to her eighth grade interviewers, "Horses are such elegant, regal beasts (although some can be quite daft, most unlike dragons), and breathtaking to watch when in full flight, that I wanted to draw from my experiences of them when describing my dragons." The close association with such large animals – especially breeding, riding, and showing of horses – contributed greatly to her eye for animal anatomy and sensitivity to their various physical needs.

In addition to horses, cats entered the mix in the form of the diminutive fire-lizards, who owe their literary conception to McCaffrey's lifelong love for felines. They are about the size of a large housecat and exhibit occasional catlike behaviors, including curling up to sleep with their paws over their faces, shoulder-sitting with their tail around the neck of their imprinted human, and an enjoyment of human contact, i.e., being petted and stroked. In *Dragonsdawn*, Bay Harkenon's bonding with the little gold queen Mariah easily resembles someone cuddling a well-fed cat. Lying along her forearm, "its hind legs dangled by her elbow, and its tail was lightly twined around her upper arm. A slight noise, similar to a snore, could be discerned. Bay stroked the sleeping creature from time to time, amazed by the texture of its skin, by the strong but delicate claws."

Creating an environment and a history within which both fire-lizards and dragons could exist for over 2500 years (turns, in Pernese terminology) required a level of world-building that Jody Lynn Nye describes as "richly textured and convincingly three-dimensional." Nye's *Dragonlover's Guide to*

Pern charts McCaffrey's created world in amazing detail, especially the science of Pernese dragons and their ancestors, the fire-lizards (dragonets). As the *Guide* demonstrates, knowledge of Pern is distributed in the stories through both science and folklore, depending on where in the Pern timeline each story falls.

This is especially effective when those two approaches intrude on each other (such a moment occurs, for example, when the present-day Pernese discover the ancient scientists' large-scale diagram of dragon DNA – a triple helix design they can't understand). A similar moment occurs when the newly discovered AIVAS computer speaks to the current inhabitants of Pern. Masterharper Robinton's remark concerning their current civilization's loss of science and technology such that "it's been reduced to myth and legend in many cases" frames the Pern history so that it comes full circle.

Fantasy-adventure writer John Marco remarks in a 1999 interview that world-building is an extremely important aspect of speculative fiction and that "many authors take a long time in creating their worlds and bringing them to life." Anne McCaffrey has been building the world of Pern for over thirty years, and her dragons have become extremely well defined, with the most well-known of them having very distinct personalities. Such a long history of writing about Pern (eighteen volumes at the time of this book) has allowed McCaffrey to build a considerable archive of lore on her dragons and their riders, which she frequently uses to add dimension to their characterization. For example, in the opening chapter of *Dragonflight*, F'lar's disapproval of the untidy High Reaches Hold makes reference to "obser-vance of the ancient Laws" and to such rituals as Search, Impression, removal of greenery from stonework, and tithing to support the single dragonweyr.

This framing folklore is embodied in the role of Harpers as archivists and transmitters of the society's knowledge through the so-called Teaching Ballads, snippets of which open each chapter and section of *Dragonflight*. Two in particular are repeated several times throughout the novel for emphasis.

"From the Weyr and from the Bowl,
Bronze and brown and blue and green,

Rise the dragonmen of Pern,
Aloft, on wing, seen, then unseen."

"Drummer, beat, and piper, blow,
Harper, strike, and soldier, go.
Free the flame and sear the grasses
Till the dawning Red Star passes." (DF, 5, 8, *passim*)

These verses reveal the most basic tenets of dragonkind on the planet called Pern: fighting dragons occur in four colors, inhabit weyrs, are ridden by men in formations, disappear through teleportation, are called to the defense by Harpers, and fight a planetary scourge by burning it with fiery breath in the sky and on the ground.

For some, such as Weyrleader F'lar, the ballads give literal guidance and should be obeyed accordingly; for others, they are merely ancient superstitions and old adages that can safely be ignored. The consequence of such ignorance sets up the tension between dragonriders and ordinary folk, which drives the basic Pern plot through eighteen novels and counting. It also serves as the vehicle for one of McCaffrey's most ardently expressed themes, the constant collision of science with superstition, of innovation with tradition. Ultimately, her dragons – adapted from native fire-lizards so the colonists can survive – must radically adapt in order to survive after Thread is permanently removed.

McCaffrey also plants puzzles in the folklore that are actually crucial plot points, as occurs in the 400-year-old ballad known as the Question Song rediscovered by Masterharper Robinton. While numerous interpretations of the ballad's verses are possible, Pern's survival rides on the one correct reading of the cryptic words: "Gone away, gone ahead,/ Echoes away, die unanswered./ Empty, open, dusty, dead,/ Why have all the Weyrfolk fled?" As readers later discover, these lines are actually instructions from the Masterharper of four centuries back on how to solve the current problem of too few dragons fighting the reappearance of Thread in the current setting – a clever use of time travel to reestablish the importance of dragons and weyrs to the planet's survival in Pern year 2505.

As mentioned above, this continually growing body of dragon folklore has been gathered and documented meticulously in *The Dragonlover's Guide to Pern*. The chapter "From Dragonets to Dragons" is the most relevant for a study of McCaffrey's dragons, for here you can find the specific alterations made by geneticist Kitti Ping (altering the original three-toed paw to a five-clawed structure more suitable for grasping, for example), along with detailed illustrations of the skeletal structure and musculature of dragons in relation to their tiny ancestors. It also graphically demonstrates the depth and breadth of McCaffrey's Pern, which began with her simple question, "What if dragons were the good guys?"

What began as an intense day's work on a new story idea in 1966 mushroomed into a world with a history spanning several millennia. Pern's society begins at a highly scientific-technological level, devolves to near-medieval standards, and then escalates to a new level of technology tempered by its previous non-scientific age. This new stage is the result of melding old and new; according to Nye, the AIVAS computer "determined that only the presence of dragons and fire lizards made it possible" to remove the scourge of Thread permanently from Pern's skies. The possibilities for plot and character development within such a world are vast, and McCaffrey has taken full advantage of this world-building role by filling in Pern's history with novels that dip in and out of the established timeline. It's a fully realized world that readers can believe in and want to spend time immersed in. Even the author admitted in a 1997 AOL Book Report interview, "I want to go to Pern as much as everyone else."

McCaffrey has said that she developed the world of Pern and its signature species (dragons) "by thinking HARD about it" – working out the details of what the dragons were and why they existed ("a renewable air force against some unknown menace"). She also drew maps of the world they inhabited and consulted experts from the fields of medicine, biology, and the hard sciences such as physics and astronomy. As Robin Roberts points out in her critical study of the science fiction framework for the Pern novels, readers are frequently reminded of the scientific basis for all the elements that would normally constitute fantasy. For example, "dragons are carefully described and their fire-breathing carefully explained as a result of their chewing a certain type of stone, firestone, so that dragons actually belch, rather than breathe fire." The scientific framework is further enhanced by the characters' gradual discoveries (and rediscoveries) of their technological heritage.

An important challenge for McCaffrey, once she'd decided to make the dragons lovable, was the question of how to establish their physical presence. How much of the traditional dragon image could be retained and what new elements needed to be incorporated into the design that would produce something of mammoth size and power, but with a love for humans rather than a desire to eat them? Such attributes as jagged scales that leak flames or poisonous breath that kills all who inhale it would not make it into the mix. When McCaffrey's first Dragonrider novels were published, her Pernese dragons were unique to the literature and established a pattern for the dragon as noble beast that many have followed since. It's interesting to see which elements of the typical Western dragon have been retained and which Eastern traits have been blended in as well. Providing the glue for these attributes was her love of animals in general and horses, cats, and dolphins in particular. For example, regardless of their tremendous size and power, her dragons love to be touched by their humans, especially to be scratched over their eye ridges and other itchy spots, just like cats or dogs begging to be petted.

The starting point, as she has Kitti Ping explain, was to derive them from a native species that had the basic body shape and personality potential already in place. Thus, regarding personality, the cat-sized dragonets (fire-lizards) discovered by Earth colonists have a temperament that makes them good pets and household guardians against livestock predators. The fact that they imprint on the first creature that feeds them upon hatching sets up the later development of empathic bond between dragon and rider so crucial to their role as planetary protectors.

Regarding their physical features, dragonets were discovered to be warm-blooded oviparous mammals, not reptiles. In terms of acceptance, it's hard to imagine wanting to cuddle a cold-blooded reptile, but relating to a warm-blooded creature that feels good to the touch is not difficult for most readers to imagine. McCaffrey makes the dragonets soft and sensual to the touch, not scaly or slimy. Their multifaceted eyes are large and beautiful, in order to serve as an indicator of mood. They are also the means by which humans easily become attached to them – looking into their eyes initiates feelings of love and mutual acceptance. Once again, McCaffrey has taken a wicked dragon trait (their gaze casts spells over their victims) and turned it upside down. She does, however, make use of the archetypal dragon's reputation for keen eyesight: "Dragons could adjust the focus of their eyes to either great distances or close inspection."

Wingsecond F'nor's discovery of the newly hatched queen dragonet on the Southern beach in *Dragonquest* provides the link between legend and science, between Harper dragonlore and the reality of knowledge from the Ancients, as the Earth colonists were dimly remembered. His realization that he can communicate mentally to the dragonet as well as witnessing her abrupt disappearance through teleportation (going *between*) gives readers solid evidence for the origin of dragons on Pern – what F'nor suspects, we instantly realize must be true. Through his astonished response to his dragon Canth ("Those legends *are* true. You were bred from something as small as her!"), depth is immediately added to our understanding of Pernese dragons and, by extension, civilization on Pern on a larger scale. Dragons roughly the size of a jet aircraft and possessed of human-type intelligence aren't simply the result of natural evolution – they are the direct result of tampering, which is evidence of advanced technology long lost to the current population of Pern.

With this realization, F'nor is able to apply what he knows from bonding with enhanced dragonkind to this new situation. He handles properly the dragonet he has inadvertently Impressed:

> "Little beauty, come where we can admire you. We mean you no harm."
> …Then the little lizard hovered at F'nor's eye level, just beyond his reach. He ignored Canth's amusement that the tiny one was susceptible to flattery." (DQ, 271)

Inverting yet another standard dragon trait, the vulnerability to flattery, in the above example McCaffrey has made it the means by which the tiny dragonet can be coaxed to accept a loving human touch.

Another inversion applies to the dragonet's ability to spit flame. Observed by the bioengineers from Earth, this ability is the primary trait that fuels their desire to make a bigger version of the creatures; basically, their intention is to create a giant blowtorch on wings that can attack Thread in the sky. Instead of a tool for incinerating knights and other adversaries, flaming becomes the means by which Pernese dragons protect humankind. It's their weapon against the forces of chaos rather than an implement of evil.

As mentioned earlier, the element of wish fulfillment gives McCaffrey's dragons their patina of fantasy. Beyond the basic fact of their physical presence wearing the form of a creature of myth, the trio of paranormal attributes (telepathy, teleportation, and telekinesis) adds to the aura of magic. When a creature vanishes suddenly before your very eyes in a true fantasy novel, magic or sorcery is usually the culprit.

The same is true if objects are made to disappear or move seemingly by unseen hands (think broomsticks in the tale of the sorcerer's apprentice). The ability to control another's mind through spell-casting has long been a staple of fantasy. In McCaffrey's world, although the dragonriders take these attributes for granted as a fact of nature, the thrill of bonding and dragonriding remains throughout their 2,500-year history. In this way, McCaffrey manages to make her dragons both believable and awe-inspiring in a non-magical setting. This will become even more apparent when we look at some of her individual dragons.

Other unique characteristics of Pernese dragons include their unusual chemistry. Their blood is copper-based, which produces the standard colors (gold, bronze, green, blue) depending, according to Nye, on the "amounts of nickel, cobalt, and iron in their makeup." Their skeletons are based on boron rather than calcium, creating a lightweight, flexible frame conducive to flight, even for a creature as large as Ramoth, Pern's largest queen (nearly 40 meters long).

Their second stomach is where chewed-up phosphine ore mixes with stomach acids to produce the gas that ignites on contact with the air, allowing them to belch fire. The fact that their dragonfire is manufactured and not a mythical mysterious ability allows McCaffrey to use an Eastern dragon element – love of and frequent immersion in water. Unlike Smaug, who fears the lake water that could quench his internal fires, Pernese dragons crave water and must be provided with sufficient bathing to preserve the health of their silky skins, which tend toward flakiness and itching as they grow.

The basic dragon personality that makes them "the good guys" is their non-territorial, non-judgmental, and somewhat literal view of life in the weyr among hundreds of other dragons and humans. They feel protective toward humans; the instinct for fighting Thread acquired from their fire-lizard ancestors has become their unquestioned role in life because it removes a threat to Pern's human population. Naturally forthright and caring of other life forms, dragons aren't wired toward deceit. In fact, they become distressed when their humans behave in ways that are unkind or dishonor-able. In *Dragonquest*, Weyrwoman Kylara's gold queen Prideth chides her mistress for mishandling a clutch of rare fire-lizard eggs ("Prideth told her that she wasn't happy that she had transported the clutch to death on a cold, alien hearth." DQ, 308). Prideth exhibits further stress as her Weyrwoman's bad behavior continues to disrupt the functioning of the weyr.

Normally placid and non-aggressive, McCaffrey's dragons don't fight among each other, with one exception – queens in heat will attack one another over their bronze suitors if left in proximity to each other. Kylara's Prideth provides a sad example: neglected by her rider, both she and a competing queen claw each other to shreds, then drag each other *between* to their deaths, leaving both riders stunned with physical pain and emotional loss. In the bigger picture of Pernese culture, the wrongful death of dragons is considered by all weyrfolk as the greatest of tragedies, sending the emphatic message of humankind's duty of care and respect toward other species and the necessity of working together for the common good above one's individual agenda.

Arguably, the most famous characteristic of McCaffrey's dragons is the ritual of Impression. Upon hatching, the baby dragon seeks the perfect match for itself among the humans presented for Impression. Once the proper candidate has been found, the dragon's mind makes itself known to its paired human, announcing its name and emanating feelings of complete love and intimacy. Engineered to be trusting and supportive of their human counterpart, dragons complete the human soul in ways that seem magical despite the fact that their empathic powers have been enhanced to this degree by highly advanced science.

There is also a dark side to Impression. The bond between dragon and rider is so strong that life without the other is intolerable. Thus when the rider dies, the dragon goes into the nothingness of *between* never to return (in essence, commits suicide), even though its natural lifespan could have been much longer. When the dragon dies first (usually accidentally), the human rider's urge is to die as well. Riders who don't commit suicide are likely to lead lives that to them seem hollow and empty. Occasionally a rider such as Lytol manages to get past that stage and pursue a productive life for himself. But even in the life-affirming roles he achieves, the sorrow over his lost companion clings to him like a shroud.

Taking all the characteristics of dragonets and magnifying them to the point where you have a beast a hundred times larger in size and sentient to the point of understanding humans sometimes better than they do themselves, but from a completely benevolent viewpoint, makes for an incomparable creature. The love and reverence so many readers express for McCaffrey's dragons demonstrate the success of her creative imagination in replacing the Western dragon stereotype with something completely different. The real challenge, once she had worked out the blueprint for her dragons, was to use it to create memorable characters. McCaffrey's Pern series includes over 200 named dragons, of which about two dozen have plot significance. I'll focus on four of the most memorable – Mnementh, Ramoth, Ruth, and Golanth – to demonstrate how she brought them to life.

Applying the Blueprint

Not an elegant stylist (although there are moments of beauty and poetry, which I'll discuss below), McCaffrey has been taken to task by critics for her romance/adventure/space-opera style of writing, which bothers her not a whit. She is well aware of her niche and proud of it: "I'm a storyteller, not a literary writer," she remarked in a 1996 interview for *Albedo* magazine. McCaffrey's writing is at its most awkward when rendering the actions and motivations of her human characters, who "snort" and "chuckle" their way through every chapter of every book, banging their fists on tables or open palms in true pulp fiction style. Likewise, her tendency to overstate the obvious hasn't disappeared from her style in over thirty years of writing novels.

Interestingly, however, her dragons rarely descend to such banalities. The moment her narration shifts to dragon-mode, her diction lifts as well. Consider this passage early in *Dragonflight*, describing Lessa's first sight of the Benden Weyr dragons.

"From behind the cliff above glided a dragon, its enormous wings spread to their fullest as he caught the morning updraft. Turning effortlessly, he descended. A second, a third, a full wing of dragons followed in soundless flight and patterned descent, graceful and awesome." (DF, 26)

The power and beauty of dragons is easily captured through this brief passage of descriptive narration from the POV of a character on the ground seeing them swoop in overhead.

To be fair, her later novels have fewer of the hackneyed phrases that cause critics to salivate and more of what makes elegant writing a joy to read. McCaffrey's own thoughts on the writing process bear this out: "Writing is never 'easy,' but you gain fluency in vocabulary and wisdom about grammar over the years of 'doing' … the hardest part is being *sure* you have the exact word that describes what you require."[2] Her true gift lies in her concept of "story," of telling a ripping good yarn with memorable characters and settings that sweep readers along on dragonback to great vistas and events. In a 1999 interview, she stated, "I become the character for as long as I'm seeing the scene through his or her eyes." It's not difficult to see that the dragons connect directly to her heartstrings, because some of her best writing and most literary passages are those centering on the minds and personalities of her great defenders of Pern.

This connection to her draconic muse is evident in the imagery used to describe the beauty of Pernese dragons. Although McCaffrey writes mostly in an unadorned storytelling style that relies heavily on dialogue, her best use of imagery, particularly similes and an occasional metaphor, is reserved for the dragons' most outstanding feature, their large faceted eyes. Consistently described in jewel-related terms throughout her novels, the dragons' eyes "sparkle," "gleam," or "flash" in the light and shine "in rainbows." Similes make vivid use of the gem imagery: their eyes gleam like "sunstruck opals" and "winking green-fired jewels" or appear in firelight "glistening like jewels."

Poetic use of metaphor presents dragon eyes as "watery jewels" seen through the thin inner eyelid when the dragon is bathing or as "opalescent pools of fire" when aroused. The image of opal is an apt simile for the dragons' eyes, which change color across the facets depending on their moods, from the blue/green of tranquility and well-being, the lavender of stress, to red/orange for arousal or anger. The gleaming dragon's eye appears in a reverse simile that describes vineflower blossoms as "glowing in the first beams of sunlight like dragon eyes."

In keeping with the science-based framework of Pern, the dragon's audible voice is pure animal noise made up of bellows, trills, croons, warbles, roars, and screeches. The intelligent conversation in perfect grammar exchanged between dragon and human is only heard in the mind, not by the ear. McCaffrey's use of metallic and musical imagery works as well to establish the dragon's call, relating it to the copper-based chemistry of their blood that produces their shining, sometimes metallic appearance. Dragons utter "fluting" noises when happy or trying to comfort their riders, but also "trumpet," "peal," and "bugle" with "brass voices," and "scream" and "shrill" when under stress, conjuring images of the brass section of an orchestra gone mad. In an effective use of metaphor, when Ramoth leaps into the air for her mating flight, the narrator says the males' answering calls are "brass thunder in the air."

With this level of detail to draw from, McCaffrey is able to make the non-human characters much more believable and interesting. As with human characters, she incorporates little touches that make each dragon an individual, often drawing the ideas from things going on around her. "While art may not imitate life, life was a major influence in Anne's art," her son Todd McCaffrey explains in his memoir of life with the "Dragonlady of

Pern." For example, her love of horseback riding and her gift of psychic ability (which she refers to as "the sight") had an obvious influence on the model for her telepathic dragons and their daring riders. Other influences are less obvious, and as she explains, can come from anywhere: "I've met a LOT of people – often displaying eccentricities which I can incorporate into new characters. Those little traits make characters seem real." The same is true of her most famous dragons, which display individual personalities in spite of their empathic bonding with specific human characters.

THE WISDOM OF BRONZE MNEMENTH. Mnementh is the first dragon we meet in the world of Pern. Unlike Tolkien's Smaug, who receives a lengthy buildup through hearsay and legend over a dozen chapters before we ever meet him in the scaly flesh, bronze Mnementh pops out of nowhere into the skies over High Reaches Hold a few pages into the first chapter of *Dragonflight*, first novel of the Pern series. Mnementh and his rider F'lar (with a "wing" of eleven other riders) take us by surprise, just as they do the ordinary folk of the hold. In this way, the dragons are introduced as powerful, mysterious, and awe-inspiring before we really know anything about them. It's through our introduction to Mnementh in these opening pages that McCaffrey establishes the ground rules for dragon/human interaction.

Bronze Mnementh is, as Pern fans all know, Wingleader F'lar's great male dragon companion. As you might expect, physically he is the most impressive bronze of Pern's dragons since he is the only consort of Ramoth, Pern's greatest golden queen. Mentally and emotionally, he exhibits the qualities of calm, wisdom, humor, and just plain good sense, all qualities that his rider must grow into as Weyrleader. He frequently advises F'lar in the right course of action for a given situation, and is not above expressing his disapproval of F'lar's hot-headed decisions. Occasionally he may even take action on his own initiative, something rare for dragonkind who normally only think in terms of the here-and-now, and not future consequences.

Mnementh is of unusual intelligence, a trait remarked upon more than once by F'lar and his mate, Weyrwoman Lessa. He and some of his offspring with Ramoth demonstrate that dragon intelligence has grown over the centuries. In fact, it has developed far beyond that of the original hatchlings created by the colonists. The limited memory and present-time thinking of the original dragons has shifted to a growing ability to plan, see consequences based on past events, and think ahead; it's most pronounced in dragons such as Mnementh, Ramoth, and Ruth.

Mnementh's colossal size in comparison to his rider is revealed in the first sentence when we're told that the rider is astride his "great neck." He must also furl his wings tightly in order to make room for other dragons landing near him in the courtyard of the hold. The perception of size is further enhanced by the fact that he must kneel in a crouch for his rider to dismount by stepping onto a foreleg. The immense size of his head is demonstrated when he must arch his neck and rest his chin on the ground in order for his standing rider to be at eye level with him. The dragon's head is clearly five to six feet in length.

In these first few pages we are also given the contrast between holders and dragonriders, a theme that runs throughout all the Pern novels. Through the omniscient narrator, we are given F'lar's thoughts regarding both the holders' fearful response to the dragons ("F'lar could not explain to the dragon the politics behind the necessity of inspiring awe in the holders") and the dragon's bemused opinion of said behavior ("The dragons could never understand why they generated such abject fear in common folk"). This statement establishes our sympathy with the dragons, which never willingly harm humans, and gives the impression it's the humans who are obtuse.

Authors deal with dragon speech in varying ways, depending on the level of fantasy established by the story. In McCaffrey's case, because her dragons are not innately magical and do have scientific reality, communication conventions must remain believable. Possibly drawing on her own stated experience of psychic phenomena, she establishes telepathy as the way in which her dragons can speak to their riders. As McCaffrey explains in the *Albedo* interview, "The whole point of the book is this marvelous telepathic communication between rider and dragon. So they speak intelligent English." This phenomenon is rendered in print in two ways: the narrator summarizes what is "heard" in the rider's mind when the dragon sends thoughts to him or her ("Mnementh informed F'lar that he had seen her…"), or the dragon's direct mental speech is printed in italics. The dragonrider's direct mental responses to the dragons are also given in italics.

> *A dragon knows what to do*, Ramoth calmly informed Lessa.
> *You could have told me*, Lessa wailed… (DF, 1320

When we first meet Mnementh, we get a hint of dragon telepathy when he rumbles in response to some plans F'lar has been considering. We're told second hand by the omniscient narrator what he thinks or what he's said to F'lar, but we don't actually hear it. At first it's all reported third-person, so the dragon's mind is kept somewhat at a distance from us. Both methods are used to indicate the dragon's mood and state of mind. Mnementh's comments are varyingly critical, encouraging, wistful, concerned, cautious, and self-satisfied, which indicates a high degree of self-awareness ("Mnementh was enormously pleased with himself and swiveled his head down for his eye ridges to be scratched").

One of Mnementh's signature personality traits is his sense of humor (he's not above making his own dry jokes and even winking like humans). He also makes rumblings that F'lar hears in his own mind as the dragon equivalent of laughter. The Weyrleader frequently receives amused yet genuine advice on his love life from Mnementh, who regrets the man's ineptitude in dealing with Lessa his weyrmate, causing F'lar to comment that "Mnementh is full of advice these days."

Mnementh on occasion takes the initiative when he knows intuitively what course of action should be followed. For example, it's the dragon and not his rider, newly installed Weyrleader F'lar, who makes the decision to end Ramoth and Lessa's rebellious first flight: "*And she is no Jora*, Mnementh reminded him pungently. *I'm calling them in*, the dragon added. *Ramoth has turned a dull orange.*" In *Dragonquest*, even F'lar is sometimes taken aback at the firmness with which his dragon makes decisions on his rider's behalf. For example, Mnementh demonstrates once again to F'lar how a leader should comport himself:

"You must be calm and cool, Mnementh said, doubling his rider's astonishment. *You must command at this meeting...*

F'lar knew that no admonitions could change Mnementh's mind when he used that firm tone. He wondered at the great beast's unexpected initiative. But the bronze dragon was right." (DQ, 224)

Thus Mnementh proves time and again that he is the perfect companion for Pern's most powerful Weyrleader, serving as mentor, advisor, critic, and comforter as his human grows in leadership. When we encounter F'lar in his sixties, in *The Skies of Pern*, still the firm leader, Mnementh reflects the same position of senior leadership. The narrator tells us that Mnementh "took a keen interest in the subtle tuition of any bronzes hatched on Benden sands," indicating that the Weyrleader's dragon had been instilling in the minds of his hatchlings that "dragons will always be needed on Pern."

THE COURAGE OF RAMOTH THE GOLDEN. Golden Ramoth, senior queen of all the Pern weyrs, is one of McCaffrey's most well-developed dragon characters. Over the course of the many novels in the series, we can observe her stages of life, from feisty youngster to regal matriarch to imperious dowager. *"Ramoth is grumpy,* Ruth said, his tone suddenly wary" when the great queen arrives at the AIVAS computer facility in *All the Weyrs of Pern;* further in the same book Ruth observes of Ramoth, *"She likes to boss me.."* She also embodies one of McCaffrey's most important themes, challenging old, hidebound traditions and modes of thought, especially concerning the role of females in society.

In what is possibly one of the most famous and widely quoted passages from the Pern books, we first meet Ramoth, the main female dragon who begins the Pern series, when she hatches from the egg: "...Lessa stood caressing the head of the most wonderful creature of all Pern, fully prescient of troubles and glories, but most immediately aware that Lessa of Pern was Weyrwoman to Ramoth the Golden for now and forever." Impressed by Lessa, McCaffrey's signature plucky heroine, Ramoth emerges with a similarly defiant sense of self. Her initial cheeky mind-speech to Lessa is given as third-person narrator reporting ("Ramoth replied: Why shouldn't she know her own name since it was hers and no one else's?"). After she has settled into her new home in the queen's weyr, we begin to hear her actual voice in italics.

As befits her role as senior queen of the only active weyr in the first of the Pern books, Ramoth's physical presence dominates the setting and strikes ordinary holders with fear and awe, weyrfolk with respect and admiration, and her weyrmates Lessa and F'lar with undying love and passionate commitment. In the eyes of young Drum Apprentice Piemur, attending his first Hatching at Benden Weyr, Ramoth is the image of dragon power: "... he'd never have ascribed maternal emotions to Benden's preeminent queen dragon. Certainly Ramoth with her yellow flashing eyes and restless foot-shifting, wing-rustling, was a far picture from the gentle concern female herdbeasts or runners showed their offspring." Ramoth grows to become the largest dragon ever hatched on Pern, half a wingspan larger than the largest bronze male, Mnementh. At 45 meters long, she's nearly the size of a 747 jetliner.

Although her first flights off the cliffside down to the feeding grounds are ungainly and awkward, she soon becomes the epitome of a healthy, vital dragon – her extremely beautiful appearance, expressive eyes, and glistening gold color are frequently commented upon by everyone from the lowest cavern worker to the heads of holds, weyrs, and crafthalls. Thus, she becomes the most critical element in repopulating the dangerously low dragon population that exists when the tale of Pern's fight for survival against Threadfall opens. As hoped, her mating flights with Mnementh produce large clutches of eggs, with several queens in each batch that can be spread among the rest of the weyrs.

Ramoth's nature is complex. She is by turns girlish and a bit of a flirt (playing the coquette with Mnementh and his rider F'lar in her early days before mating), proud and cheeky (continually interrupting her rider's thoughts with tart comments of her own), demanding and a bit whiny as she continually complains that she's dying of hunger or her itchy skin needs bathing and oiling. There are occasional flashes of irony in her wheedling, as she can appear simultaneously childish and supremely self-aware.

Her pride (encouraged by her rider's complete adoration of her greatness) is at times endearing in its naiveté (as a growing youngster, she dominates the feeding ground with the unapologetic observation that "she was queen and had priority"), but can also be selfish. She dominates the weyr as senior queen – for example, "her full-throated brassy bugle" echoes throughout the weyr as she informs all the dragons of Threadfall, and she oversees the initial flight of the runt Ruth, keeping him on a short leash and commanding him to land after one short circle of the courtyard.

McCaffrey allows Ramoth to change over the years, however, and the great dragon's domineering pride gives way as the queen learns some humility from a lowly green (the dragon type lowest on the pecking order). Having led the courageous rescue of Golanth (which I'll discuss in detail below), Ramoth's natural instinct is to crow over her exploit (*"But it was I who timed it to save Golanth from that last feline. Only I could have done that."*). Uncharacteristically, she follows this with a chagrined admission that *"today I learned something from a green dragon… I have told the others what Zaranth showed me how to do, how she pushed felines away,"* referring to a newly discovered draconic skill, telekinesis. As if amazed by her own admission, hours later Ramoth is still pondering the fact that *"I had not thought to learn from a green dragon. I have."*

As Ramoth matures and establishes herself as senior queen, one of the defining traits by which all know her is her temper, which no one wants to get on the wrong side of. This aspect of her personality lies dormant until she goes into her first heat, which changes her from a sweet, flirtatious youngster into a teeth-baring, flesh-ripping demon. Some readers have quipped that after her first mating flight, Ramoth stomps around in a perpetual state of PMS, which is an exaggeration, but it does give you an idea of how she rules the weyr.

Ramoth's temper (fanned to flames by Lessa's own fury) becomes a serious issue when "Oldtimers" from another weyr steal a queen egg from one of her clutches. Both Ramoth's and Lessa's bloodlust for revenge against Southern Weyr nearly precipitates the horrible taboo of dragon fighting against dragon. The unexpected return of the egg cools her wrath, but ever afterward Ramoth guards her eggs with such red-eyed fury that she barely allows Impression candidates to approach them at hatching. Lessa must remind her forcefully to back away and allow Impression to take place.

She seems to have Lessa's malicious sense of humor coupled with shrewd resourcefulness. More than once she initiates prankish behavior that gets them both in trouble with trainers trying to teach them how to behave. For example, her hasty jump without proper visualization during lessons on flying *between* causes even the normally unflappable Mnementh to display exasperated fury. This particular episode also sets up the fact that as a dragon/human pair, Ramoth and Lessa are as brave as they are headstrong, leaping into the unknown with a trust that they will be able to protect each other in any situation.

This combination of courage and seeming foolhardiness is what's required for them to make the terrifying decision to jump back four hundred years to the time when all the weyrs were populated with Thread-fighting dragon troops. But once they've made the jump safely, an even greater challenge for Ramoth and Lessa is to convince the "Oldtime" weyrs to come to the aid of the single depleted Benden Weyr by following the pair on the long jumps into the distant future. The fact that Ramoth and Lessa decide on their own to make the unprecedented trip with no assurances that once they get there anyone would come back with them further attests to their great courage and skills of persuasion.

Through many situations that reveal Ramoth's resilience and utter faith in her rider, McCaffrey has prepared her two heroines for this momentous act of bravery. So astonishing is the event in Pern's history that it becomes part of the legendary tales recited to AIVAS by the Harper Piemur; even the artificial intelligence seems impressed: "'A spectacularly brave and daring exploit, clearly of epic proportions despite the considerable risk she ran in losing both herself and the queen Ramoth. The results clearly justified the journey,' AIVAS stated. It was more praise than Piemur had expected."

Ramoth's rebellious nature is proud and headstrong, like that of her rider Lessa, but it's those very qualities that McCaffrey puts forward as enabling both of them to achieve greatness. Born into the only weyr on Pern at a time when the vitality of dragonkind is at its lowest ebb, Ramoth Impresses the one female human with the guts to take on years of tradition that limit the role of queen dragons and their riders. Lessa and Ramoth innately know that Weyrleader R'gul's teachings are antiquated and actually untrue.

His dogged insistence that queens should not fly except to mate and that they especially don't fly in Thread-fighting squads is just the fuel required to fire Ramoth and Lessa's desire to prove him wrong. Over the course of the Pern series, Ramoth proves that not only can she fly (further and higher than most males), she repopulates the failing weyrs and leads the "queen's wing" of female dragons during Threadfall. She is both feared and revered among dragonkind, who acknowledge her as the greatest of her species.

THE HEROISM OF WHITE RUTH THE UNDERDOG. As a small white dragon, Ruth is a sport (non-reproductive mutation) of the dragon species from the line of Ramoth and Mnementh. In size, he is a throwback to the first dragons that were not much bigger than a large horse. But in intelligence and independent thinking, he is light-years away from them. Ruth's uniqueness sets him up as both underdog and ultimate hero (one of McCaffrey's favorite themes).

Ruth and his rider Jaxom, orphaned lord-in-waiting of Ruatha Hold, are well matched – in Jaxom's words at Impression, "You want to get born. Just like me. All you need is a little help, same as me," uttered as he breaks the shell open for the tiny dragon, runt of the clutch. Jaxom's unexpected Impression of a runt who should have expired in the shell takes place near the end of *Dragonquest* and sets up *The White Dragon*, third book of the Dragonriders of Pern series. The larger issue of the unlikely hero appearing when least expected and when the times call for it is suggested through Jaxom's POV; he observes that life on Pern is out of balance:

> "Everything was going wrong on Pern. Dragon queens killing each other, Weyrleaders dueling in public, Thread falling here and there, with no rhyme or reason. Order had slipped away from life; the constants that made his routine were dissolving, and he was powerless to stop the inexorable slide." (DQ, 430)

Ruth's spurious Impression of the youngster Jaxom (who is neither weyrbred nor a candidate for Impression) seemingly adds to the complication (runts who can't open the shell are traditionally allowed to die), yet as he begins to thrive against all odds, we readers realize that his rescue by Jaxom was meant to be, on many levels. As we come to see, this underdog pair rises above everyone's expectations, fulfilling their destiny not once (in *The White Dragon*), but twice (in *All the Weyrs of Pern*).

In *How to Write Science Fiction & Fantasy*, Orson Scott Card discusses this layering of cause and effect through which "the characters – and the story – become richer, deeper, more complex, and potentially more truthful and insightful." If Jaxom hadn't sneaked onto the Hatching Ground with Felessan and touched Ruth's egg, hadn't impulsively helped the runt out of its shell, and hadn't moved the dragon into his quarters at Ruatha Hold away from the established weyrs, the means to avert disaster among dragonkind and ultimately accomplish AIVAS' plan to conquer Thread would not have been possible.

As the Weyrleaders try to sort out the consequences of Jaxom's Impression of Ruth, it's Ramoth who first states a kind of prophecy: "Ruth will prosper," causing Lessa to wonder "Did the dragons know something she didn't?" In *The White Dragon*, this aura of destiny is sensed by Jaxom ("He was moving in inexorable steps toward a predestined event and nothing could stop him now. So he mounted Ruth calmly, trusting as he had never done before in his dragon's abilities."), but also by the Harper Menolly ("When Jaxom influences what happens to Pern, then he becomes Harper business") and AIVAS, who confirms Ruth's uniqueness.

Ruth's physical traits immediately set him apart from other dragons. When full-grown, he is about half the size of a standard dragon and slightly larger than the largest of the original hatchings engineered by the colonists, a throwback to the original dragons. At twenty feet, Ruth is only slightly bigger than dragon males from the first clutches. Although small by Pern's current standards, Ruth is perfectly proportioned and properly muscled for flight; as Fort Weyrleader N'ton observes, "He may be small, Jaxom, but he's a fine-looking fellow!" This fact will play a very important part in Ruth's ability to carry out both of his heroic missions: the return of Ramoth's stolen egg so a dragon war is prevented, and teleportation onto the bridge of the ancient colony spaceship to begin preparation of AIVAS' plan to remove

Thread permanently from Pern. He also leads the wings of dragons needed to move the Red Star out of orbit.

N'ton also notes that Ruth isn't completely white – his coat is faintly dappled with all the possible dragon colors (green, blue, brown, bronze, and gold), again a reference to the original blueprint. Wild fire-lizards flock to him because he activates in them a shared ancestral memory of the first dragons and the colonists who were their riders. This is an important planted plot device, for the fire-lizards will give Ruth clues in finding both Ramoth's stolen egg and the long-lost plateau where the colonists made their first habitation and where the AIVAS computer lies hidden in buried ruins.

A drawback of his striking white coat is that it shows dirt easily, thus Ruth is fastidious, like a cat that continually cleans itself. He must have his daily bath and scrub, and when he kills food beasts, Jaxom is struck by the neat and tidy way in which he dispatches and devours the kill. His landing on the grass is "dainty." Everything about Ruth is compact and neat, which makes him the perfect choice in situations where larger dragons are not appropriate.

Ruth's personality in his early years is sweet and naïve, in a childlike literal-minded way. He states simply what he sees, in short sentences that go right to the heart of the matter. For example, on discovering the colony shuttlecraft buried under volcanic debris, Jaxom's urge is immediately to go inform his comrades and the Benden Weyrleaders. But Ruth's cheerful observation, *"They are asleep. Benden is asleep. We are the only ones awake in the world!"* allows him instead to stop and savor the moment, letting the immensity of his discovery sink in quietly. Ruth's simple yet accurate announcements tend to confound Jaxom who too often is prone to over-analyze and worry about decisions. On their first flight together, monitored by Ramoth, Jaxom worries that he will be too heavy for Ruth, who simply states, *"Flying you is no strain. It is what I want to do. She says we may fly a little farther every day. I like that idea."*

As Ruth matures, his speech pattern changes, such that he speaks in longer, more complex sentences that use humor and irony instead of simply reporting what is observable. In *All the Weyrs of Pern*, we hear him advising his rider *"You'd better not say that to Sharra* [Jaxom's wife]," when Jaxom remarks that life could use some excitement, a joke Ruth would never have conceived of expressing as a youngster. More than once, riders and holders mention Ruth's intelligence and unique ability to understand abstracts (especially his spatial and temporal navigation sense).

One aspect of the underdog theme McCaffrey frequently makes use of is one character helping another so that both can rise above their present downtrodden state. As a pair, Ruth and Jaxom combine their abilities to achieve greatness. Jaxom is characterized as a bit too cautious, taught by his guardian Lytol to be logical and think things through perhaps too much. However, his one act of impulse (stepping onto the Hatching Ground to rescue Ruth from the unbroken shell) changes his life. Ruth gives him confidence and the ability to finally stand up for himself against his detractors who treat him like a child and doubt his suitability to become Lord of Ruatha Hold.

Ruth is much less bothered by taunts about such things as his size or sexual immaturity or insults that he is an overgrown fire-lizard instead of a genuine dragon. Ruth is supremely comfortable with who and what he is, and he attempts to instill this innate self-awareness in his rider as well (*"I am a dragon. You are my rider. No man can change that. Be what you are. I am."*). When Jaxom finally confronts the bullies with conviction – "I am the Lord of this Hold … I am Ruth's rider. He is unmistakably a dragon." – he has learned his lesson well.

Chafing under the protective constraints imposed on himself and Ruth, Jaxom complains that neither has been allowed to become who they really are and take the risks necessary to discover their true strengths. Toward this end, Ruth's demonstration of his ability to chew firestone and make flame in the air allows him and his rider to achieve success in Thread-fighting because his smaller size allows a maneuverability the larger dragons don't have: *"We fought well and no Thread passed us,* Ruth said in a hopeful tone. *I was quite comfortable sustaining my flame … This is the most firestone I have ever chewed!"* Ruth's self-confidence and sense of accomplishment allow his rider to begin to feel the same.

What truly sets Ruth apart, however, is his greater than normal dragon intelligence, far beyond instinct and typical shortened memory. He always knows WHEN he is as well as WHERE he is when he jumps *between*, even without mental images and coordinates telepathed from his rider. This single gift allows him to accomplish both his extraordinary acts of heroism. The first act involves going back in time to find Ramoth's stolen egg hidden by its thieves in a location from the past, and then teleporting himself, his rider, and the egg into a small hidden recess of the Hatching Ground cavern where it must be returned unseen. By doing so, Ramoth's rage for revenge is cooled, and the horror of dragons killing each other in a firefight is avoided.

Ruth also shows an occasionally alarming tendency to make decisions on his own. He knows what's best for his rider and doesn't ask first when he decides to act, a trait that saves Jaxom's life when he becomes ill with a life-threatening fever. Ruth decides on his own that his rider is ill and summons the appropriate healer by mentally sending her a distress call. N'ton expresses his respect for Ruth's intelligence to Jaxom after the young man is able to get up:

> "You owe your life to Ruth, you know. F'nor says Ruth has more sense than most people. Half the dragons on Pern wouldn't have known what to do with their rider delirious; they would have been totally confused by the confusion in their riders' minds." (WD, 651)

It's evident that he thinks ahead like a human, demonstrated by his concern over the future of dragons. When Jaxom tells him that AIVAS' plan could eliminate Thread, Ruth voices what others have quietly been thinking: *"If it can, that means dragons won't be needed anymore, doesn't it?"* Such behavior leads Jaxom to realize just how unusual Ruth really is:

> "He was always being told that dragons had no ability to understand abstract concepts or complex relationships. Too often Ruth surprised him by remarks that cast doubt on the theory. Dragons, particularly Ruth in Jaxom's biased opinion, obviously perceived far more than others credited to them." (WD, 515)

In another example of initiative that shocks everyone who witnesses it, in *All the Weyrs of Pern*, Ruth teleports by himself from outside the computer complex up to the airless bridge of the colony spaceship *Yokohama*, with no instruction or command from his rider. He simply perceives the problem: AIVAS cannot explain to the less intelligent fire-lizard how to go there to activate the life-support system she has learned to do with a dummy control panel. Ruth realizes the solution (if he goes there, the fire-lizard can mentally follow him) and implements it: "*As you understand, so do I. Ruth's tone was almost accusatory. It is not really a very long way between but it is up far.* Although Jaxom leaped to his feet, shouting "No, Ruth, no!" he was too late."

Ruth's smaller size allows him to materialize on the bridge with just enough wing clearance. Once he is there, the fire-dragon easily follows him. The only explanation Jaxom can offer is "Ruth's got a mind of his own!" The humans are dumbstruck at the dragon's seeming irresponsibility, but they have to admit their problem is solved – neatly. As a result, AIVAS is able to depend on Ruth and Jaxom to perform a far more risky role in the plan to blow the Red Star out of its orbit. AIVAS dryly explains, "Jaxom is the most adept computer operator, and Ruth is the most courageous of the dragons."

THE TRAGEDY OF BRONZE GOLANTH. I mentioned near the beginning of this chapter that McCaffrey's style and tale-telling abilities have matured over the course of her career. The story of bronze Golanth and his rider F'lessan, Weyrwoman Lessa and Weyrleader F'lar's only son, well illustrates this shift toward more weighty material and an elevation of diction.

Consider what it would be like to have everything that defines you as a vital, active being (dragon or human) suddenly taken away in one brief horrific event. But rather than embracing death, you must live and deal with the loss, which means trying to figure out what is left for you to do with your life. This theme of dealing with a life-altering handicap has been touched on with the character of Lytol (who lost his dragon to an accident), but his loss is given mostly through second-hand reference. We don't live its tragedy fully, as we do that of Golanth and F'lessan. To grasp fully the depth of this sad tale from McCaffrey's 2001 *The Skies of Pern*, it's necessary to look briefly at McCaffrey's setup of F'lessan before he Impresses Golanth.

We are introduced to Felessan early in the Pern series, just before the episode of Jaxom's unexpected Impression of Ruth, detailed in *Dragonflight*.[3] A youngster at the time, it's Felessan's exploration among the unused cave tunnels of Benden Weyr that brings the boys to a secret spy hole just above the Hatching Ground sands. McCaffrey uses this scene to contrast the Weyrleader's unfettered son with the inhibited Jaxom, who as we know is overly cautious and obedient to authority. His younger pal Felessan is just the opposite.

We're given the impression of an adventurous, impish, exuberant, fearless personality who embraces life, especially its physical side. He's intelligent but not studious, and would rather be on dragonback than in a classroom. The fact that he shouldn't be wandering around in deserted tunnels or spying on Ramoth's precious clutch of eggs adds spice to the adventure from his point of view. It is typical of Jaxom to express a bookish curiosity over why there are so many empty corridors and how they were carved in the first place. Typically, as the omniscient narrators informs us, that "[c]learly the matter had never troubled Felessan." Like a dragon, his consciousness exists in the here and now. Older weyrfolk refer to him as "young scamp" and "wher-whelp." The dragon he Impresses, Golanth, matches him in all aspects.

When he impresses a bronze dragon at a young age, his parents are duly proud – we're told that among the anxious candidates he alone showed no fear or nervousness. Having grown up around dashing dragonriders and their equally impressive beasts, Felessan's future as a dragonman is easy to predict. Together, bronze Golanth and F'lessan ("his name after Impression) make a formidable pair, excelling at all aspects of dragonflight. Their prowess at fighting Thread and their exploits in all things daring and dragony become the stuff of legend among friends and younger riders, especially when F'lessan becomes Wingleader of the Benden Weyr riders. He's sociable and well-liked, a bit of a Don Juan (reflected in Golanth's taste for randy green dragons), but has no aspirations to succeed his father as Weyrleader. He and Golanth would rather go exploring over the wide continents of Pern, free from boring responsibilities and duties.

The narrator tells us "the son of F'lar and Lessa took nothing very seriously except his dragon, Golanth." Bronze Golanth is everything one would expect of the companion to F'lessan: large and powerful, capable of winging over stretches of the vast uncharted Southern continent for hours without tiring, proud of his physical strength and virility (*I'm big and strong*, he boasts to F'lessan, who has been thinking about their uncanny ability to avoid injury while fighting Thread). The fact that for all his suitability Golanth has not mated with a queen from any weyr reflects the fact that his rider refuses to settle down with any of the women with whom he has fathered children. He's also a bit of a clown. A standout example is the scene in which he makes a vile-smelling mush of some trundlebugs while attempting to learn green Zaranth's telekinetic ability. The scene is not there just for laughs, however; Zaranth's special skill is the only thing that will save Golanth's life when tragedy strikes.

It's during an exploring expedition in *All the Weyrs of Pern* that Golanth and F'lessan successfully locate the ancient settlement of Honshu, which sets the stage for the tragedy waiting to happen in the following book, *The Skies of Pern*. On this reconnaissance mission for promising weyr locations, Golanth and his rider are absent from class with AIVAS under false pretenses, in essence, skipping school. Typically they're doing what they love best, and Golanth's enjoyment of flying is so complete that F'lessan doesn't allow himself "unnecessary remorse" for flying high instead of attending a Hatching at Benden Weyr (where AIVAS understood he would be).

The totally carefree tone of this scene is in stark contrast to the fate that Golanth and his rider will endure when they pick Honshu as a suitable habitation for themselves and others like them. On this fateful scouting flight, McCaffrey specifically emphasizes two qualities of Golanth that he will lose in the feline attack at the lake just below Honshu: his masterful ability to fly and his acute eyesight. His joy of flight, climbing thermals and gliding high over peaks and valleys, is detailed here exuberant detail:

"Golanth began to stroke the air, beating upward. *Thermal*, he said cryptically, and F'lessan leaned down against the great bronze neck so as not to impede the ascent... Golanth flattened out and set his wings to glide on the hot air." (AWP, 249)

Several times in this joyous flight F'lessan comments on Golanth's extremely acute eyesight, praising his ability to see far in the distance, and ultimately to pick out the anomalous shapes of ancient buildings hidden under vegetation far below them. He wonders, as do we, what it would be like to have such great faceted eyes – "*I can see anything you wish…*" Golanth responds. We are told further that the dragon's sharp eyesight locates the cliffside entrance to Honshu. F'lessan's suggestion that large "felines" (vicious lion-sized mutations left behind by the colonists) might wander the property provides the final setup for the event that robs Golanth of his glory. Golanth asserts, "*No feline would challenge me!*" Sadly, this will not hold true.

What makes the attack of the feline pack on Golanth and F'lessan so wrenching is that disaster strikes not during an event such as a hunt where you'd expect physical danger and injury, but rather during an unguarded moment of peace and tranquility. The attack itself occurs through Golanth and F'lessan's careless sense of security as they doze on the riverbank under the stars with their chosen mates. McCaffrey's sense of the dramatic is used to excellent effect here and produces some of her most powerful writing. As the atmosphere of contentment shifts suddenly to terror and pain, readers are catapulted from an idyll into a death struggle. McCaffrey's taut, vivid prose describes the struggle from a cinematic point of view, such that the reader watches with held breath as the struggle unfolds over several pages:

> "Spotted, striped, and tawny hides, assaulting him from three directions, abruptly covered the bronze. He reared to his full height, front legs clawing the air to remove the one that had sunk teeth in his left eye ridge. He tried to whip free of the one on his tail ... to buck against the others racing in from the thick shrubs that bordered the river. Feline jaws clamped harder, determined to retain their hold." (SP, 358)

> "Trapped on one side by the terrace, Golanth had no way to unfurl his right wing. With his rider in peril, he would not go *between* where he could have shed the felines in the great black cold ... One feline was attempting to shred Golanth's left inner wing sail and others, sinking talons deeply into tough dragon hide, climbed all over him." (SP, 359)

If you've read McCaffrey's short story titled "The Impression," which details F'lessan's Impression of Golanth, its loving description of his perfect "transparent sails" makes the above passage all the more disturbing. Just as it looks as though all is lost, McCaffrey makes use of the dragon talent of telekinesis, planted earlier, to dispatch the attackers. Thus the skill AIVAS predicted emerges during extreme need: Ramoth and other dragons who come to the rescue discover their own ability, flinging felines away from the victims without actually touching them.

Golanth and F'lessan survive the assault severely damaged, the extent of which is brought home to readers through the POV of F'lessan's new weyrmate. In her anguished appraisal, Golanth "seemed smaller somehow, diminished by the absence of his characteristic vitality: like rider, like dragon. She pushed that thought away." Just how much of their former brilliance has been lost is not evident until the two are healed enough to get up and move around; then the full scope of their individual losses becomes apparent. Golanth is blind in one eye and will never fly again; likewise, his rider will be lame for the rest of his life. Given what we know about these two, their gradual realization of what these losses will mean to them in the future becomes the stuff of tragedy.

A dragon that can't fly cannot mate; likewise, a dragonrider whose dragon can't fly cannot be Wingleader. A dragonman whose mobility is severely limited is only half the leader he needs to be, as F'lessan realizes with a shock: "A dragon must be in the air to 'fly' his mate. He could not suppress his anguish at that realization. Hard enough to lose his right to lead, but to lose the ecstasy, too?" The narrator's observation that "[b]eing Wingleader suited F'lessan's blithe personality" now rings hollow.

One is led to wonder what was going on in McCaffrey's own life at the time this story was written. When she wrote the novel *The Ship Who Sang*, it was because she "wondered how a handicapped person could live a useful and meaningful life." In 2001, McCaffrey was confronting those issues in her personal life as well. In a 1996 interview, she mentioned arthritis in all her joints curtailing her ability to travel, and by 1999 she had endured replacement of both her right knee and hip. The joint in Golanth's damaged wing heals in such a way that he can't open it fully, preventing full flight. We know from Todd McCaffrey's biography of his mother and from her interview admission that "there's no doubt that what's happening in the world around me creeps into what I'm writing"

McCaffrey's career-long interest in victims who become survivors receives its best expression in the story of Golanth and F'lessan. To regain some control over their lives, they must rely on others to help them fly, literally and figuratively. Golanth's mate Zaranth lifts him into the air through telekinesis; he can't fly under his own power but he can glide down to the water with his rider for a somewhat ungainly landing. Once fiercely independent, F'lessan must now limp about with a cane and allow others to catch him when he falters. But by the end of the novel, he is able to look beyond this handicap to the challenge of restoring Honshu to, ironically, a seat of learning, something he would never have imagined himself doing. Golanth and F'lessan find hope for their future in science and technology, especially useful for dragonriders in post-Thread society.

The important message in all this is that rather than giving in to despair and choosing suicide, the pair accepts help from others and begins to learn ways to make a different life together. For Golanth, sadly, that new life no longer means being a handsome bronze dragon in prime condition with an admired Wingleader for a rider. Regarding this compelling theme, McCaffrey has said, "People, and the daily struggles they overcome, inspire me to write," and she knows that struggle firsthand. Wheelchair-bound these days, McCaffrey still manages to travel, attend conventions in a specially designed three-wheeled motorized cart, and surround herself with the horses she once rode. It's no great stretch to say that F'lessan and Golanth mirror McCaffrey's own experience.

In Conclusion

In the final analysis, what do dragons represent for her? Most obviously, the love and respect for animals and the need for compassion and empathy for others, of any species. The joy such loving partnerships offer elevates humans above their petty squabbles and ambitions; love does indeed transcend all in McCaffrey's novels. On a larger scale, the dragon/human society demonstrates the way in which working together toward common goals succeeds much better than isolated, single efforts.

In a recent review of *Dragonquest* for The Reading Nook, Conan Tigard encapsulates all this quite well: "Once again, Anne McCaffrey proves that no one else can touch her when writing a story about humans and dragons living in harmony. The world of Pern that she created in the late 1960's is one of the most fascinating landscapes for a fantasy story ever created…. McCaffrey shows how all people are dependent upon all others to survive in a trying time."

Notes

AWP – All the Weyrs of Pern
DDn – *Dragonsdawn*
DDs – *Dragon Drums*
DF – *Dragonflight*
DQ – *Dragonquest*
SP – *The Skies of Pern*
WD – *The White Dragon*

1. This particular interview, consisting of e-mails from eighth graders at Thomas Jefferson Middle School in Garfield, New Jersey, has some of McCaffrey's most candid answers to the frequently asked questions that show up in most interviews.

2. This 1999 Internet interview for *Corridors of Communication* catches McCaffrey in an introspective mood, with some revealing comments on style, character, POV, and her own literary legacy.

3. McCaffrey herself suggests reading her books in the order in which they are written rather than in Pern history timeline order as some readers are inclined to do.

Chapter 4

Terry Pratchett
Funny Side Up

"ON THE DISCWORLD we know There Be Dragons Everywhere. They might not all have scales and forked tongues, but they Be Here all right, grinning and jostling and trying to sell you souvenirs."

Thus spake Terry Pratchett in the 1989 Introduction to the reprint of his first Discworld novel, *The Color of Magic*. When a satirist such as Pratchett trains his sights on something as big and mythically imposing as a dragon, you know you're in for a wild ride. In Pratchett's world that could mean a trek to Valhalla, with a side trip to the moon and other outlandish ports of call. Just about anything is possible in the Discworld multiverse, and, of course, There Be some side-splitting dragon escapades.

As discussed in Chapter 10, as early as 1898 the dragonslayer motif took a right-angle turn into comedy with Kenneth Graham's *The Reluctant Dragon*. Since then, dragons have been used for comic effect by all sorts of writers, and perhaps none better than Pratchett. But simply to say that his dragon creations are comic doesn't go nearly far enough.

What Kind of Fiction Is It?

Ask Terry Pratchett what kind of fiction he writes and he'll simply say that it's fantasy. But we aren't going to let him off that easily – the more appropriate question is, what kind of fantasy is this Discworld cosmos? More specifically, what kind of humor does he write so dependably, book after book: parody, farce, lampoon, biting social commentary? Is he a satirist, humorist, master of the sub-sub genre now referred to as comic fantasy? In interviews, he claims to prefer the term "resonances" rather than parodies. In a 1999 interview, he explained that "none of the books is a parody in the sense that, say, *Bored of the Rings* was a parody of *The Lord of the Rings*. I prefer the term 'resonance.' Put Discworld people in, say, a movie-making setting and they'll resonate with every Hollywood cliché that ever was." Perhaps that makes him the Resonator.

I remember hearing a radio interview with Pratchett several years ago in which he admitted having parodied (resonated?) most of the fantasy genre's well-known writers somewhere along the Discworld timeline. In terms of dragons, that clearly must include "Dragonlady" Anne McCaffrey, and indeed it does, as we'll see. Le Guin and Tolkien come in for their share of good-humored roughing up as well, not to mention those great icons of science and invention, Isaac Newton and Leonardo da Vinci. Many sources of inspiration are tossed in the blender of a Pratchett opus. "I look upon the parody structure as a vehicle for other things," says Pratchett. Science and fantasy fall in step on Discworld without missing a beat, all the while treading continually on each other's toes. Poking fun at fantasy conventions and assumptions – for example, the physics of dragonflight – is a Pratchett staple.

Rather than a simple one-to-one send-up of a single topic or object of amusement, Pratchett-style humor is a complex and wide-ranging though skewed vision of human society. According to Pratchett, "a lot of Discworld humor – in fact the basis of Discworld humour – is not 'wacky thinking' but entirely logical thinking … Discworld deals with the world as perceived," what people think they know about the world. Much of the fun resonates with the "huge body of movies/fiction/folklore" that makes up our cultural knowledge base. As you can tell from the chapters in Part 2 of this book, the received knowledge base concerning dragons is quite large, and Pratchett mines it as well as anyone, to great comic effect.

The fantasy lexicon on dragonlore is also full of some of the most recognizable clichés in the genre, and Pratchett takes full advantage of the grist from that mill. You can find most of these clichés catalogued in Diana Wynne Jones' truly funny *Tough Guide to Fantasyland* ("[Dragons] are always very old. Most of them seem to have flown to Fantasyland aeons ago across the void."). Even Pratchett, the master satirist himself, can be discovered among the entries. See her entry on "Alleys" and you will immediately recognize Ankh-Morpork, the greatest and vilest city of Discworld, as well as the "Invisible College," which brings to mind Pratchett's Unseen University, which is itself a humorous take on all magical institutions of higher learning (Le Guin's wizard school on Roke, which refused to enroll a female shape-shifting dragon, comes to mind). There will be, of course, more on dragons invading the grounds of wizarding schools when we get to the chapter on J. K. Rowling.

To discuss Pratchett's dragons (and to get at the heart of his skill as a writer), we need to apply a few definitions from Chapter 1, specifically parody, satire, farce, and irony – what Mary Ann Rishel calls "the rich variety of humor."[1] In most humorous fiction, a basically simple or linear storyline is torqued and twisted through many complications; in comic fantasy, the possibilities are even greater. Comedy thrives on opposites and reversals, on the unexpected turnaround that puts the reader off-balance in a non-tragic way. Probably the first things readers detect when reading a Pratchett novel are the obvious jokes and parodies, but there is much more to Pratchett's comic technique than that.

The important question is, is it funny even if you don't know the inside joke or recognize the specific comic references? For humor really to be effective, you must have contrast between the light and the dark – that is, the degree to which the funny stuff is peppered with serious moments gives you a means by which to measure the depth of the humor. You can't just depend on a string of pratfalls and non-stop one-liners to create true comedy; if you do, you don't have a story, you have a standup comedy routine. "In any case, there's got to be more to a book than that," Pratchett tells his interviewers.

Pratchett's ability to weave a complex storyline involving three-dimensional characters that readers bond with enough to care if they get crisped by dragon fire puts him at the top of the comic fantasy heap.

As The Wyrm Turns

Discworld dragons come in two flavors, *Draco nobilis* (true dragons), ridden by dragon lords, and their much lesser cousins, the diminutive swamp dragons that most people treat as pets or nuisances.[2] Exactly how these two strains are related is open to debate, but they share the basic attributes of flying and flaming. From that point on, they are quite different. Fundamentally, the difference between swamp dragons and noble dragons is that one is the "exploding sort" and the other is the "killing people kind."

Dragons are introduced in Pratchett's Discworld fiction in the first novel of the series, *The Color of Magic*, specifically in Chapter 3, "The Lure of the Wyrm." They are more fully developed in a later novel, *Guards! Guards!*, but our first meeting with them early on establishes them as creatures of both parody and burlesque – parody specifically of Anne McCaffrey's Pernese dragons (with spicy dashes of Tolkien and Le Guin for good measure) and burlesque of the high fantasy style in general. Before exploring the parody of Pern, it's worth taking a quick look at some general examples from *The Color of Magic* to see how Pratchett's comic fantasy technique is both subtle as a whisper and blatant as a pie in the face.

Pratchett has the comic technique of playful incongruity (or humorous contrast, if you prefer) nailed. Playful incongruity occurs when something contradicts the expected, especially as a turnaround at the end of a line. For example, as the city of Ankh-Morpork goes up in flames, the aristocrats "on the far bank were bravely responding to the situation by feverishly demolishing the bridges." This technique also shows up in individual phrases: the city is "blazing merrily," and its "merry burning" is seen for miles.

Throughout the novel you will find examples where a passage of mostly concrete imagery ends in one great abstraction, usually capitalized for added comic effect. In the Prologue, we are given the cosmic setup for Discworld in a style that begins with a call to attention, echoing Tolkien's saga-style "Lo!"

"See …

Great A'Tuin the turtle comes, swimming slowly through the interstellar gulf, hydrogen frost on his ponderous limbs, his huge and ancient shell pocked with meteor craters. Through sea-sized eyes that are crusted with rheum and asteroid dust He stares fixedly at the Destination." (CM, 1)

Pratchett is also a master of the ironic reversal: "… on the disc, the Gods are not so much worshipped as blamed." This inversion of expectations, in which characters as well as the narrator may lead you in one direction while implying another, occurs continuously in any given Pratchett novel. It gets a workout in this first outing of Discworld dragons, where their entire existence depends on a discrepancy between appearance and reality – if you have the Power (not merely *power*) to visualize a dragon, you can make it real, but not really. If the magic-wielding dragonrider who conjures up such a beast happens to lose his or her focus, *poof!* – the dragon (which may be your airborne vehicle) is gone.

Shifting focus is another comic technique Pratchett uses to keep the reader off balance and chuckling. At the end of a particularly vivid description of the consequences of defying the gods, the inept wizard Rincewind asks, "Got any food?" We immediately deduce from this that no matter how dire the consequences, the wizard's immediate concerns are never far from his stomach.

Another way to manipulate comic focus is through incongruous metaphor and simile. In stating that the great fire and ensuing flood that levels Ankh-Morpork did not "mark its end," Pratchett carries this idea further in a series of outrageous metaphors that play on the word "mark": "Rather it was a fiery punctuation mark, a coal-like comma, or salamander semicolon, in a continuing story." Such witty wordplay perfectly suits the dialogue of the wry and cunning Patrician, lord of Ankh-Morpork. Responding to a blatant lie from Rincewind, the Patrician says, "Indeed? Then if I were you I'd sue my face for slander."

This punning wordplay is laced throughout the Discworld tales, not only in dialogue, but in character concept as well. A good example is the character Twoflower. He's the Discworld's first tourist; but besides that, he's a walking disaster of clumsiness. Thus he is literally an "accidental tourist" – the first bumbling thing he does is burn down the oldest, largest, most important city on Discworld. It's this glib facility with words that makes Pratchett's treatment of both McCaffrey's invented world of Pern and her particular writing style a clever parody on the intellectual level as well as a hilariously broad farce.

In the realm of satire, one of Pratchett's most formidable tools is the use of opposites, in which contrast in achieved through layered exaggeration and overstatement (what Rishel calls "topping the joke") or understatement (the equivalent of deadpan delivery on paper). A good example is the description of the two Ankh-Morpork beggars whose names are the opposite of their behaviors. Blind Hugh watches with keen vision the tourist Twoflower's display of gold coins and sends Cripple Wa "scurrying off" to set up an ambush of the rich stranger.

Even Pratchett can't resist the old theme of the magic fading away. Tolkien used it to bittersweet effect; it forms the basic premise and plot of Larry Niven's 1989 novel *The Magic Fades Away*. In the "Wyrmberg" chapter of *The Color of Magic*, the magic literally fades away out from under the dragonriders because these dragons are imaginary. Before explaining the nature of magic on Discworld as we contemplate the awesome spectacle of the Wyrmberg (spoofing McCaffrey's dragon weyrs located in volcanic calderas), the narrator informs us, "The magic never dies. It merely fades away." Adding to the humor, however, is the ongoing analogy of magic to radioactive fallout, so that after the disastrous Mage Wars the residual magic releases "decayed myriads of sub-astral particles" causing a distortion of reality around all sites that took direct hits.

This fact has a direct bearing on Discworld's *Draco nobilis*, the so-called "true" dragons, as opposed to swamp dragons which are considered vulgar, illegitimate. Unlike McCaffrey's dragons, which are completely real and non-magical, Discworld's noble dragons are total figments of the imagination – literally. They are conjured up and given substance by their dragonriders, as well as the highly imaginative Twoflower, inside the intense magical field surrounding the Wyrmberg cone (invert the image of a volcano, and you have it).

In his spoof of Pern, Pratchett approaches the parody on several levels, giving us both specific and general swipes at the original. Parody involves imitating and riffing on characters, plot, dialogue, exposition, and diction of the original work, with some elements kept the same and others exaggerated, changed, or caricatured. Part of the fun comes in seeing how the stylistic conventions of the original work are reworked into something wickedly similar but telling in its difference. For example, Pratchett copies the convention of contracting Pernese dragonrider names (F'lar, F'nor, etc.), but he does it with a different punctuation mark stuck at random into the name, suggesting an interesting but unpronounceable glottal stop (Lio!rt, K!sdra).

In defining literary parody, Jerome Stern advises that it "requires great skill as a stylist, otherwise it falls flat or is just too obvious to be funny," the correspondences becoming mechanical rather than inventive. "Once readers get the joke, the parody has to stay interesting" – the imitation of style has to be imaginative and as original as, well, the original. Pratchett's skill as a satirist and savvy wordsmith lets him succeed on all fronts, and one of the ways he keeps the parody fresh is to spice it up with infusions from other sources in addition to the main one being parodied. In the lengthy "Wyrmberg" section, we follow the exploits of Liessa Dragonlady, ("Dragonlady" being one of McCaffrey's nicknames), who strides and snorts and tosses her mane of wild hair like her Pern counterpart. As a dragon lord's daughter, she rides the gold dragon Laolith (a male version of Ramoth) in a society of dragonriders immersed in a leadership succession problem (a typical Pern occurrence), but also worked into the story are jokes, caricatures, and parallels from Middle-earth, Earthsea, and other fantasy locales.

Psepha, an aggressive bronze dragon belonging to dragonrider K!sdra, reminds us of bronze Mnementh of Pern, whose name is similar in its use of a "silent" consonant at the beginning. Psepha gives Rincewind his first ride on dragonback at K!sdra's command in a very funny reversal situation where it's debatable who has captured whom. In a hilarious parody of the Black Sword Gurthang from Tolkien's *Silmarillion*, Rincewind at one point finds himself bossed around by Kring, Hrun the Barbarian's magical Black

Sword made from a thunderbolt that has a mind of its own and a cheeky attitude toward cowards. The fact that Rincewind would rather run away than rescue his companions creates a very humorous situation in which the sword takes possession of him, making the quaking wizard force K!sdra at sword point to fly him directly back to the dragon stronghold of Wyrmberg – exactly the last place Rincewind wants to be.

Pratchett keeps McCaffrey's convention of telepathic dragon speech rendered in italics, but he also uses it for exposition, given in the present tense. The effect is absurd and funny. Inside the hollow core of the Wyrmberg, dragons hang upside down from hooks like giant bats (of course Pratchett doesn't fail to point out the patina of dragon poop on the cavern floor, similar to guano that carpets bat caves). The cavern's ceiling is dotted with hooks "huge as rainbows, rusty as blood. From them ... *The dragons sense Liessa's presence. Air swishes around the cavern as eighty-eight pairs of wings unfold ... Moving with the easy gliding movement that is second nature Liessa sets off toward her own dragon, Laolith, who turns his great horsey head toward her. His jowls are greasy with pork fat.*" This misuse of McCaffrey's dragon-speech convention combined with Pratchett's ability to create similes so incongruous they inspire outright guffaws, capped with one of his trademark reversals in tone at the end of a line, introduces the Wyrmberg dragons. The mock-heroic diction of this passage that degenerates with the last sentence is mildly amusing in and of itself, but for readers familiar with Pern and McCaffrey's writing style in general the humor is greatly magnified.

The third Wyrmberg dragon we meet is Ninereeds, created from Twoflower's vivid imagination and named ironically for the plodding master accountant who was "everything that dragons were not." The passage in which Twoflower accidentally creates Ninereeds is packed with comic references to Le Guin, Tolkien, McCaffrey, and any number of novels with standard Western dragons. Twoflower's temporary inability to think because his mind is "awash with dragons" reminds us of Arren's confused state in Le Guin's *The Farthest Shore* when his long day had been filled with dragons. Ninereeds echoes McCaffrey's white dragon Ruth in his obedient temperament and literal-mindedness, but physically he pays homage to Tolkien's "green great dragon."

Disappointed with the size and shape of the Wyrmberg dragons, Twoflower longs for something more magnificent: "Dragons ought to be big and green and clawed and exotic and firebreathing – big and green with long sharp…" The noise we hear in the dark recesses of the dungeon cell is, naturally, the perfect wish fulfillment of everyone who has ever desired dragons. Twoflower knows what they should look like from having seen them illustrated in *The Octarine Fairy Book* (a nod to Andrew Lang's *Red Fairy Book*, which contains the story of Sigurd the Dragonslayer that captivated Tolkien).

Pratchett's noble dragons as imagined by Liessa and her riders are highly dangerous and menacing. Although partially transparent most of the time, Liessa has the Power that makes them solid – strong belief in their existence plus a powerful surrounding magical field. The flames they spit out leave real burns on humans and scorch real furrows in fields, but they wink out of existence the moment the mind conjuring them becomes disengaged or incapacitated, somewhat like McCaffrey's idea of going *between*. But the *between* where Pratchett's noble dragons lie hidden is packed like sardines with the beasts in a kind of comic one-dimensional Flatland.

The element of farce brings the Wyrmberg sequence to an end. In a grand finale, we have all three main characters of the Wyrmberg saga soaring into the upper atmosphere aboard Ninereeds. But you can guess what happens when the lack of oxygen causes Twoflower to lose consciousness. From this unexpected predicament, two completely farcical events occur. Farce, you'll recall, includes outrageous coincidences and deus ex machina inventions, both of which Pratchett uses with relish in this emergency situation that imperils his characters.

Liessa and Laolith suddenly come soaring up under Hrun the Barbarian, saving his hide and sealing his role as consort with a kiss. Rincewind, finding himself riding the thinnest of air instead of Ninereed's sturdy back, is forced to try conjuring up his own imaginary dragon. And here is where Pratchett's comic genius kicks into high gear – unable to imagine dragons because he doesn't believe in them, what the failed wizard's panicked imagination produces is a warp in the time-space continuum that lands him in a metal fixed-wing version of a dragon: a modern jetliner! Both his and the readers' minds are blown until the narrative catches up to the point where the cosmic ripples send the wizard, Twoflower, and his enchanted suitcase simply known as "the Luggage," back into the Discworld universe along with a label bearing the "powerful traveling rune TWA." This is the laugh-out-loud humor that makes Pratchett unique among writers of comic fantasy.

Errol and the Dragon of Ankh-Morpork

In Pratchett's 1989 Discworld novel *Guards! Guards!*, on the surface we are treated to a classic hero vs. villain plot structure with the twist that both hero and villain are dragons. One is a seemingly indestructible monster and the other is a seemingly weak runt of the litter. As you might expect from Pratchett, neither is what he seems, and there's a lot more going on in terms of structure than the elementary plot mentioned above. In typical Pratchett fashion, *Guards! Guards!* contains varying levels of parody and satire, some specific and some general, and discovering the jokes is only part of the fun.

The very first sentence of the novel tosses us right into the whole question of dragons: "This is where the dragons went." You know right from the start what's waiting – dormant dragons about to be awakened. You can almost hear the ominous music building in the background. Then you remember that this is Discworld, and in order to awaken dragons that are "huge and scaly and proud and arrogant," the bumbling summoners are going to enact some priceless Monty Python moments. They are also going to pay dearly for their exploits in finest sorcerer's apprentice mode. You just *know* the dragon they attempt to conjure will flap out of their control, and Pratchett does not disappoint.

Also in the mix is Lord Vetinari, a Machiavellian both feared and appreciated by the citizens, who rules Ankh-Morpork through concealed despotism. By skillfully manipulating all the factions of the great sprawling city, he maintains an equilibrium that allows the city to *work*. He uses practical tyranny, in which he "sorts out" anything that interferes with the day-to-day working of the city. Thus the Dragon of Ankh-Morpork becomes his adversary, because the beast disrupts everything on a grand scale. The struggle for power becomes one of the main themes of the story, on both slapstick and bitingly satirical levels. In one of the grander understatements of the book, we read, "'Power,' growled the Supreme Grand Master [who orchestrates the summoning of the dragon], 'does not come cheap.'"

This theme is demonstrated with a serious bite at the same time the action around it is comic. On the dark side we have the magical dragon that terrorizes the city and his human summoner, the Supreme Grand Master of the Elucidated Brethren, and on the side of light and right we have the swamp dragon Errol, an underdog hero, and his companions, several human don't-want-to-be heroes. Carrot Ironfoundersson (a strapping hero reared as a dwarf) represents good so literal and unflinching that he could easily be drawn as a two-dimensional cartoon in lesser hands than Pratchett's. There's also Vimes, the captain of the City Watch, who begins the story in the gutter (literally) and redeems himself (sort of) by solving the mystery of the marauding dragon.

The first dragon to enter the tale is the villain, the Dragon of Ankh-Morpork, conjured into reality through the focused ill-willpower of a coven of misfits called the Elucidated Brethren, led by the self-styled Supreme Grand Master. The discovery of how an extinct dragon from another dimension has suddenly appeared in the skies over Ankh-Morpork is treated within the framework of a crime novel, with Captain Vimes as the dragon detective. His logic (with a nod to Sherlock Holmes) is relentless: "Once you've ruled out the impossible then whatever is left, however improbable, must be the truth." Much like the venerable television detective Lt. Colombo, he chews over all the details that others, in their shock at the dragon's appearance, have failed to see. He notices, for example, that the dragon's tracks lead out of a dead-end alley, but not into it, suggesting it could only have got there by magical means. This narrows his search to wizards and disgruntled conjurers.

The crime novel framework with its emphasis on governance, laws, civil disobedience, and the nature of society at large gives Pratchett an arena for social satire in which the dragon threat brings out the best and worst of the city's citizenry. We see how the highly dangerous and malevolent *Draco nobilis* is summoned by drawing on the dark, nasty, mean-spirited thoughts of the Brethren. "It's a metaphor of human bloody existence, a dragon," observes Captain Vimes, who regards most of humanity as the bottom of the barrel and could be seen as the voice of the author. Through biting humor and outright slapstick Pratchett tackles the theme of abuse of power, especially who has it and who wants it. Power becomes a drug to the conjurer bringing the dragon across from another dimension:

> "Easier every time. He could feel the scales, feel the rage of the dragon as he reached *into the place where the dragons went* and took control. This was power, and it was his." (GG, 162)

This passage sounds deadly serious, but before you get swept away, notice the parody in the italics, which echoes McCaffrey's concept of *between* (always italicized), where Pernese dragons go when they teleport out of the material world.

The fact that the Supreme Grand Master turns out to be the Patrician's sycophant Wonse (a wicked parody of Tolkien's Gríma Wormtongue) makes the sorcerer's apprentice motif more significant. It's not just some bumbling hooligan or Unseen University dropout trying to work magic – it's the personal representative of the city's ruler. The extent to which he enjoys manipulating the simpletons who comprise the Brethren and controlling the summoned dragon invites disaster in numerous ways. Resonance with the folktale motif of the consequences of inviting a demon over the doorstep provides grim humor of the most delicious Pratchett variety. Infuriated at being summoned with magic and then summarily sent back where it came from, the dragon follows the scent trail of Wonse's thoughts back into the Discworld reality on its own initiative. The ensuing complications provide great opportunities for comic development of plot and characters.

The framework of a mystery built around tracking an unseen assailant who commits crimes such as reducing citizens to piles of charcoal provides Pratchett with some clever ways to introduce his main dragon character. He builds suspense by first showing us the "crime" in progress (the Brethren calling up the dragon) and then plants evidence of the dragon's presence, but withholds actual face-to-face confrontation with it to build up expectations. When we finally do meet the dragon in the scaly flesh, the effect is quite spectacular.

For its first appearance, we don't see it; we experience it. The moment the summoning spell is said, the reader is catapulted out of the Supreme Grand Master's mind and into the dragon's:

> "The words. Oh, yes ...
> He looked down, and spoke them aloud.
> Nothing happened.
> He blinked.
> When he opened his eyes again he was in a dark alley, his stomach was full of fire, and he was very angry." (GG, 36)

We realize the summoner has suddenly become joined in consciousness with the dragon as it materializes. But Pratchett maintains taut suspense by letting us observe only the effects of the dragon's actions (the stone wall glowing red where the first victim had been standing, his mortal remains turned to a small lump of charcoal), but not showing us the dragon itself. Suspense continues to build as the dragon is spotted intermittently from a distance or fleetingly before it flames someone. Even when one of Vimes' own Watch sees it face to face, we still aren't given details of what he sees, even though we are looking at it from his point of view: "There's a dragon on the roof! It's looking right at me, Nobby!"

Likewise, the great beast is sensed by the little swamp dragons inside Lady Ramkin's kennel, but not seen; they all silently stare up at the ceiling, "bright-eyed and watchful." Throughout the city this air of tense watchfulness is stretched to the snapping point as citizens line the rooftops, trying to catch a glimpse of the fabled extinct creature as dusk falls: "The city waited. A few stars came out ... Half an hour went by. Hails of arrows greeted a passing cloud, several unfortunate bats, and the rising moon." Anyone who's spent time staring at the sky for sign of a reputed meteor shower will relate to this scene with chagrined amusement.

Continuing his burlesque of the mystery genre, which has been smoothly laid over the comic fantasy novel foundation, Pratchett describes Vimes' musings about the mystery dragon in typical crime novel style, from his assertion that a "handful of high-temperature murders was only the start of it" to the moment he puts on his rain cape and steps "out into the naked city." Through increasingly dire encounters with the dragon, the methodical Vimes keeps a notebook of "Ityms" that he tics off as events roll toward a climax wherein the mystery of who conjured the dragon and why is finally exposed. In hilarious faux Middle English spellings, he wonders, "Itym: Can a dragon be destroyed into utterlye noethinge? ... Itym: Whyfore did it Explode that noone may find It, search they greatly?" As Vimes tries to figure out the mystery, readers are given doses of dragonlore from ordinary citizens who parrot the hackneyed standard legends, as well as dragon science from the breeders' perspective, which is just as outlandish and comic.

Standard beliefs common to the fantasy fiction dragonlore and allusions to traditional dragonslayer myths are pontificated by the members of the Watch, including such pearls of wisdom as dragons needing to live in high places far away from cities where there's plenty to eat. The Patrician adds his own bit of Discworld dragonlore, asserting that dragons are mythical, having been extinct for thousands of years, and solitary, not urban. But contrary to this "party line" regarding dragons, the Dragon of Ankh-Morpork decides to make its home in the Patrician's palace instead of a high crag in the wilderness, creating a situation both highly comic and dramatic.

The dragon has its own store of ancestral memories about dealing with humans, especially regarding St. George-type heroes and edible maidens. Pratchett offers the amusing possibility that there could be scenarios in which "the shape of someone on a horse holding a sword clicked a few tumblers in a dragon's brain." After the dragon has flamed the pretend king to a cinder and taken over the city itself, turning the wrecked Patrician's palace into a cavern suitable for building a hoard, it reverts to standard dragonlore to exert control, informing Wonse that the traditional virgin sacrifice must be observed to keep it from incinerating the metropolis.

Pratchett further manipulates the level of tension by stopping the action right at the moment when the dragon and the hero on horseback finally confront each other in the town square. The next sentence jumps ahead to the following day, where the confrontation is given as a mental flashback by Vimes ("What a day! What a fight!"). The events of the encounter are cleverly disclosed to the reader by having Vimes puzzle over each thing that happened as he writes his list of "ityms" that don't add up, from the lawman's standpoint. We begin to sense that the reason things don't add up is because the entire dragon saga is a setup job.

The resolution of the dragon problem comes in one of Pratchett's trademark surprise endings, i.e., multiple surprises emerge. The Patrician was in on the plan to conjure up a dragon all along; Wonse is Supreme Grand Master who does the actual summoning (hence the dragon's evil delight in personally tormenting him); the totally inept Sgt. Colon and the swamp dragon runt Errol play their parts as true heroes; and the Dragon King turns out to be a queen.

Pratchett's characterization of the Dragon of Ankh-Morpork (also referred to as the King of Ankh-Morpork) is as good as anything you will find in serious fantasy fiction. This *Draco nobilis* is the blazing, raging archetype of Western dragons – reptilian, malevolent, dangerous, with a cold alien intelligence that immediately figures out how to feed on magic for its power supply. We are definitely not dealing with the Eastern "Dragon King" folk figure. This dragon king is the embodiment of ruthless power run amok. In fact, Pratchett's description of this *Draco nobilis* is so convincing you may well forget you're reading a comic tale at all.

The dragon's physical description is kept a mystery at first. Readers are given clues little by little, starting with the ghost of the first person who encounters the monster as he discusses the event with Death: "I mean, it looked like a bloody dragon! What's a man to do? You don't expect to find a dragon around the corner! ... A bloody dragon ... Fire breathing, too. Did I suffer much?" We add a few more details to our dragon data bank when the Supreme Grand Master comes to his senses trying to "shed the feeling that he weighed several tons and was covered in scales."

The sound imagery is particularly important in establishing the dragon's fearsomeness. The noise of it flaming a victim (still out of sight) gives a hint of its size and threat: the sound is *volcanic*, like a *boiling geyser*, with a *roar* like a *bellows* or *forges of the Titans*. Like Pernese dragons, this one drops off a high perch and glides out into the air currents seemingly light as a bird, but the sound of its dragonflight suggests otherwise; it soars "as though the air was slowly and carefully being torn in half." Its wings "hammer" and "pound" the air like "potted thunder." In one outrageous passage the sound metaphor for the dragon's movement ("the great dragon reared up with the sound of a dozen anchor chains being thrown into a corner") is resonant of the metallic similes associated with Le Guin's immense Earthsea dragon Kalessin.

Corporal Nobbs adds more details with his observation that it has "great big wings," and that it's a reptile with scales: "It's a bloody great lizard ..." When Pratchett finally allows us to see the Dragon of Ankh-Morpork, it's rendered in non-comedic exposition with imagery that vividly evokes the creature:

> "The great dragon danced and spun and trod the air over the city. Its color was moonlight, gleaming off its scales. Sometimes it would twist and glide with deceptive speed over the rooftops for the sheer joy of existing." (GG, 109)

Eventually we learn that it has "magnificent bronze scales," "horse-like features," red reptilian eyes, that it's "long as a street" and the size of a barge, with wings big as sails and talons the length of a man's reach. Meeting the monster face to face through Vimes' and Errol's POV as they stare at it crouched on the roof above them, readers realize that its head is taller than a man's and that its terrible reptile gaze is merciless, ancient, and cold. The metaphors describing its intelligence are simultaneously amusing and chilling: it had "been long basted in guile and marinated in cunning."

In *Guards! Guards!*, only the *Draco nobilis* has the intelligence and power of communication with the humans it terrorizes. The little swamp dragons make various animal noises such as yammering, whining, keening, and howling, and seem to understand what the humans try to say to them, but they don't actually speak. Pratchett makes use of italics to show the dragon's mind-to-mind communication with its chosen mouthpiece, the Patrician's personal councilor Wonse.

The dragon takes great malicious delight in tormenting the man's mind for his audacity in attempting to command it from the dimension where it lay dormant. It speaks only through Wonse, who experiences the dragon's commands viscerally rather than merely hearing its words in his head. Its thoughts play his nervous system like a plucked bowstring. Its possession of Wonse is truly frightening at the same time it carries the social satire, demonstrating the subtle depth in Pratchett's writing. You could lift those passages straight out of the comedy and have them work on a dead-serious level.

The dragon communicates in a tone that's imperious and demanding (*"There is nothing I mustn't!"*), but also a bit peevish. The dragon's thoughts reveal both its wicked nature and its total ignorance of modern Discworld society. In a hilarious reversal, the dragon is horrified when it learns that the denizens of Ankh-Morpork typically treat each other worse than any outside threat such as itself could ever do. It also realizes with rage that the age of dragonslayers is gone (*"There will be no mighty warriors sent to kill me?"*). This discovery does nothing to improve its disposition, and cements its anger at being yanked into a domain that doesn't appreciate its noble dragon status.

These glimpses we get of Discworld from the dragon's point of view give Pratchett his best opportunity to inject scathing satire of Ankh-Morpork society (and by extension, humanity in general). It's also a chance for readers to feel the malevolence of the alien dragon mind. Our very first impression of the dragon is from inside its head, where we instantly feel its disorientation and anger. Its alien thought patterns reveal how dangerous it is:

> "It wouldn't play with you, or ask you riddles. But it understood all about arrogance and power and cruelty and if it could possibly manage it, it would burn your head off. Because it liked to." (GG, 166)

Depth is added by its reaction to the Supreme Grand Master's (Wonse's) presence in its own head; it doesn't even recognize the summoner as a human being, just as a tiny mind with a thought trail it can follow. The fact that it can "smell" its invader's thoughts makes Wonse regret the day he ever considered fooling around with magic books and summoning spells. We're made aware that it has thoughts beyond mere animal instincts. It thoroughly enjoys the "feel" of the new world into which it has been summoned and is infuriated by being sent away just as it's getting the hang of flying and flaming. Its unwilling role of vanishing dragon in Wonse and the Patrician's scheme to install a seeming dragonslayer as king backfires, of course, in ways that are both hilarious and chilling (especially in the way it toys with its victims, "giving terror time to mature").

The level of parody in *Guards! Guards!* spreads over a wide range of familiar fantasy icons. Le Guin's imagery in which dragons look like pieces of masonry from a distance is referenced several times (in particular the Dragon of Pendor and the dead dragon on the beach in Earthsea). The moment Sgt. Colon asks what's odd about the top of Unseen University's Tower of Art, we can guess what's coming. By the time Vimes and Colon resolve their argument over whether it really is a dragon perched atop the turrets or just "shadows and clumps of ivy," it's almost too late to avoid being crisped. Pratchett ramps up this image yet again (topping the joke, in comedy terms) when he has the bumbling members of the Watch climb up the dome of the Small Gods temple, only to find that what they thought was a slate rooftop is actually the crouching dragon's back.

References to Tolkien and McCaffrey abound as well. Like Smaug descending on Lake-town in fire and then circling around for another pass, the Dragon of Ankh-Morpork "turned in a tight circle, pounded the air a few times to build up speed, and came back." Pratchett also pokes fun at typical fantasy dragons that hover on the wing. He puts these sentiments into the mouths of Captain Vimes and Lady Ramkin, who decide the dragon is operating against laws of logic and nature. Imagine Le Guin's Orm Embar floating over a raft in order to converse with the wizard Ged, and you may agree with Vimes that "[f]or something the size of a barn with an armor-plated hide, it was a pretty good trick." On the ground, the noble dragon is heavy and ungainly, dragging itself over the cobblestones like Le Guin's Kalessin. Fans of Earthsea will no doubt sniff out the Le Guin resonance in the following passage:

> "Somehow the dragon was worse on the ground. In the air it was an elemental thing, graceful even when it was trying to burn you to your boots. On the ground it was just a damn great animal." (GG, 189)

One of the most farcical attempts to rid the city of the dragon involves Sgt. Colon and his lucky arrow. Early on, Pratchett sets up the fact that Colon was once pretty good at archery, which leads to his decision to try to shoot it out of the sky. The reference to Bard the Bowman in *The Hobbit* who mortally wounds Smaug with his lucky ancestral arrow can't be missed. The scene in which the members of the Watch debate Colon's chances of hitting the dragon in its "voonerables" is a prime example of Pratchett's ability to turn logic inside out and stand reason on its head. All are agreed that million-to-one chances always work. (By these standards, Bard's chance of killing Smaug was bound to succeed because he was relying on the "last desperate million-to-one chance" that always works in fantasy stories.) But if it's only "999,943-to-one, for example," all bets are off. Their attempts to adjust the odds back to a million devolve into the kind of total slapstick that readers of Discworld books have become gleefully accustomed to.

As with most fantasy dragons, we learn many of the details about their powers from what others say about them. As a fount of dragonlore, Lady Ramkin supplies the intricacies of swamp dragon anatomy, but she also explains the origins of *Draco nobilis*: that it's an extinct species of great dragons that vanished into another dimension. This knowledge allows Vimes to reach the conclusion that the Dragon of Ankh-Morpork is obviously a creature of magic and therefore must feed on raw magic to remain substantial (a "thaumivore," according to Lady Ramkin).

In confirming what Vimes has begun to suspect, that Lord Vetinari the Patrician is at the root of the scheme to threaten the city with an extinct noble dragon, Wonse informs us that the creature turned out to be beyond control because of its superior cunning. It has a mind like the Patrician's, but "with all the brakes off." Thus it has the power temporarily to terrorize the city, take over the palace, and begin creating a hoard through fear and extortion. Initially it's summoned and commanded by Wonse, but once it sorts out who brought it across the dimensions, the tables are turned.

The plot significance of the Ankh-Morpork dragon is that it plays the villain, demonstrating the abuse of power. But even as the villain, Pratchett gives it some shadings of gray; observing the rooftops full of archers and spearmen ready to attack, the narrator suggest you might almost feel sorry for it. This sentiment is short-lived, of course, because it wreaks total devastation and demands human sacrifice – the essence of the evil Western dragon. As a threat to the equilibrium of Ankh-Morpork, it provides the city with a graphic example of leadership they *don't* want. "There's no truce with dragons," Vimes exclaims. Thus, anything else looks much better, which is exactly what the Patrician had in mind. Counter to what Wonse may have expected, the dragon rules the skies over Ankh-Morpork until Errol, an unlikely swamp dragon with the unwieldy breeder's name of Goodboy Bindle Featherstone, challenges him. Which brings about the one thing that's considered taboo on both Pern and Earthsea: dragon fighting dragon.

Errol, so named for Nobby's brother who is also long in the nose, has every strike against him for the role of hero. In Errol's first appearance, we hear the swamp dragons before we see them (they bark and whistle, but don't have the power of speech). In the kennel, we meet our unlikely hero, the runt of the litter. At this point, let me remind you of another dragon runt who eventually saves the day, McCaffrey's Ruth. We'll return to Ruth in a moment. Swamp dragons are small enough to be pets, about two to three feet long. As opposed to a thaumivore (eater of magic), swamp dragons are omnivores; so much so that Errol provides an ongoing joke as to what he has consumed: coal, fire irons, doorknobs, cobblestones, broken bottles, inkpots, and a tin of armor polish, just for starters.

Swamp dragons in Discworld are non-magical and are referred to as pets or pests, depending on one's inclination. Among the pet fanciers we find Lady Ramkin and her clique who breed the species like fancy kennel dogs (a parody of British dog and horse breeders that provides a large part of the book's comedy). Swamp dragons don't talk; instead they make animal noises such as yammers, keens, and howls, but those close to them swear they can understand what's said to them. For the most part, they are small, harmless, animal-intelligence-level versions of the greater beasts.

The one thing they do have in common with the noble dragons is their ability to produce flame. Like the dragons of Pern, Discworld's *Draco vulgaris* produces a lethal mixture of volatile gases in its various stomachs that ignites upon contact with the air. In a hilarious turn on that concept, the unstable digestive systems of swamp dragons often cause them to explode when they flame. As the old joke goes, any swamp dragon can flame once.

The animal breeder jokes begin with Vimes' first meeting with Lady Sybil Ramkin at her swamp dragon kennel and provide examples of several comic writing techniques at which Pratchett excels (punning wordplay, parody, burlesque, farce, and caricature). He completely skewers the pedigree naming style with monikers such as Lord Mountjoy Gayscale Talonthrust III of Ankh. The story's unlikely dragon hero Errol staggers under the weight of his pedigree name of Goodboy Bindle Featherstone of Quirm, especially ridiculous given that he's a misshapen runt who can't even remain aloft long enough to mate (like Pernese dragons, swamp dragons mate on the wing). More breeder jargon wordplay occurs in the invented names for gender stages of swamp dragons, such as cobbs, hens, pewmets, cocks, snoods, and dams, as well as highly evocative group terms such as a *slump* or an *embarrassment* of swamp dragons. Lady Ramkin herself is referred to as the "dragon lady" and is highly resonant of that other "Dragonlady" with her horse stables and Pernese dragon species.

Swamp dragons are consistently referred to in doggy terms and imagery, so that exaggeration and outlandish metaphors focus the humor on the dog-breeding world. Lady Ramkin's wildly inappropriate suggestions for reacting to the Dragon of Ankh-Morpork's presence are pure farce, in which absurd humor, non sequitur, and illogical reasoning are the order of the day. In addition to not showing fear, she urges Vimes to give it a "good sharp 'no!'" and take away its food bowl or give it a swat on the nose with a rolled-up newspaper.

In a humorous imitation of everyone's family spaniel, Lady Ramkin's aged house dragon Dewdrop Mabelline Talonthrust the First plops his drooly jaws into Vimes' lap and stares at him with soulful eyes. Lady Ramkin's cheerful acknowledgement of Vimes' predicament adds further mirth to the situation: "No fire left now, poor soppy old thing. He likes his belly rubbed." Topping the joke yet again, Vimes' unsuccessful slapstick attempts to dislodge the old dragon end in a totally icky image as it gives him a toothy smile, rolling "back the corner of its mouth, exposing a picket fence of soot-blackened teeth."

Errol is consistently described in humorous doggy terms. At their first meeting, his intelligent soulful gaze reminds Capt. Vimes of wanting to own a puppy as a child. Like anyone who has seen that doggy in the window of the pet shop and couldn't leave without it, Vimes can't refuse. Vimes' adoption of the forlorn stunted dragon and his attempts to settle it in at the Watch headquarters open more chances for comedy. For example, Errol pees on the floor like an excited puppy. Vimes later attempts to use him as a bloodhound to track down evidence in the mystery yarn, and apologizes to Errol near the climax for treating him "like a dog," which readers have been laughing at all along the way. Clever readers may discover the implied pun embedded in the event when Errol rearranges his internal plumbing to act as a ramjet flaming from the rear. It gives literal meaning to the concept of reverse engineering.

By shifting his plumbing into a sort of bionic rocket – the first dragon to ever flame backwards – Errol embodies pure Pratchett slapstick. Quick and agile in the sky once his physical properties are transformed, Errol's scrappy nature takes over. Everyone assumes it's because he's trying to be a brave little hero and drive away the big nasty magical dragon, but you must pay attention to the hints Pratchett has dropped early in the book in order to guess Errol's true motivation. Swamp dragons become very aggressive and show no fear during mating behavior. As we find out in the hilarious reversal of expectations at the end of the novel, the noble dragon is a female and Errol has been courting her!

As Errol goes through his transformation, he becomes frozen white, then silver like a rocket. It's suggested he may be a throwback to the ancestral proto-dragons who may have originated in space where this was their usual method of propulsion. The little silver/white dragon who overcomes his runt status and saves everyone's skin strongly suggests McCaffrey's Ruth, who is also a sport or throwback to the original dragons of Pern. In both cases we witness the triumph of the underdog. After the irony of the Dragon King (or Queen) getting blown sky high when its own pure plasma flame hits a distillery, Errol finds his chance to shine. He disarms the noble dragon in a completely unexpected way – he'd rather court than fight. The old mantra "make love, not war" becomes Discworld's message to the world.

Dragons in Space

In 1991, Anne McCaffrey launched dragons into space (an idea some readers found unintentionally humorous); in 2001, Terry Pratchett did the same thing, with fully intentional hilarity. *The Last Hero* finds the dragon-powered *Kite* (a Rube Goldberg-type contraption designed by Leonard of Quirm, a parody of Leonardo da Vinci) launched over the Discworld rim into space. Readers of McCaffrey's *All the Weyrs of Pern* cannot miss the parody of her space-faring dragons and humans from Pern.

To figure out how to launch teams of hundreds of dragons into space on a mission to save the world, the Pern dragonriders have the AIVAS (Artificial Intelligence Voice Address System) computer, an artifact of the original colonists. Equally formidable, Discworld has Leonard of Quirm, all-around artist and deep thinker, "... the cleverest man alive, if you used the word 'clever' in a specialized and technical sense." Pratchett's send-up of the great inventor and artist Leonardo da Vinci provides ample opportunity for comic understatement, said both by him and to him.

This technique provides the perfect contrast to the over-the-top, slapstick action that will be required to put Leonard's inventions into use. For example, to his query on the relative importance of the quest over the rim into space, he receives from Lord Vetinari the Patrician the following dry response, "If it is not successful, the world will end." "Ah. Quite vital, then," he acknowledges. The Patrician's complaint about the cost of construction and his demand that there be something to show for all the expense receives an equally dry response from Leonard, "The continuation of the species, perhaps."

The AIVAS plan requires three teams of two hundred dragons each to move the colony spaceship engines onto the barren "red star" in order to blow it out of its current orbit, thus saving Pern from Threadfall. Likewise, Leonard decides he will need two hundred dragons ("to be on the safe side") to power the space contraption he has in mind to save Discworld from Cohen the Barbarian's plan to attack the Gods. Parodying Pern's collaboration of Masterweavers and Mastersmiths who create space suits and new technology to implement AIVAS' design, Leonard demands "the help of, oh, sixty apprentices and journeymen from the Guild of Cunning Artificers."

In both these stories, dragons are chosen for the quest into space because of their unique attributes. AIVAS' daring scheme can work only because the dragons can wink *between*, essentially the same vacuum as space, for up to fifteen minutes with no harm. Hilariously, Leonard of Quirm realizes the swamp dragon's ability to flame backwards is the propulsion mechanism needed for his space-faring ship, the *Kite*. He even suspects that their ancient origins may have been in an environment where their anatomy as a "living rocket" would be more suitable. Turns out, he's right.

The dragon species discovered on the Discworld moon is leaner and sleeker than their swamp dragon descendents – "... they were so silvery that they looked like moonlight hammered into shape." They also jet about with rearward flaming as efficiently as any rocket, roaring off into the thin atmosphere "vertically on a needle of blue flame." The crew of the Kite now recognize that Errol, the underdog hero of *Guards! Guards!*, is not some new kind of dragon, but is actually a throwback to the silvery, streamlined moon dragons.

In Conclusion

In comparing all the dragons we've discussed up to this point, the power to flame provides the most consistent basis for comparison. For Tolkien and Le Guin, that power is purely magical and is endemic to their imaginary world. In Le Guin's case, it's not just a magical power the dragons possess – it's their essence; her dragons are elemental creatures of fire and air. They exude heat and just to touch them invites physical damage. Earthsea dragons consume fire for sustenance. For McCaffrey, the Pernese dragons' ability to flame is purely physical and scientific. They chew a specific type of rock and produce gases that ignite on contact with air. For the dragons of Discworld, Pratchett employs a little of each. Swamp dragons are non-magical animals, and the combination of what they eat plus their ability shift their intestines around produces the dragon flame. *Draco nobilis*, however, are creatures of pure magic. They can only manifest solidly in the Discworld environment through *belief* in them. They consume magic to maintain bodily form.

Looking at Pratchett's style as a fantasy writer, lest you get the impression that he's only a writer of jokes, consider this description of the

Discworld concept as a "small traveling circle of firelight in a chilly infinity."
Beautiful. An even better example of his non-comic style with its excellent
command of visual imagery is Twoflower's rescue of the wizard Rincewind
from the Wyrmberg on the tourist's own imagined (and fully realized)
dragon:

> "... A pair of arms locked around his waist and the whole world jerked
> sideways as the dragon rose out of its long dive, claws grazing just for a moment
> the topmost rock of the Wyrmberg's noisome floor. Twoflower laughed
> triumphantly.
> 'Got him!'
> And the dragon, curving gracefully at the top of his flight, gave a lazy flip
> of his wings and soared through a cavemouth into the morning air." (CM, 135-
> 6)

That passage could sit easily within the confines of any serious fantasy
fiction. The spare, specific imagery puts us right in the saddle with Twoflower
as he experiences the sheer joy of flight. This command of the language lifts
Pratchett's abilities above the label of mere fantasy humorist and into the
realm of master stylist.

In her essay, "From Elfland to Poughkeepsie," Le Guin praises Kenneth Morris and James Branch Cabell for their mastery of the "comic-
heroic" style in which the grins and laughter of readers are achieved through
"an eloquence, a fertility and felicity of invention that is simply overwhelming. They are outrageous, and they know exactly what they're doing." I can't
think of a better description for the art of Terry Pratchett.

Notes
CM – *The Color of Magic*
GG – *Guards! Guards!*

1. If you want to delve more deeply into theories of literary humor, the best
place to start is *Writing Humor: Creativity and the Comic Mind*, by Mary Ann Rishel, from
Ithaca College's Department of Writing faculty. Originating from her seminal
classes on literary humor and its finest exponents, *Writing Humor* goes a long way

toward explaining *why* something strikes readers as funny and *how* skilled writers employ (consciously or unconsciously) these techniques.

2. For a thorough discussion of the types of Discworld dragons and their separate attributes, you should consult *The New Discworld Companion*, a collaborative effort of Terry Pratchett and Stephen Briggs. As of this writing, the types include *Draco nobilis*, *Draco vulgaris* (of which there are now 37 subspecies), and a new type of star-voyaging dragon, *Draco stellaris nauticae*.

Chapter 5

Ursula K. Le Guin
Wild Spirits of Earthsea

" . . . THINGS CHANGE:

authors and wizards are not always to be trusted:

nobody can explain a dragon."

The above quotation from the 2001 volume *Tales from Earthsea* is typical Le Guin – cryptic, suggestive, an Earthsea Zen koan of a statement that takes you lightly, teasingly, by the fingers as it leads you over the cliff. There is no net. To understand and enjoy Le Guin's high fantasy world of Earthsea and its complex inhabitants, readers must engage their thinking brains as well as their capacity to be entertained by "what if." Yes, there are swords and sorcerers, but these are tools for accessing the larger moral and ethical issues that underpin the Earthsea novels. Author Neil Gaiman describes the magic in Earthsea as "primal"; that label defines her dragons as well, for they are the essence of magic.

As of this writing, two separate trilogies comprise the Earthsea cycle: *A Wizard of Earthsea*, *The Tombs of Atuan*, and *The Farthest Shore* (1969-1972); and *Tehanu*, *Tales from Earthsea*, and *The Other Wind* (1999-2001). While the world of Earthsea remains the same in both sets of trilogies, Le Guin's approach and technique shifts considerably from the first set to the second. The dragons, however, change very little.

In Tolkien's Middle-earth, the Firstborn are elves; in Le Guin's Earthsea, the Firstborn (also called Eldest, Elder Children) are dragons. Although dragons are not major characters in the Earthsea novels, and occasionally make fleeting appearances (ferrying human characters from one place to another, passing on messages of high importance, and coming to the rescue at the last possible moment), the emotional and intellectual impact they have on the narratives themselves is profound. They embody ideologies and themes, providing some of Le Guin's most visual and epic images and some of the best dragon-human interaction in fantasy literature.

It's questionable whether they are allies or enemies of humans. On one level, they seem above such cut-and-dried categories and deal with humans reluctantly. They are iconic. What contributes to this sense of distance is the fact that Le Guin doesn't enter into the actual minds of the dragons; they are indeed alien. As the wizard Ged observes, "dragons have their own wisdom." We experience them as others see them or as the narrator describes them, but we don't "hear" them thinking. Some are wise beyond measure, while others are brute beasts. On the occasions when they attack humans, the reasons are widely varied and complex, having as much to do with their species' evolution as with their distrust of human motivations.

The named dragons of Earthsea include Kalessin (Eldest), Orm (a dragon we meet only in legends recounted by other characters), Orm Embar (offspring of Orm, friend of the Archmage Ged), Ammaud (the marauders' spokesdragon), and Yevaud (Dragon of Pendor). However, the two we get to know best, on a very personal level – Orm Irian and Tehanu – are actually shape-shifters, dragons wearing female human bodies for most of the tales in which they appear (the short story "Dragonfly" and the novels *Tehanu* and *The Other Wind*); they are misfits in human society seeking their true identities.

Le Guin uses the shape-shifter motif to demonstrate the divided species of dragons and humans and the difficulty each experiences trying to fit into human society. Irian's nature is fierce and extroverted with a quick temper, whereas Tehanu is shy and nearly tongue-tied around others. Irian has a wild beauty that both repels and attracts her suitors; Tehanu's beauty has been disfigured by fire, making her an object of scorn and fear. Both characters call to mind numerous Eastern myths and folktales of dragons living in human form. One such is the tale of Shen Lang, a dragon in human form, who married the Chief Judge's daughter. A local magistrate spies on him, discovering his secret. His challenge to Shen Lang, "Dragon, how dare you hide yourself there under a borrowed form?" illustrates the reaction the Summoner gives to Irian when she invades the Roke School.

The transformation and redemption of these two hybrid characters add depth to Le Guin's portrayal of both humans and dragonkind. This tactic opens up many possibilities for character development at the same time it imposes limitations on their relationships with the humans around them. Orm Irian and Tehanu experience a range of suffering that is both mental and physical, gradually forcing the dragon persona to the surface. In both cases, the first actual demonstration of their dragon selves comes in response to a threat from human magic. As their separate stories progress toward the inevitable change into permanent dragon form, they achieve freedom both for themselves and humankind. When these two characters reappear in *The Other Wind* (the sixth Earthsea book), they come as empowered dragonkind wearing their human bodies as saviors rather than victims.

Philosophical Worldbuilding in Earthsea

Eastern thought, particularly a reverence for the Taoist teachings of Lao Tzu, permeates much of Le Guin's fiction. Introduced to the *Tao Te Ching* (*The Book of the Way*) at an early age by her father, Le Guin's intellectual curiosity about this nearly three-thousand-year-old compendium of wisdom led her into a lifelong connection with its precepts. Also helpful in grasping the truths contained in this document is the *I Ching* (*The Book of Changes*). As "one of the first efforts of the human mind to place itself within the universe," the *I Ching*'s discussion of ethical values through commentaries on the oracle's trigrams and hexagrams inspired some of Lao Tzu's most profound observations. The two books together provide further insight into Le Guin's incorporation of Eastern philosophical thought into her fiction.[1]

Naturally, this influence is present in her concept of dragons. They represent the creative force of life: unpredictable, spontaneous, and ultimately beyond explanation. An explication of the first *I Ching* hexagram, the Ch'ien (the Creative), is also the essence of Earthsea's dragons: "... primal power, which is light-giving, active, strong, and of the spirit ... its essence is power or energy ... represented as unrestricted by any fixed conditions in space and is therefore conceived of as motion" (from Cary F. Baynes' English translation). Le Guin's dragons exist on the wing and consume fire as their sustenance. Unlike its generally evil Western counterpart, the Chinese dragon evokes electrically charged power of creation, dynamic motion, the spark of life breathed into the making of the world by the creator (Segoy, in Earthsea's mythology).

Balance and natural law, referred to in the Earthsea novels as Equilibrium or the Pattern, are the basic structures that underlie Le Guin's invented world. The dragons are living examples of this balance and harmony of creation. We are told by wizards and other practitioners of the Art Magic that the dragon race doesn't just use the Old Speech or Speech of the Making; they are living embodiments of that speech uttered by Segoy that lifted land from the oceans and breathed wind into the skies. In *A Wizard of Earthsea*, it's said, "The dragons do not dream. They are dreams. They do not work magic: it is their substance, their being. They do not do; they are." In the Old Speech, the word and the act are one. The dragons don't have to learn the Old Speech, as do wizards; they come into existence knowing it – it's not the means by which they cause things to happen, it's their essence. It distinguishes them as highly evolved creatures of accumulated wisdom rather than dumb beasts. Le Guin's interpretation of the first chapter from the *Tao Te Ching* reflects this idea:

"The way you can go
isn't the real way.
The name you can say
isn't the real name.

Heaven and earth
begin in the unnamed:

name's the mother

of the ten thousand things." (*A Book About the Way*, 3)

The dragons serve as a barometer of the Equilibrium. In *The Farthest Shore*, when the breach between worlds created by the wizard Cob begins to pull apart the very fabric of magic that underpins Earthsea, the dragons become "mad or bewildered," exhibiting the "dumb terror" of mere beasts. They fear what's "outside of nature," a corruption of the pattern on which life itself is founded. A similar situation in *The Other Wind* finds the dragons attacking human communities as retribution for having created the Dry Land in their misuse of the power of the Making. The words of Orm Irian, standing before the king's council in human form, put it bluntly: dragons "fear nothing in the world, except your wizardries of death... We fear your spells of immortality." Her challenge to the council – "You have unmade the balance of the world. Can you restore it?" – is the quest of the novel and more broadly the guiding theme of the second Earthsea trilogy.

Le Guin's concept of Equilibrium in Earthsea also represents the Way, the Tao, in which seeming opposites such as light and dark, good and evil, are but aspects of the whole, integrated into one, as depicted by the yin/yang image. As embodiments of this unified existence, her dragons are beyond the human compulsion to divide life into opposing choices of good or ill. When the dragons allow the evil of men to sway them into killing each other as well as invading the eastern territories traditionally inhabited by humans, they come under the yoke of choice, a human attribute. To right this wrong, the pattern of life itself must shift. The wisest of dragons, Kalessin, confirms this, stating at the climax of *The Other Wind* that "the balance changes," offering dragonkind three choices: "... to fly on the far side of the world, on the other wind [where dragonkind fly free]. Or stay and put on the yoke of good and evil. Or dwindle into dumb beasts."

A second philosophical thread that surfaces in Le Guin's fiction is the Jungian notion of dream, the collective unconscious (the subconscious archetypes we all "know"), and what it means to be an artist in human society. Beginning with the observation that "the human psyche is the womb of all the sciences and arts," Jung's explanation of the role of the artist and of the artistic process fits Le Guin's best fiction well. Her tales are character driven, she insists, not plot driven. Thus, they often unfold slowly, with less plot-based action and more character-based thinking – less doing and more being. Says Jung in *Modern Man in Search of a Soul*:

> "A great work of art is like a dream; for all its apparent obviousness it does not explain itself and is never unequivocal ... It presents an image in much the same way as nature allows a plant to grow, and we must draw our own conclusions." (172)

We can apply this to Le Guin's dragons in *The Farthest Shore*. The younger dragon Orm Embar tries to *do*, while the ancient Kalessin simply *is*. Involved actively in the struggle with men and wizards, Orm Embar loses his life. In contrast, Kalessin reclines Buddha-like at the edge of a stream, unmoving, barely visible through the mist. From the young apprentice Arren's perspective, it could have been crouching there for days or even centuries. It offers no advice, leads no attack against the wizard's enemies. But with the single word "Mount!" it offers rescue to the battle-weary humans.

Le Guin recasts some of these ideas in her own words during the wizard Ged's discourse on balance and immortality with his young companion Arren, king-in-waiting, during their voyage to the dragon realms. Ged makes the distinction between the proper cycles of existence and the false immortality Cob has conjured: "In life is death. In death is rebirth. What then is life without death? ... What is it but death – death without rebirth?"

Ged and Arren witness the horrific death of dragons resulting from the wizard Cob's disruption of natural law. In addition to draining the power of magic from witch and mage alike, it removes the dragons' higher intelligence and connection to the Speech of Making, leaving them in a state of bestial wildness where they prey on humans and kill one another. The terrifying result is rendered in some of Le Guin's most graphic and moving prose, painted in imagery that sears the mind. What Ged and Arren take to be a fortress wall along the shoreline is actually the carcass of a ravaged, dying dragon:

"The long snake-body lay full length on the rock and sand. One foreleg was missing, the armor and flesh were torn from the great arch of the ribs, and the belly was torn open, so that the sand for yards about was blackened with the poisoned dragon-blood. Yet the creature still lived ... The green-gold eyes were open, and as the boat sailed by, the lean, huge head moved a little, and with a rattling hiss, steam mixed with bloody spray shot from the nostrils." (FS, 196)

Dreams and their meanings haunt the philosophy of Jung and, to a great extent, the fiction of Le Guin. "The great fantasies, myths and tales are indeed like dreams," Le Guin wrote in her book of essays, *The Language of Night*, where "Fantasy is the language of the inner self" through archetypes and symbols. Le Guin described the meat of most high fantasy as the "journey toward self-knowledge, to adulthood, to the light." Add to this Jung's notion of archetype, "structural forms of the stuff of consciousness," and you have a good idea of the type of fantasy Le Guin writes. The mythmaking faculty of the writer applies the collective archetypes to new material, turning the shadow world of psychoanalysis into high truth where epiphanies can take place.

How does this apply to the Earthsea dragons? While her dragons are elemental creatures, embodiments of fire and air, they can also be seen as symbols of the dark side of the conscious mind, "something not known and not expressible otherwise than symbolically." Le Guin explains in *The Language of Night*, "It is the animal who knows the way, the way home. It is the animal within us, the primitive, the dark brother, the shadow soul, who is the guide." For the child Therru and the rustic young woman Dragonfly, embracing this dark, powerful animal self makes them whole. Both of them go into the spiritual darkness of the Dry Land to restore the balance distorted by magic and perverted by hubris and greed. The sorcerer Alder's nightmares become the practical means by which souls are liberated.

To generalize Jung's approach to dream analysis, we can say that in addition to treating various neuroses, it provides rational insight into psychic causality. This second aspect of dream analysis forms the basis for Le Guin's sixth Earthsea novel, *The Other Wind*. Solving the mystery of the sorcerer Alder's terrifying dreams about the Dry Land becomes the means for saving

Earthsea itself. Once the sages to whom Alder turns for help agree that his recurring grim dream experience isn't just the product of grief over the death of his wife, they begin to look more deeply at where the cause really lies. Le Guin's invention of the Dry Land, where shadow and dream create a frightening, disorienting realm of the seeming dead, owes much to these Jungian ideas on the nature of the psyche. This hellish afterlife is a human construct that exhibits all our worst misunderstandings of power and immortality. Dragons fear it with good reason; madness lies there and in it, the magic of creation fades away.

Integration of one's shadow self, which underlies the structure of both *A Wizard of Earthsea* and *The Other Wind*, applies to dragons as well as wizards. When Ged finally realizes that the shadow demon he has pursued through most of the first Earthsea novel is part of himself, balance is restored – "Light and darkness met, and joined, and were one." This is especially true of the several rare dragon-human hybrid characters that suffer as humans until they can achieve a unity with their true nature. It's in the shadow worlds, whether on the magical Knoll of Roke Island or the false afterlife realm of the Dry Land, that the human dragons emerge, then fly free.

Interestingly, Le Guin's two philosophical influences (Lao Tzu and Jung) are brought together in Jung's 1949 Foreword to the 1950 edition of Wilhelm's translation of *The I Ching or Book of Changes*. Jung's pronouncement on the use and understanding of the *I Ching* perfectly describes Le Guin's mysterious Immanent Grove, the center of power in Earthsea:

> "The I Ching does not offer itself with proofs and results; it does not vaunt itself, nor is it easy to approach. Like a part of nature, it waits until it is discovered ... To one person its spirit appears as clear as day; to another, shadowy as twilight; to a third, dark as night." "(*I Ching*, xxxix)

The Master Patterner who inhabits the Immanent Grove exhibits these same qualities of approach: passive acceptance of gradual understanding and grasp of the greater whole rather than active demand for specific answers to immediate problems. This Taoist attitude defines the period Dragonfly spends with the Patterner as she gradually comes to the realization of who and what she is: Orm Irian, a red-gold dragon of great power and beauty. In an especially moving scene from "Dragonfly," Irian begins to look at herself and the world around her from the ancient dragon perspective rather than from that of an uncouth country bumpkin:

> "She felt herself larger than he was, larger than she was, enormously larger. She could reach out one finger and destroy him. He stood there in his small, brave, brief humanity, his mortality, defenseless. She drew a long, long breath. She stepped back from him." (TE, 269)

In that instant, the dragon exercises restraint, taking full responsibility for its might and power. According to Margaret Mahy, "the inner theme of the books, she [Le Guin] says, is the balance between power and responsibility." Says Ged to Arren in *The Farthest Shore*, "I know that there is only one power that is real and worth the having. And that is the power, not to take, but to accept." Humans don't handle power nearly as well as dragons in Le Guin's Earthsea; the sorcerer's apprentice archetype applies to fledgling wizard Ged as a warning that "danger must surround power as shadow does light," illustrating how humans wield power poorly. This contrast between wise dragons and unwise humans plays out through most of the Earthsea novels.

Another familiar theme, "the magic fades away," provides a bittersweet effect similar to that which permeates all of Tolkien's Middle-earth. Here, it's more that the magic has shifted into something more mundane and at the same time more focused; the innate magic of dragons becomes separated from the learned magic of humans once and for all. Sacrifice is required. The sorcerer Alder consciously chooses to lose his power in order to become the instrument for change that resets the Equilibrium. In this act, he emulates the Archmage Ged, who also sacrificed his great powers to mend the evil created by the wizard Cob. This acceptance of responsibility and its complicated results is what makes Le Guin's characters compelling and her themes thought provoking. The wizard's discussion after the Dry Land has been dismantled emphasizes all these points:

The Doorkeeper shook his head. "I think maybe the division that was begun, and then betrayed, will be completed at last," he said. "The Dragons will go free, and leave us here to the choice we made."

"The knowledge of good and evil," said Onyx.

"The joy of making, shaping," said Seppel. "Our mastery."

"And our greed, our weakness, our fear," said Azver ...

"What I fear," said Gamble, "... is this: that when the dragons go, our mastery will go with them. Our art. Our magic." (OW, 199)

Magic in Earthsea derives from language, more specifically, the language of dragons – the Old Speech or Speech of the Making. There is no religion in Le Guin's Earthsea, but there is innate spirituality and understanding of life as it was intended by the maker, Segoy. All the peoples of the Archipelago honor the solstices and the turn of the seasons; all celebrate "the Long Dance" on the longest night of the year, no matter what island or culture they belong to. The dragons express their own version of the Long Dance, circling in joyful spirals in a mass winged dance of pure existence, at one with air and breath. When the young prince Arren sees them in their great aerial dance, he experiences a brief moment of ecstasy, knowing that "all the glory of mortality was in that flight" which demonstrates pure strength, wildness, grace, and intelligent communion with each other. "Arren did not speak, but he thought: I do not care what comes after; I have seen the dragons on the wind of morning."

Balanced between the ungoverned Old Powers of the earth and the carefully structured, taught skills of the Art Magic that require mastery of the language of Making, Earthsea magic is as endemic to the world as music. In fact, Le Guin has used this analogy to explain how magic works in her invented world: magical ability is like perfect pitch; some don't have it, some have it a little, and some are gifted with it in high degree. "Wizardry is artistry," she explained in *The Language of the Night*. Dragons don't have to learn magic or the language with which it is practiced, they *are* it, Le Guin stresses through her characters who try to explain dragons. But we already know her opinion on that: "Nobody can explain a dragon."

Ursula Le Guin's Earthsea dragons are a fascinating mix of Eastern and Western models, mostly the former, but with some significant touches of the latter. "My dragons are not the conventional ravening hoarding beasts," Le Guin emphasized to interviewer Margaret Mahy. If anything, they are more like elementals, creatures of fire and air representing unfettered freedom, earthbound only to lay their eggs. Earth and water are not their elements, and they don't cross the open waters of the Archipelago willingly. Occasions where we do encounter them making long flights over water involve great need. Examples include Orm Embar coming to enlist Ged's help against Cob, Kalessin responding to Tehanu's cry for help, and Kalessin carrying Ged and Arren back from the land of the dead.

Le Guin gives many clear, vivid descriptions of her dragons. In shape and form they most resemble Eastern dragons with their long sinuous bodies and short crooked legs with enormous talons on their clawed feet. Clumsy and heavy-bodied on land, they're graceful and swift on the wing. The ancient dragons of Earthsea's uttermost West (a nod to Tolkien's West, where Valinor and Middle-earth's higher beings reside), being creatures of the air, have wide membranous wings that seem to fill the sky when one of them hovers overhead.

They breathe fire and, in fact, seem to be a sort of organic internal combustion engine, with banked flames encased in metallic bodies. Heat radiates out from their plate-like scales and the touch of their hide can burn a human, as Azver discovers when he reaches out for Irian's hand just as she shifts into dragon form: "She reached out and touched his hand. He drew his breath sharply ... A curl of fire, a wisp of smoke drifted down through the dark air. Azver the Patterner stood with his left hand holding his right hand, which her touch had burnt." Likewise, when the dragon/human child Therru tries to comfort Moss, the dying witch's response is "You're like fire, child, your hand burns me."

The size of the ancient dragons of the West is large, some so great that puny humans mistake their bulk lying on land for castle walls and towers. In challenging the old Dragon of Pendor to come out and fight, Ged realizes with a shock that "what he had taken for a part of the tower was the shoulder of the Dragon of Pendor as he uncurled his bulk and lifted himself slowly up," revealing himself to be "higher than the broken tower's height, and his taloned forefeet rested on the rubble of the town below." In another astonishing image, Orm Embar, hovering over the rafts of the ocean people, measures ninety feet from wing tip to wing tip. Two devolved branches of dragon beasts are much smaller. The mountain creatures are perhaps a yard long, and those of a related strain are tiny enough to ride on their owner's wrist. But more about them in a moment.

Although as Elizabeth Cummins points out, Le Guin's dragons are "more Oriental than Occidental," certain aspects of the Western dragon model are just too effective to jettison, especially the poisonous nature of dragon's blood and the danger of looking directly into the dragon's eyes (which are catlike, with green or yellow vertical irises). Throughout the Earthsea novels, characters remember to avert their gaze when confronting dragons, even when they are cloaked in their human forms. Le Guin also preserves the tricky, coldly intelligent, devious mind of dragonkind, best expressed in her portrayal of the Dragon of Pendor. Such a dragon loves to toy with humans, entrapping them in clever dialogue while it decides whether or not to crisp them. Le Guin points out that her dragons don't feed on humans (as elemental creatures, they consume fire), but they will harass farms and cities when they feel humans have wronged them in some way.

Le Guin summarizes the nature of Earthsea dragons in Ged's dialogue with the youthful Arren, who clearly desires to see dragons as much as we do. Ged warns Arren about the dragons' venomous blood and basilisk gaze, as well as their pitiless, treacherous nature, but he refuses to condemn them: "But are they evil? Who am I, to judge the acts of dragons? … They are wiser than men are." Clearly these are not pre-Christian chaos dragons, nor are they Christian-era agents of Satan. But they are fearsome.

The first dragon we meet in Earthsea, Yevaud the Dragon of Pendor, exhibits all these delicious "dragony" attributes. He is, in fact, the most Western of Le Guin's dragons and pays no small homage to another fantasy dragon of great repute: Tolkien's Smaug. First conceived in the 1960s in a short story called "The Rule of Names" published in *Fantastic* magazine, Yevaud was a comical dragon in disguise as a Mr. Underhill (a wink at Frodo that one might expect from Pratchett rather than Le Guin). However, in *A*

Wizard of Earthsea, the reader's first impression of Yevaud leaves no doubt as to his affinity with the wicked worms of the West. The Low Torning islanders' warnings regarding the dragon do little to dissuade Ged from his intent to challenge the beast, but they give readers a very clear picture of the type of dragon we can expect.

> "... none had sought to revenge the Lord of Pendor, after the dragon came suddenly out of the west upon him and his men where they sat feasting in the tower, and smothered them with the flames of his mouth, and drove all the townsfolk screaming into the sea. Unavenged, Pendor had been left to the dragon, with all its bones, and towers, and jewels stolen from long-dead princes of the coasts of Paln and Hosk." (WE, 85)

This is as close as Le Guin comes to creating a ravening, treasure-hoarding saga dragon; the rest of her dragon characters – Orm Embar, Kalessin, Orm Irian, Tehanu, and Ammaud – are a bit different. As befits his sinister role, Yevaud's coloration is grey-black like burned stone, and his brood of dragonets are black-winged and "worm-thin," with black blood that "scalds" Ged's hands on contact. Yellow smoke trickles from the monster's nostrils when he laughs. Like Smaug, he enjoys toying with his prey and is amused by what he regards as a pitiful match against him. His weapons are talons like steel "as long as a man's forearm" and "withering fire" held ready in his throat; his defenses are a hide hard as stone and wits honed from centuries of deceitful manipulations.

The dragon-magic Ged anticipates is also typical of the Western model, "guileful in a sorcery like and unlike the sorcery of men." He is just quick enough to avoid the dragon's "oily green gaze" that can entrap the unwary, and he knows that dragons are legendary for being able to twist "true words to false ends, catching the unwary hearer in a maze of mirrorwords." As one would expect, this dragon makes use of taunts and temptations to confuse his adversary, first offering something he knows the wizard probably won't fall for: an invitation to come ashore and inspect his hoard. Typically, the dragon has a trump – information that Ged badly wants – which he saves for last.

The dragon plays this trump card with typical reptilian flair, eliciting from Ged an unguarded reaction of admission in much the same way that Smaug tricks information out of Bilbo about the dwarves and their mission. The fact that the wizard has his own secret trump, the dragon's true name, is pivotal. By cleverly setting up a way to bring the contest to a stalemate, Le Guin initiates the chain of cause and effect that creates the history many Earthsea legends refer to in subsequent novels. By speaking his true name, Ged can force the dragon to swear never to maraud the human lands east of Pendor; thus the Archipelago remains dragon-free until the events recounted in *The Other Wind.* In spite of the dragon's terrible rage and hatred toward the mage, "his oath held him." This episode demonstrates the main convention in Le Guin's Earthsea world: magical power is inherent in names from the Language of Making.

The Dragon of Pendor aside, Le Guin's other dragons present a number of parallels with the Chinese mythological dragon, which is not the same as the somewhat destructive and capricious folktale Dragon King. The Chinese equivalent of a celestial divine being is the sky dragon *tianlong* (*tian* meaning both physical sky and heaven, *long* meaning dragon), who regulates life on earth through sun and rain and is seen in cloud shapes as well as in the wind and lightning. The natural world to the Chinese mind is "filled with the divine majesty of the transcendent, of absolute reality," which is the precise quality with which Le Guin's elder dragons are endowed, particularly Kalessin, who is Eldest and wisest, and Orm Embar, who sacrifices his life to enable Ged's quest to succeed.

Le Guin has mentioned in interviews and essays that the *Tao Te Ching* has been a guiding influence in her writing, and indeed her dragons owe much to that philosophy. The Chinese mythological dragon is a noble creature of benevolent power and wisdom, much like Le Guin's Kalessin. Elizabeth Cummins' study of Le Guin makes an interesting point that's relevant here. Characters earn the epithet "Dragonlord" in the world of Earthsea not because they have slain a dragon, but because dragons will talk to them in their own language, the Old Speech of the Making. Confucius, it's said, had a similar experience when he first encountered the sage Lao Tzu. Unlike ordinary animals, said Confucius, the Dragon exists in its own plane of being: "I don't know how it rides on the wind or how it reaches the heaven. Today I met Lao Tzu. I can say that I have seen the Dragon" (as recounted in *Shiji – Records of the Historian*). The Taoist dragon is charming yet dangerous, undermining authority simply by its state of being in which all creatures are equal, master of none and mastered by none; it is ultimately unfathomable.

So, how did Lao Tzu's wisdom translate into dragon imagery, and more to our purpose, how did that imagery enter Earthsea? We'll have to go back to the *I Ching* for clues. Consider the six unbroken lines of the first hexagram, representing primal power, creativity, continuity, harmonious transformation; these are also the qualities of the ancient dragon species brought into being by Segoy, Earthsea's creator. The hexagram lines that invoke the power of dragons are as follows: 1 (Hidden Dragon – holding power in check with calm strength), 2 (Dragon in the Field – light-giving power appears, creative potential is unfettered), 5 (Flying Dragon in the Heavens – great good fortune; all things flow freely in harmony, the joy of life and movement).

All six unbroken lines together: "a flight of dragons with no leader – good fortune." The six dragons fly wing to wing, guided by the self-sustaining invisible force of creation itself. Thus the entire hexagram is in motion, changing into the Kun hexagram (the Receptive), whose character is magnanimity. Compare this with Ged's vision of the dragons dancing together: "They fly on their great wings in spirals, in and out ... like a storming of yellow leaves in autumn," he tells the young priestess Tenar, his staring eyes "seeing the open sea stretch unbroken to the sunset, the golden dragons on the golden wind."

As the dragon symbology moves through the lines of the hexagrams, unbroken lines manifesting positive dynamic energy and broken lines suggesting the opposite, we realize the potentiality of the image. Change is always possible, even probable. The Chinese spiritual dragon demonstrates the continuous transformation of one force into the other – yin continually balances yang. Le Guin has clearly incorporated these elements into her concept of dragonkind. Tenar confirms to King Lebannen that dragons are "the sacred sign and pledge of death and rebirth," Acknowledging this draconic integration of yin and yang, he tells his people "when the dragon comes, do not fear it, do not fight it, do not flee it, but welcome it in the Sign of Peace. Greet it as you would greet a great lord come in peace from afar." In her retelling of the *Tao Te Ching*, Le Guin calls these interactions of yin and yang "the great reversals that maintain the living balance of the world."

Under the Hood: Le Guin's Technique Revealed

Says Le Guin scholar Charlotte Spivack, "Le Guin's mythopoeic imagination is gracefully fulfilled and embodied in her elegantly precise style." Nowhere is this gift of language better demonstrated than in her descriptions of dragons. Although the diction, narrative style, and point of view vary significantly across the Earthsea cycle, the dragons are always breathtaking (compare, for example, the high saga style of *A Wizard of Earthsea* with the despairing reality of *Tehanu*)..

Le Guin's elegant, flowing prose can be lyrical and poetic as well as stark with epic grandeur. She has in abundance what many writers lack: a keen "inner ear" for the way language sounds in the mind, particularly the cadence of syntax, the inevitable rise and fall of sentences and paragraphs, the absolute rightness of names. In her essay "Dreams Must Explain Themselves," she addresses the issue of choosing names, explaining that "I hear them." The analogy of music used earlier to explain magical talent in Earthsea applies equally well to the writer herself. It's the difference between a wordsmith who is tone deaf and one who possesses perfect pitch, Le Guin being one of the latter.

Naming and the use of true names is the means by which magic is acquired as a high art form in the Archipelago; likewise, it's how Le Guin applies fictional magic to her characters. The dragons' names are evocative. As examples of the Old Speech, they conjure up transitory visual as well as auditory images: Kalessin, Orm Embar, Yevaud. You can almost hear the hiss of smoke escaping from jaws and nostrils, see the glowing embers of dragon fire, feel the hardness of stone-like scales. Masters of elevated style such as E. R. Eddison, Kenneth Morris, Lord Dunsany, and J. R. R. Tolkien were her early touchstones, and it was through appreciation of such works as *The Worm Ouroboros* and *The Lord of the Rings* that she began to find her own voice.

Her essay "From Elfland to Poughkeepsie" is an amazingly funny rant on the abuse of high style in fantasy writing, in part because it's dead on target for all the pitfalls that type of style invites. Good prose, in her estimation, is "exact, clear, powerful. Visually it is precise and vivid; musically – that is, in the sound of the words, the movement of the syntax, and the rhythm of the sentences – it is subtle and very strong." She could have been describing herself writing the following scene in which Kalessin makes his first appearance. Emotionally and physically spent after escaping from the Mountains of Pain, Arren looks across a stream and realizes he is being watched:

> "Its head, the color of iron, stained as with red rust at nostril and eye-socket and jowl, hung facing him, almost over him. The talons sank deep into the soft, wet sand on the edge of the stream. The folded wings were partly visible, like sails, but the length of the dark body was lost in the fog.
>
> It did not move. It might have been crouching there for hours, or for years, or for centuries. It was carved of iron, shaped from rock – but the eyes, the eyes he dared not look into, the eyes like oil coiling on water, like yellow smoke behind glass, the opaque, profound yellow eyes watched Arren." (FS, 248)

Several of her trademark devices are displayed in that passage. In spite of its simplicity of diction, we find alliteration, retarding devices of repetition, apposition, and parallelism, and figures of speech such as simile and metaphor.[2] Dissecting the passage, you'll notice that alliteration occurs in "red rust," "oil coiling" and "soft ... sand." Devices that retard or regulate the movement of the lines include exact repetition ("the eyes, the eyes") and repetition with variation ("for hours, or for years, or for centuries"). Likewise, we find the wavelike motion of parallelism ("carved of iron, shaped from rock"). There's an appositive (parenthetical) construction as well in the first sentence. Similes include wings "like sails," eyes that reflect like oil on water and "yellow smoke behind glass." It's revealing to note that these are also key elements of the Eddic poetry Tolkien knew so well. It shouldn't surprise anyone that Le Guin has published numerous volumes of poetry as well as prose.

Le Guin's dragon imagery is consistently sensory, with references to smoke, fire, burning, heat, and metal too hot to touch. Kalessin, perched on a chilly windswept mountain ledge, demonstrates this effect when the narrator tells us that the "heat of the dragon's body beat through the cold sea wind" Also in *Tehanu*, when Ged returns home to Gont on the dragon's back, Tenar feels the "heat of its body" just standing nearby. Through her POV, we see details of the creature's alien body so close we feel the urge to back away from its "mailed flanks" and "armored carapaces," its "scythe-blade talons" and "fuming nostrils." Olfactory images etch the picture more precisely; we can almost smell the "coils of smoke fading behind it in the air" as the "stink of burning filled the wind." She is close enough to see its fiery tongue and hear its smoky voice.

Even speaking the dragon's name after it has gone calls up this imagery of heat and flame. Tenar forms her mouth around the sound of Kalessin's name, "making her breath soft fire." The dragon/human child Therru responds to the sound of Kalessin's name with a "wave of warmth, heat" flowing out around her like a fever. Her name itself means "burning, the flaming of fire," which has a double meaning that doesn't become apparent until near the end of the novel. On the surface, the name references her disfigurement by burns from a campfire, but the name is also a foreshadowing of her true nature. At the moment she embraces her dragon form, fire runs along her body and into her hair, blazing "up into great wings above her head," as she rises in flight, "a creature all fire, blazing, beautiful."

Dragon hide colors are metallic hues: iron gray or black, rust, or gold. The description of Kalessin's scales as "iron-dark" with rusty touches around the eyes and mouth and his dark red wings the color of rust or blood give the sense of great age and weight. Irian's shift from vigorous young woman to dragon reveals a vibrant red-gold form. Orm Embar is the epitome of beauty and power with his undulating golden body and huge golden wings swimming through air in glittering movements. Le Guin emphasizes the impact of his death by shifting this color imagery – struggling out of the surf on Selidor, Arren sadly notes the hulking grey body of the dead dragon that was once golden Orm Embar.

With carefully chosen sound imagery (my boldface added) describing Kalessin's rescue of Tenar and Ged from the wizard Aspen, Le Guin implies the immense size and threat of the great dragon "as the **roar** of fire went over them, the **rattle** of mail and the **hiss** of wind in upraised wings, the **clash** of the talons like scythblades on the rock." Similes are used with poetic skill to emphasize size and weight; for example, Kalessin's huge head is described with "nostril pits, big as kettles, bright with fire." A passage introducing the dragon Ammaud employs metallic sound imagery to similar effect: "... those wings were fifty feet from tip to tip, and as they beat they made a sound like kettledrums or rattles of brass."

Talking with Dragons

Orson Scott Card said in his book on writing fantasy that if you intend to write about aliens, you have to figure out how to communicate with them and how humans will relate to them. He included dragons in the alien category.

The simplest approach is the way in which Tolkien deals with dragon dialogue: treating it the same as human speech with no typographical peculiarities or specialized dragon language. He lets diction – mere word choice – indicate the dragon's mood and intelligence. McCaffrey, you will remember, presents her direct dragon speech as telepathic, rendered in italics, because the only audible communication her dragons can make are animal chirps and bellows. Le Guin's dragons communicate audibly in speech, but the rendering is more complicated than Tolkien's.

The basic convention Le Guin establishes is that her dragons can vocalize. They also make shrieks, hisses, and cries like animals, but they definitely talk to humans in an audible, not telepathic, language. What complicates rendering this in print is that they only communicate in the Speech of the Making, the Old Speech. Thus we have two additional conventions: Old Speech (her invented words, not English) is always printed in italics, but when we are told that the dialogue is taking place in Old Speech by both parties, English in regular type is used. In many of these latter instances, the archaic pronouns *thee, thou,* and *thine* are used to indicate the ancient tone of dragon speech.

In chapter 5 of *A Wizard of Earthsea*, the entire exchange between Ged and the Dragon of Pendor, two adversaries speaking the Language of the Making, is given in print as normal dialogue, with no italics or need for translations. "'You are a very young wizard,' the dragon said, 'I did not know men came so young into their power.' He spoke, as did Ged, in the Old Speech, for that is the tongue of dragons still."

The combined approach occurs frequently in *Tehanu,* for example. Early in the novel Kalessin delivers Ged to his mountain retreat and encounters Tenar, who doesn't understand Old Speech. Thus all Kalessin's words are rendered in italics, with no translation, to let readers experience the dragon's bemused attempts to make her understand what is needed ("*Ahi eheraihe, Ged!* said the dragon, a little louder"). When she finally hears a word she recognizes ("'*Sobriost,*' it said"), the narrator includes a translation ("That word of the Language of the Making she knew ... Go up, the dragon said: mount!"). In the final chapter, we first hear Kalessin address Therru/Tehanu in Old Speech: "*Aro Tehanu?*" However, the remainder of the exchange between the child and Kalessin is rendered as normal human dialogue with no italics, while the narrator informs us "she spoke in the language of the dragons, the words of the Making."

In some instances this approach to dragon speech can be frustrating for the reader, a problem that is related directly to how point of view is handled. We almost never enter into the dragon's minds and hear their words directly from their POV, with the exception of the shape-shifters Tehanu and Orm Irian, whom we know as human characters. Often, we don't hear the direct speech of the dragons at all; instead, the narrator tells us that the dragon spoke or a character translates what they supposedly have just said. While this approach requires the reader's imagination to fill in the gap, it also creates distance. Perhaps Le Guin's intention is to emphasize that the dragons are ultimately unknowable and remote, in essence, alien.

A good example occurs in *The Other Wind*, when the king rides out to discover why dragons have begun marauding the lands of men. Tehanu's call to the dragon leader Ammaud is shown in Old Speech first: "'*Medeu!*' Tehanu called, and the answer came like an echo prolonged: *'Me-de-uuu!'* 'What does it mean?' Lebannen asked, bending to Onyx. 'Sister, brother,' the wizard whispered." In a visually stunning scene, the massive dragon swoops down to hover just above the woman as she reaches up to it. It's a scene of tremendous drama and tension, and the reader is anxious to participate in their dialogue, to hear how the dragons phrase their anger toward humans in general but with respect for the half-human woman who is their translator. But we are denied that experience. Instead we read, "Tehanu spoke, the dragon spoke, both briefly, in their cymbal-shiver voices. Another exchange, a pause; the dragon spoke at length. Onyx listened intently. One more exchange of words ... She spoke clearly two words. 'Bring her,' the wizard translated in a whisper." Those two words are all we are given, second-hand, of this important human/dragon interaction.

In contrast, the actual sound of dragon voices is appropriately described with imagery drawn from the ingredients already associated with dragons: metal and fire. In *The Farthest Shore*, we hear what the dragon's voice sounds like ("soft and hissing," "terrible music"), but not what was said. Some of Le Guin's best metaphors and similes describe the draconic voice: "a whisper of steel sliding over steel," "like the dry roar of a kiln-fire," "like a broom of metal dragged across a gong," "like the noise of an avalanche, stones falling among mountains," "high, metallic," "cymbal-shiver," "like a sea of cymbals." The child Therru's unearthly voice – "a metal brush drawn across metal, like dry leaves, like the hiss of fire burning" – foreshadows the emergence of her true dragon form.

How humans relate to dragons and vice versa provides a great deal of the substance with which the world of Earthsea is shaped. Le Guin has been praised consistently for her mythmaking ability – building a very convincing secondary world, with pseudo-historical details about dragons in the form of legends, old ballads and sea chanteys, homilies and charms, figures of speech, municipal sculpture, ship's prows, and libraries filled with histories and rune books. We learn early on in the first novel that dragon references are ubiquitous to Earthsea, and that their very real existence isn't questioned by the people of the Archipelago. Those lands farthest from the western dragon realm, the Kargad Lands, have had no direct contact for many centuries, but ironically have preserved the earliest myths of the origin of dragons (which they take to be symbolic rather than literal).

General dragonlore is sprinkled throughout the stories. For example, the first two hints of the existence of dragons in Earthsea come in the first chapter of *A Wizard of Earthsea*: on the first page the narrator informs us this is a tale of a man who is both Archmage and dragonlord; later the narrator briefly draws the reader's attention to a village chanter singing the *Deed of the Dragonlords* at Ged's naming ceremony. Somewhat later, when the main port of Gont is described as having great dragons carved on the pillars of the landgate and the ship on which young Sparrowhawk departs has a carving of the Old Serpent of Andrad on its keel, we start to get the idea.

All over the islands of the Archipelago, dragon-related sayings abound. Some of the best ones include "better guarded than a dragon's den," "the hunger of a dragon is slow to wake, but hard to sate," "bright as the prize of a dragon's hoard," "hoard it, as a young dragon hoards up its fire," "where mages argue, dragons may be wise," "what dragons hunt, they find," and my personal favorite, "The question is always the same, with a dragon: will he talk with you or will he eat you?" which immediately begs the question, are Earthsea dragons allies or foes? The answer is *both*, depending on the circumstances.

Since we don't enter the dragon's thoughts directly, we learn most of our Earthsea dragonlore from what others say about them. Characters comment on them, or we observe their behavior through others' eyes, with additional interpretations coming from the narrator. Which characters give us the best information? Mainly the Dragonlords, humans to whom the dragons will speak. Ged, of course, as Le Guin's chief wizard has met more dragons than anyone else, so his understanding of them is valuable. He's well aware of all the warnings and dangers inherent in dealing directly with them, as we know from his successful entrapment of no less than Yevaud of Pendor, a dragon renowned for subtle duplicity and bloodthirsty inclination. More important, the ancient noble dragons know Ged and treat him with respect, as they do also for Arren (King Lebannen), who has interacted personally with Ged's closest dragon friend Orm Embar, as well as the Eldest, Kalessin. The dragons also speak to Tenar of Atuan (eventually Ged's wife) and their foster-child Therru/Tehanu.

What we really see through the eyes and ears of others is how the Earthsea dragons sort out as friend or foe. Legend tells us that dragons are aloof and hold their race apart, living beyond the Far Reaches in the West, and when they do clash with humans, the outcome is unpleasant. The greatest legend of dragon vs. human is that of the ancient dragon Orm and hero Erreth-Akbe, a mage-king. Both perished in the conflict, but their fame lives in song and sword (an artifact ensconced on the palace tower). The Dragon of Pendor, as we've seen, represents foe of the most typical kind, and his brood eventually would have preyed on the livestock of the islanders if Ged hadn't killed them.

Creating an alliance with dragons is chancy: you can't master a dragon because they have no masters; they decide if they will talk or fight. They may be wise, but they aren't kind. To creatures who live a thousand years, the life of a human is like a moth or insect in their scheme of things. Only on a grand scale (undoing the balance of Earthsea) are they moved to get involved.

Dragons are beyond good and evil. They are the integration of all existence, with the knowledge that the universe is impartial. Their utter wildness is balanced by their ancient wisdom; between the two, they are simply expressions of the universe. The dragons affected by Cob's evil magic turn into voiceless brutes, attacking Ged and each other. They are unbalanced. The raft people who witness Ged's interaction with Orm Embar can't tell if it's an ally or an enemy. Ged clarifies that the dragon was angry and afraid, and chagrined to have to ask a human for help.

Orm Embar is unique among dragons in that he is straightforward in dealing with humans and hides nothing, not even his true name. He genuinely tries to communicate with Ged truthfully with no typical dragon deviousness. Having once shown mercy to Ged by saving his life and telling him how to restore the Ring of Peace, Orm Embar presents the Archmage the opportunity to repay the debt. Ged tells us that this is a watershed event. This is an open alliance of human and dragon initiated at the dragon's request. It's interesting that the effort of speaking with Orm Embar, who is genuinely friendly toward Ged, drains the wizard's strength, even in the context of allies working together to right a universal wrong.

Even when dragons try to "talk straight" to humans, they aren't sure how it should be done. Thus Ged has difficulty determining how much of what the dragon says is metaphorical or equivocal and what is literal. Ged also takes a calculated risk in introducing another human to him, given the capricious nature of dragons. Ged's act displays trust toward the dragon, assuming it will see Arren is another ally, the future king fulfilling a prophecy of which the dragon would be aware.

What truly sets Orm Embar apart is his almost human display of heroism during the confrontation with Cob. The dragon willingly and deliberately places himself between Ged and potential death from Cob's staff. This sacrifice displays an uncommon alignment of dragonkind with human agendas, making choices that revolve around the concepts of good and evil. The dragon's motives are complex as well; his death impaled on the wizard's staff is deliberate, not accidental. This act does several things. Although it doesn't kill Cob, it successfully disables him, giving Ged a momentary advantage that might be enough to defeat the evil wizard and repair his rift made between worlds. On a more personal level, though, Orm Embar has sacrificed himself to protect his human friends, something no one in Earthsea would have expected.

The truce between dragonkind and humans brokered by Lebannen and Orm Irian pays back Orm Embar's sacrifice. The young king he protected is now in a position to restore the balance disrupted by the existence of the Dry Land, created by human magic in imitation of dragonkind's life beyond death, on "the other wind." Irian parlays on behalf of Ammaud and his followers who honor Kalessin. She's relaxed, almost jovial, at the court of Havnor while in her human form, which is a far cry from her grim, commanding behavior witnessed just before her transformation on Roke Island. However, the seriousness of her mission as Kalessin's emissary is paramount.

Her eloquent explanation before the king's council of the nature of the conflict clearly spells out how dragons regard humans. They don't enjoy preying on human settlements and don't particularly want to kill them, but they do want to stop what they perceive as human encroachment into realms where they don't belong. Dragons have long lives and ancient memories, so they remember the original bargain between dragons and humans, while humans have lost the knowledge almost entirely. The militant dragons believe humans should be put in their place, but what really is their place and who's to enforce it? This brings us to Kalessin, also called Eldest, and the most important question regarding dragons in Earthsea: what are they and where did they come from?

Origin of the Species

Possibly the most intriguing element of Le Guin's dragons is hinted at in the first trilogy and fully revealed in the second: dragons and humans were originally a single species. This knowledge was planted early in the first Earthsea trilogy, and plays out dramatically in the climax of the second.

As Eldest, knowledge of this fact of origin resides with the ancient dragon Kalessin. The patriarch of his species, Kalessin is introduced to us first by hearsay and rumor, building up our expectations before his stunning appearance in the flesh. The narrator mentions that both Kalessin's age and gender are indeterminate. Because Le Guin refers to him with masculine pronouns, I'll follow that convention as well.

The first mention of him is at the beginning of *The Farthest Shore* in which the narrator informs us that Kalessin is the only dragon besides Orm Embar that knows the Archmage Ged's true name. Kalessin is next mentioned by Ged once the quest to save Earthsea's magic is well underway. Encountering the maddened dragons and the slaughtered beast on the shore near the reefs known as Dragon's Run, Ged laments the shame of the sight, wondering aloud where Kalessin has taken refuge. The reader now wonders as well, and we might expect him to come thundering to the rescue to defend dragonkind, but that would be too easy, and Le Guin is a more subtle writer than that.

The human-friendly Orm Embar gets directly involved in the fight with Cob, whose rogue magic has devised a way to cheat death and steal the knowledge of the Making from dragons, reducing them to terrified wild beasts. Kalessin's appearance out of the mist when Ged and Arren return to the land of the living accomplishes several things. He comes back to the edge of the human world from the uttermost West to ensure the restoration of each survivor to his rightful place: Ged to his homeland of Gont and Arren to his destiny as king in Havnor. It's Kalessin who witnesses Ged's shift from powerful mage to spent old man and Lebannen's transformation from boy to man and king. Kalessin's presence at this point in the story confirms the success of the quest and in a sense bestows the blessing of the Elder race on their estranged cousins.

Kalessin is the only dragon that transports human riders. In oriental dragon mythology, this is regarded as a privilege of rank or a sign of divinity. Chinese poetry and visual art from the Warring States Period in Hunan Province or Eastern Jin Dynasty are full of images of humans ascending to the heavens on a regal dragon or in a carriage drawn by flying dragons. Ged may be humbled by the total loss of his magic, but he's honored that the greatest of Earthsea dragons is willing to deliver him in safety to the one place where he can be healed, his mountaintop retreat where Tenar waits. The care with which the great dragon lifts his wings and crouches in preparation to lift off so that its tiny helpless riders won't be unseated is yet another indication of the respect given them. In spite of all, Kalessin regards the scene calmly with "ancient laughter" in his expression as if to say, "yes that was a horrible experience, but now you will ride on a dragon's back – such is life." I could be convinced that somewhere in Le Guin's imagination Kalessin has Buddha-nature.

We see a repeat of this attitude when Kalessin deposits Ged safely on the Gont cliff ledge in front of a shocked Tenar. The dragon laughs in a "great 'Hah!' of orange flame" when he encourages Ged to dismount. His mouth seems set in a perpetual smile as he waits for Tenar to figure out how to get the unconscious Ged down off his back. As before, his manner is passive, mild, and gentle with the puny human creatures, taking care to move his huge taloned feet away from Ged's sprawled body before launching back into the air.

Kalessin is anything but gentle, however, when he comes flaming out of the sky in a power dive that destroys the evil wizard Aspen. What rouses him to intrude into the affairs of humans once again is a call for help from one of his own, the burned child Therru, who is then revealed to be a dragon in human form. Kalessin acknowledges her as his own, calling her daughter. The unfathomable dragon's nature is again demonstrated by his response to her decision to remain behind with her human family awhile longer. "Kalessin turned aside to give that immense furnace-blast of laughter or contempt or delight or anger – 'Hah!'" What this scene accomplishes besides the obvious rescue of Ged, Tenar, and Therru is that the dragon child has embraced her true nature by calling out to her great sire, who comes at her beckoning. And most important of all, he gives her true name to her – Tehanu, literally "white star." Tehanu's importance to the history of human/dragon evolution is that she is the final such hybrid that will be born among humans. The final split of the two species is about to be accomplished, at which time Kalessin will come to collect her permanently. But before we see how dragons and humans are sundered permanently, we need to look back at how the first split occurred.

Le Guin creates at least three major retellings of the creation myth, each with a slightly different slant, each adding more detail and filling in missing pieces. Leading up to it she plants several strong clues along the way about this monumental fact of dragon/human evolution. The first is in *The Tombs of Atuan* where the young priestess Tenar discovers the Painted Room among the tunnels of her underground domain. On its walls are depicted "men with long wings and great eyes, serene and morose." The fact that neither Tenar nor anyone among her retinue knows what these paintings mean or who put them there shows how long the truth has languished among the civilizations of humans. Her uneducated guess that they are spirits of souls who can't reincarnate is closer to the mark than she can possibly know. Readers won't find out how accurate she is until the last book of the second trilogy, *The Other Wind*, where it's revealed that souls from lands of wizardly magic end up trapped indefinitely in the mage-created Dry Land.

When Ged encounters Tenar, he's a maturing wizard at the height of his powers. Even so, the dragonlore he shares with her is missing this key fact. His little lesson on dragons shows how much respect he holds for them and perhaps how little they have toward humans. "Dragons think we are amusing," he says, but then qualifies that assessment with the legend of Erreth-Akbe. In *The Farthest Shore*, Ged tells Arren that humans are "mayflies" in comparison to the longevity of dragons. It's easy to see why dragons might not take humans seriously, but the disruption of the Equilibrium forces all Earthsea inhabitants to look back at the beginning and see how the original division of the species has been corrupted.

Tenar gives readers the first full explanation of how Segoy created the creatures and places of Earthsea by telling Therru the story of creation told her by Ged's teacher Ogion. Tenar's plot significance throughout the story is important because it touches on all the strands of human-dragon interaction that are pulled together in the second trilogy. She begins by telling the child what a shape-changer is, which leads to an explanation of how wizards of great power can become another creature, not just look like one in an illusion. From there, she tells how Ogion heard an old sea chantey with a refrain about "dancing on the other wind" that led him to an encounter with someone who was two beings at once, something not even the greatest of wizards could accomplish. This Woman of Kemay, according to Ogion's account, appeared to him in the doorway as a dragon with golden scales surrounded by an aura of flame, which she quickly cloaked with her human form. In answer to Ogion's question "Are you woman or dragon?" she offers to sing him a story.

It's in this story that Le Guin plants the creation of the first beings. She has Tenar tell it to Therru, so that we start out the novel *Tehanu* knowing these fascinating facts about the original dragon people:

- At the beginning of time, Segoy raised up the land and made the first living creature.
- The first beings were all one race, dragon and human combined.
- They had wings and spoke the Language of the Making.
- They were "beautiful, and strong, and wise, and free."
- Over time, they began to separate into two very different groupings: those who loved wildness and flight, and those who loved gathering wealth and learning and living on the ground in enclosed dwelling.
- Flying wild dragons inhabited the western islands and beyond as their numbers dwindled.
- The grounded people lost their wings but increased in numbers in the eastern Archipelago.

- The two groups constantly made war on each other.
- A small portion of the grounded humans preserved their knowledge of the Old Speech and became wizards.
- A small portion of the original unsplit dragon-people disappeared to the other side of the world where they continue to live in harmony, as they began.

We now have part of the backstory in place, although there are still some points yet to come to light. The creation account from the Woman of Kemay is a basic, somewhat biased version and doesn't include such things as the bargain agreed to when the dragon-people divided into two different species. But as Tenar's tale reveals, clues have been laid all along the way that point to the fact that Therru is one of these rare double beings, half-human/half-dragon. As we've already discussed, at the climax of the novel, the leader of all dragons bestows both her name and identity on her, calling her daughter and admitting "I have sought thee long." However, it isn't until the third novel of the trilogy, *The Other Wind,*" that we discover why these very rare hybrids appear in human populations. That tale is reserved for Kalessin.

In *Tales of Earthsea*, Le Guin introduces a second double being, the rustic young woman named Dragonfly, who becomes the dragon Orm Irian. She's been discussed previously concerning her role as shape-shifter, but her introduction in *Tales of Earthsea* provides the "bridge" to the culmination of dragon history presented in *The Other Wind* where she delivers the second telling of the dragon/human species split. But before that, her story in "Dragonfly" delves at length into the interaction between dragonkind and human wizards, giving a narrative told from the human-dragon's point of view as well as that of the wizard's.

Humans tend to treat these human/dragon women as stupid, demonstrating through both irony and abuse that these are inferior beings. Both Tehanu and Dragonfly seem simple-minded at first, but as we see, they think with a higher, half-alien mind. One convention of Earthsea magic is that humans can't lie or deceive using Old Speech, which explains why both shape-shifters seem literal-minded to the point of slowness. As we discover with both, however, they see a different reality. For example, the story

"Dragonfly" allows Le Guin to pull off one of her effective character reversals that is both subtle and surprising when it happens.

All along it has seemed that the manipulating sorcerer Ivory is pulling the strings and using the lovely bumpkin Dragonfly for his own selfish agenda, which first involves getting her into his bed but rapidly morphs into a scheme for revenge on Roke School for expelling him. But when his joke of getting her admitted to the all-male wizard school backfires, and the Doorkeeper actually lets her in, she says simply that she used the wizard Ivory in order to get to Roke where she hopes to learn her true identity. This turnaround deftly illustrates the way in which half-beings are treated in the human world. Ivory has assumed Dragonfly is stupid because she takes what he says literally and doesn't seem to be interested in his petty flirtations and games of manipulation. But as we now know, her agenda is much loftier than his and brings about a change that shakes Roke's gender-biased wizard institution to its foundations. This "thoughtful feminism" is a message Le Guin began incorporating into her fiction from the mid-eighties onward.

Irian's return as fully empowered dragon in *The Other Wind* commands respect and some nervousness from the humans who witness her arrival in majestic red-gold dragon form. No longer is she testy and ill at ease. Now she knows who and what she is and adopts the amused benevolence toward humans displayed by the elder dragons. Her appearance at the Dragon Council as participant in the final quest to restore the Balance of Earthsea provides the second lengthy retelling of the creation myth. Her slant on the story is given mostly in a second-hand telling of Kalessin's words. He explains the reason shape-changers like herself are born into human communities: because once dragons and humans were one people, "in sign of that, in every generation of men, one or two are born who are dragons also." The reverse is also true, that a human is occasionally born into the dragon population. But now, because of the current quest that will change the Balance, no more will come. Kalessin's words come in the form of an oracle: Irian and Tehanu are the last of the shape-changers, and their role is to be messengers of choice for dragons and humans.

The three choices Kalessin's message stipulates are these: (1) dragons who wish to regain their ancient heritage can go beyond the West to the other wind (which he chooses himself), (2) dragons who choose to stay in human lands will put on their "yoke of good and evil," and (3) some who stay may dwindle further into dumb beasts, such as exist in the mountains of the Kargad Lands. With the listing of these three options, Le Guin pulls together the plot strands that have threaded their way through both trilogies. It's clear that Kalessin represents the first choice, as do the two messengers Irian and Tehanu. Yevaud and his brood, as well as the young marauding dragons of *The Other Wind*, represent the second choice. The third choice is embodied in the sacrifice-eating dragon beasts of the Kargad Mountains and to some degree in the tiny dragonets called *harrekki*, which humans use as house pets.

Irian's council declaration also tells how the bargain made between the separating species has been broken. "Men in their envy of us long ago stole half our realm beyond the west from us and made walls of spells to keep us out of it." We know what this place is: the Dry Land, where Cob tried to manufacture his immortality. According to Kalessin's lore, "Long ago we chose. We chose freedom. Men chose the yoke. We chose fire and the wind They chose water and the earth." The oath sworn that each group will go its own way (dragons to the skies of the West and humans to the eastward lands) was broken when ancient mages, envious of the dragon's immortal life on the other wind, tried to create a parallel place for humans using a piece of that space. Irian also warns that after Tehanu makes her transformation, the way west into the other wind will be closed forever, by which readers realize this is the approaching climax of the Earthsea cycle.

The Kargad princess adds the final version of the myth, the *Vedurnan* (Division), which has been preserved by the Kargad people among their ancient rituals. She tells of the devolved dragons of the Kargad Mountains, the puzzle piece that explains what happened to the dragons that kept their animal form in human lands. They have stubby useless wings and crawl down the slopes once a year along a beaten track known as the Dragon's Way. Here Le Guin incorporates a Western dragon trait (eating sacrificial maidens) into her dragonlore, but with a twist (echoing Buddhist dragon legends of mountain *nagas* that were dangerous and feared by villagers). They are wild beasts that have learned a behavior pattern humans continue to placate, not the intelligent dragons of the original Making.

When Lebannen shares her tale with the masters of Roke, they contribute a few additional details, thus tying the immortality theme into the creation myth. Here Le Guin injects the concept of reincarnation: humans who lost all knowledge of the Old Speech die and are reincarnated as dragons or humans. But those humans who kept knowledge of the Language of the Making and developed sorcery from it get stuck in the Dry Land when they die; in essence, they can neither die or nor return to the living. Righting this unnatural state of imbalance is the driving force of the second trilogy, but as the wizards suspect, removing the Dry Land and freeing the souls trapped there will change the nature of the Equilibrium.

The result is a Tolkienesque departure of magical beings into the West; those who remain will diminish and devolve. Unlike Middle-earth's passing of the elves and wizards, however, Earthsea gets to keep its wizards and their magic even though the dragons are gone for good. Says the Roke Master Doorkeeper as the walls of the Dry Land are being dismantled, "We made it [knowledge of the Language of the Making] ours. It can't be taken from us. To lose it we must forget it, throw it away." Perhaps Ged's pithy statement at the end of the novel encapsulates Le Guin's Eastern worldview best of all: "We broke the world to make it whole."

In Conclusion

Like ripples in a pond, Le Guin's human characters act and create consequences that are judged as good or evil; her dragon characters look on with enigmatic internal laughter and depart into "the other wind," beyond the yoke of choice. In Taoist terms, humans do, dragons are. Le Guin's admission in interviews that her primary focus is on emotional relationships between characters, with all their attendant arrogance and humility, applies to her dragons as well. The same comparisons of selfishness and selflessness can be made between Yevaud and Kalessin. In addition, the complicated relationships of the half-dragon women with their human families and their dragon brothers and sisters carry as much emotional impact as does the journey of Tenar and Ged from adversaries to soul mates.

The popularity of Le Guin's invented realm of Earthsea lies clearly in what she describes as the appeal of fantasy to readers: In our dynamically impermanent modern society, "we also long for the unalterable ... So people turn to the realms of fantasy for stability, ancient truths, immutable simplicities." Yet even in the world of Earthsea, the Balance can be changed, which infuses her secondary world with the "intellectual and ethical complexity" missing from much of what Le Guin labels "commodified fantasy." The tales of her humble heroes and Zen dragons do not fall into that lamentable category.

An elegant, graceful stylist as well as a skilled storyteller and mythmaker, Ursula K. Le Guin has won many Nebula and Hugo Awards, as well as a National Book Award, a Pushcart Prize, the Harold D. Vursell Memorial Award of the American Academy of Arts and Letters, a Newbery Honor, and the World Fantasy Award for Life Achievement. It's not difficult to see why.

Notes

FS – *The Farthest Shore*
OW – *The Other Wind*
T – *Tehanu*
TE – *Tales of Earthsea*
WE – *A Wizard of Earthsea*

1. Authorship of *The Book of Changes*, also called the *I Ching*, is open to debate. It is likely a compilation rather than the single work of one person, not necessarily all written down at one time several thousand years ago. However, it's certain that Lao Tzu was aware of it and studied its precepts, which appear in much of his own philosophy as expressed in the *Tao Te Ching*, also referred to as *The Book of the Way*.

2. To get a detailed understanding of Le Guin's writing techniques – down at the sentence and word level – let me recommend her volume of exercises and discussions on writing titled *Steering the Craft*.

Chapter 6

Jane Yolen
Poetry and Pit Dragons

"MAYBE WE can't have real dragons roaming the earth, fire-belching monsters a hundred and fifty feet long, with hard green scales and long serpentine tails ... But in our stories—both old and new—these dragons live, they fly, they fight, and sometimes, they die. In so doing, they touch the magic spot deep within us that does, indeed, desire dragons."

Jane Yolen's introduction to *Fire and Wings: Dragon Tales from East and West* (from which I've quoted above) suggests that so many readers and writers remain fascinated by dragons because "there is something seductive, something wonderful, something both scary and enlightening" about these creatures and the type of stories one can build around them. As one of the most admired and prolific of fantasy writers for the young adult (YA) market, Jane Yolen incorporates her love for dragons into her novels, short stories, essays, and poetry.

In fact, some of the best fantasy/scifi dragon tales can be found in the Young Adult section of libraries and bookstores, with many respected writers connected to the genre – Robert Asprin, Patricia Wrede, Andre Norton, Patricia McKillup, Laurence Yep, Susan Fletcher, Barbara Hambly,

Robert Stanek, the team of Tracy Hickman and Margaret Weis, Diana Metz, Kenneth Grahame, and Yolen are among the most prominent. Many of these authors enjoy crossover audiences of adolescents, teens, and adults. Among their widely varied approaches to fantasy in Young Adult fiction, you'll find dragons that are comical, sentimental, and serious, whose stories range from hilarious to heart breaking.

I've plucked Jane Yolen out of this pack for a couple of reasons. I was intrigued by Yolen's idea of pit-fighting dragons as her basic dragon environment (based on the illegal sports of cock and pit-bull fighting, which she abhors). In her invented world of Austar IV, an ex-penal colony planet, pit-dragon fighting is a legal government-endorsed part of the economy, but that still doesn't make it "right."

Her condemnation of the way humans subjugate and abuse dragons, which are treated as dumb animals but are gradually revealed to be a sentient species, is woven in both blatant and subtle ways throughout her Pit Dragon series of novels. A doctor advocating societal change labels the fighting pits "symptoms of a sick society." Inside the Pit arena itself, the wasteful death of a prime fighting dragon hamstrung in the ring and then sent immediately to the nearby slaughterhouse sears the emotions of Jakkin as he experiences its death-sendings. Here is Yolen's style at her most poetic and poignant:

> "... there was an agonizing streak of bright yellow pain. It blotted out all other colors, all other sensations. Then the yellow began a slow leakage off to the left-hand side, draining away to a somber grey background. Only one small, bright, flickering bit of yellow remained in the center of the grey, a candle flame that suddenly guttered and went out, leaving a wisp of lighter grey in the dark, like smoke from a candle snuff." (HB, 136)

This moral conflict is a constant that surrounds the boy Jakkin and his imprinted dragon; he loves her more than anything in the world yet rigorously trains her to fight in the pits (to severely injure other dragons and be injured in turn). He is both proud of her record of wins in the pit, yet hates putting her in harm's way for money. Observing the network of scars on her wings at one point, Jakkin "could read the history of her fights in those scars, and he loved and hated every lesion."

The theme of exploitation runs like a drumbeat throughout the series. As Heart's Blood begins to win her bouts, the heated argument between Jakkin and his sponsor about the true purpose of dragon fighting presents this theme from two perspectives. First, we have the boy on the verge of manhood who sees the pit tournaments in life and death terms. In counter-argument is the jaded dragon breeder who insists that the real issues are power and dominance, and all that implies for the planet's economy.

The theme is also carried by the motif of the mute: (1) Heart's Blood is bred specifically to be a mute, which gives her an advantage in the pit, but it robs her of her natural voice; (2) the cave people who trap Jakkin deliberately suppress their voices from infancy in favor of total telepathic connection, which becomes their means of dominating and controlling their dragons and each other. This opens the question of just who is really civilized? Jakkin's sympathies lie with the dragons.

Also attractive to me is the way in which Yolen's dragons communicate with each other and with linked humans. The dragon's actual voice is purely animal, huffing and grunting, "thrumming" in a type of dragon purr, or roaring that begins as a "deep bass note" and escalates into a piercing scream "beyond human hearing." But as young Jakkin discovers when he imprints a stolen hatchling (a rare gift among dragon trainers), a rich silent language awakens when the dragon and its handler share blood. These communications appear in the mind visually as landscapes of color; Yolen relies on her skill and practice as a poet to paint these images for the reader. The similarities with McCaffrey's Pernese dragons and their bonded riders are obvious, but Yolen does have some intriguing twists on the human/dragon relationship that are her own.

For example, the experience of color-telepathy has a deeper, semi-magical level that is only evident after a human is immersed in the blood of a dead dragon (live dragon blood burns human flesh on contact, like acid). The idea that bathing in dragon's blood or partaking of the dragon's body will confer special powers is an ancient concept (the Norse hero Sigurd understands the speech of birds after tasting the worm Fáfnir's heart, for example), but Yolen puts her own spin on the idea by having the two young protagonists shelter from the freezing night inside the dragon's body. This act is symbolic on several levels, for the dragon saves their lives both in life and in death. She puts her body between them and the gunfire of the enemy, giving them a brief moment to escape, and afterward her dead body protects them from the freezing After-Dark, but more significantly, transforms them into neo-humans who have dragon powers (the ability to withstand freezing cold with no adverse effects, as well as expanded senses that include the ability to see in the dark and deeper psi-level links).

This act embodies for the young pair of human heroes in the Pit Dragon series both a physical change and a mythic rite of passage. They are literally and figuratively reborn. Yolen says in her essay "Here Be Dragons" that "while dragons are mythical, they are also metaphoric. They stand for something beyond the page and beyond the actual story." This is the premise behind the plot of these novels. Beyond flesh and blood beasts to be trained and fought in the pits, the notion of dragon as "other," as something alien to be faced and embraced in order to attain mastery (to grow up, if you will) is the larger thematic fabric of Yolen's Pit Dragon series.

Heart's Blood and Her Offspring

Physically, Yolen's pit dragons are more in the Western than Eastern mold, and for most of the pit fighters, their temperament is Western as well, although this perception will change as we get to know the main dragon character, Heart's Blood. Pit fighters are selectively bred animals, not magical creatures in the sense that Kalessin and the Dragon of Ankh-Morpork are magical. Descendants of a nearly extinct indigenous feral species on the planet Austar IV, they have much more in common with the dragons of Pern. Warm-blooded reptilians, the largest are the size of elephants, with a body shape that's basically saurian (as opposed to serpentine). The somewhat crocodilian head is armored with two horns. Two large talons ("lanceae") on the paws of shortened front legs provide weapons for shredding an opponent's scaly hide in a manner that may bring to mind the terrifying velociraptors of the film *Jurassic Park*.

Pit dragons acquire the ability to breath flame by eating specific plants ("blisterweed" and "burnwort"), which must be consumed in large amounts to generate significant flame for fighting and defense. They are scaled in maturity, with back scales that can be sharp-edged enough to cut those who touch them. Their tongues are rough and thick rather than forked or snaky, and their totally black opaque eyes shine with menacing red sparks called "dragons fire" when they are aroused. Their eyes are generally reptilian, with a second membranous lid.

Their large ribbed wings, with taut membranes stretched across the wing frame and fleshy "feathers" that are really wing scales, can span twice the length of the body. Interestingly, Yolen has chosen to design her flying dragons such that they cannot carry human riders. Dragon nurseries maintain meticulous bloodlines to bring out traits valued in the fighting pits; females are called hens and males are cock dragons, further carrying out the cockfighting reference. Fighting temperament is linked genetically to scale color, which can shift until the dragon matures. Yolen allows an interesting variety of colors and splotch patterns in her dragons, including gradations of gray, brown, yellow, mustard, orange, and red, with deep wine red being the most desirable as it indicates the strongest fighting spirit. The quality of dragon scales can range from dull and spotty to highly iridescent with the gleam of mirrors.

General personality characteristics of pit dragons include a volatile temper and a vicious craftiness, especially among the dominant fighters, as their names imply (Murderer's Row, Blood Bath, Bloody Flag, Blood Brother). Not linked mentally or emotionally with their handlers and trainers, they know only anger, fighting lust, and hunger. Some regard humans with a deep-seated mistrust and fear, for if they fail to perform up to expectations or become unable to fight, they are immediately sent to the slaughterhouse.

Beyond this pit mentality, however, lies a sentience that's above the level of dumb beasts and only slightly below human intelligence. Readers discover along with Jakkin, as he bonds with his stolen hatchling, that dragons can reason and make decisions on their own. They are self-aware. Ultimately, Yolen reveals that the human-linked dragon can be fiercely loyal.

Halfway through her Pit Dragon series, she kills off her main dragon character in a desperate scene that comes as a shock to both readers and Jakkin. Heart's Blood deliberately sacrifices herself to save the two humans she loves. Yolen's command of the language is displayed in the dragon's death scene,[1] where shock, sorrow, and poetic beauty are all evoked in a single passage when, shot in the neck, the beast dies on top of those she tried to defend:

> "A third [shot] hit Heart's Blood in the throat, the unblemished, unscarred throat with its tender neck links of dark red scale. A bright flower seemed to bud and bloom there. Then, slowly falling, falling as though the world were ending, the dragon collapsed on top of Jakkin, on top of Akki, pushing them into the rock-littered ground. The rainbow of her mind went out color by color: red, orange, yellow, green, blue, indigo jewels fading one after another until all that was left was a faint violet glow." (HB, 327)

Heart's Blood's sacrifice plays directly into the larger theme of the series, that of a sentient race enslaved for base motives by an opportunistic race that cares little for their ultimate welfare. Humans on the planet (both primitive cavemen and sophisticated city dwellers) have enslaved and abused the dragon race. The former have bred and ritually killed them mainly through superstitious tradition, and the latter raise them for sport, meat, leather, and neutered, stunted pets. In a metaphor for the larger issue of the dragon species' enslavement, Yolen creates a subplot in which rebels attempt to unseat the planet's governing faction while spouting slogans about freedom and throwing off the yoke of oppression. The rebel plots are mainly misguided and destructive, while the race that really should be freed is ignored.

The book offers hope that this can be changed. The two human heroes, Jakkin and his female companion Akki, seem destined to create a new race for the planet, a dragon/human meld in which both species share consciousness. As mentioned earlier, the dragons of Austar IV aren't magical, and yet, when the two young humans shelter inside the dead dragon's body (specifically the egg chamber), something magical happens to them. They're transformed, physically and mentally. They emerge from the dragon's body (out of Heart's Blood, like the pit dragon genealogies) with dragon senses and imperviousness to the deadly cold of Austar's pre-dawn deep freeze. As Jakkin observes at the end of the second novel, "He guessed he was part man – and part dragon. And though he did not fully understand the changes that had taken place, he knew that he was something new, the first true human Austarian."

Their heightened dragon senses involve telepathic communication with each other and with all dragons, even tiny rock lizards, and their ability to see the color emanations given off by the environment that are invisible to ordinary human sight, especially in the dark. Telepathic messages are "sendings" in the form of shifting landscapes of color with fleeting images that represent emotions and concepts. The dragons that live in caves produce sendings in shades of gray, not color. Words in language are also possible in limited syntax, written in italics (as are the human telepathic communications).

Individual personalities of the character dragons are vibrantly drawn, with detailed visual imagery. Our first introduction to the pit dragons is a frightening experience in which the dragons are brought to life through detailed physical description as dangerous, unpredictable, barely control-lable beasts with their feral ancestry lurking not far beneath the surface. Their handlers routinely endure risk to life and limb as they feed, bathe, and maintain the pit fighters at the breeding farms. Yolen introduces this concept in a graphic sequence early in *Dragon's Blood* (first book of the series) when a maddened old fighter has to be put down.

> "Blood Brother backed out of the stall screaming ... The scarred wing scraped past a pair of hooks, and one hook caught the tender membrane, ripping it open. Frantically the dragon tried to shake his wing loose, screaming his fury over and over into the cavernous barn ... Blood Brother gave one last mighty pull and his wing tore free, the hot blood dripping down onto the dust, burning the floorboards where it fell." (DB, 42-3)

Some censors have complained that such passages are too graphic. *Dragon's Blood* was, according to Yolen, "taken off the shelf before I came to visit a school, and all copies to be sold were hidden away by the librarian who felt the book's dragons were too graphically real ... Well, perhaps that is the hallmark of good writing: making the unreal – the not-real – real."[2] It's definitely one of the reasons Heart's Blood and her offspring are such memorable dragon characters.

Heart's Blood, the main dragon of the series, embodies everything the young hero Jakkin wishes for in life. On a shallow level, that means having a fighting dragon good enough to pay for his freedom out of the bondage class and into the status of master, or free citizen. This dream comes to pass, but the greater gifts the splendid red dragon offers him are things he didn't even realize he needed: pure love, communion with another soul in total honesty with no deception, complete loyalty, bravery, and ultimately, life itself. She is the draconic representation of all those qualities and teaches him what it means to have compassion for another creature, as well as how to deal with the loss of love through death.

In this respect, Jane Yolen offers to younger readers what Anne McCaffrey offers to adults: the wish fulfillment of having a dragon as your closest companion and friend, your soul mate. "Be thou ever my friend," Jakkin whispers to Heart's Blood, as he begins to realize that she is more than just an impressive fighter or producer of prize hatchlings. "She was – his other self, he supposed."

What he learns through his relationship with the dragon transfers to his understanding of the need for love and freedom among humans as well, particularly his chosen companion Akki. The gift of rebirth that Heart's Blood bestows on both Jakkin and Akki makes her death all the more intense for readers vicariously experiencing Jakkin's grief over her murder. Heart's Blood is more than just a magnificent fighter and loyal friend. She's the means by which a new breed of human can emerge, one willing to free the enslaved race of dragons from their pit bondage.

We know from our first impression of her as a hatchling that she's unusual. Yolen introduces her as an anomaly, an uncounted tenth dragon in what is listed on the hen's stall as a litter of nine. It's also made clear that

Jakkin the lonely bonded servant is himself unique, with the ability to bond with dragonkind on a much deeper level than that experienced by trainers with their assigned beasts. The moment where this becomes clear occurs when the newly hatched dragon licks his blood pooled from a scratch caused by the sharp eggshell. Yolen's description gives us one of those suspended moments when something almost magical happens: the wobbly hatchling licks at the blood and then stares at him with its jet-black eyes; the telepathic connection is made.

In this pivotal moment, Jakkin's instinctual use of the honorific *thee* and *thou* to address the creature and the tiny dragon's telepathic response reveals the starting point for a type of dragon-human linkage currently unknown on Austar. This is Yolen's first opportunity to show us the color-based telepathic sending of a genuine mind-to-mind connection: "'*Thou*,' he said again in a hushed voice, and suddenly felt a small rainbow moving in his head." As the two stare eye to eye, "[t]he rainbow in his head danced, shooting off pale bursts of color." In Yolen's world, a dragon's gaze is not something to be feared; rather, it's a link through which dragon and human share their thoughts.

The linkage is not as complete and instantaneous as occurs with McCaffrey's Pernese dragons when the gaze of a newly hatched dragonet binds it for life to the human of its choice. Having no model to follow, Jakkin must feel his way into the dragon's mind gradually and accustom himself to the meaning of the rainbows and color bursts it projects into his own mind. For example, approaching the oasis where he has hidden the dragonling, "a cascade of muted colors burst into his head," by which he knows the tiny dragon has sensed his approach and recognizes him. On another occasion when Jakkin appreciates the dragon's healing a wound on his wrist with its saliva, he's overwhelmed by the force of the dragon's joyful response, by the "great rising bursts of color that came into his head, reds and oranges and shining golds. He stumbled and put his hand to his temples."

As their relationship matures, each learns to moderate and better focus the sendings so that specific meaning is conveyed rather than merely super-saturated emotions laced with color and light that are too intense for Jakkin's human mind. When Jakkin and Akki, the two human protagonists, acquire dragon-induced telepathy, they must go through a similar process of learning to bank the intensity of their sendings to avoid "shouting" in each other's heads.

Once the main point-of-view character's mind is opened to dragon thoughts and emotions, we learn through him that each dragon's sending has its own color signature and pattern (Heart's Blood's signature is bursts of rainbows), recognizable even over great distances. Like Lessa of Pern, Jakkin realizes that he can read the telepathic sendings of all dragons, not just his own chosen one. This ability makes him a formidable trainer and opponent in the tournaments, but it has grander implications for his survival when Heart's Blood is killed in the second book, and her full "dragon sight" is transferred to her.

Here's a sampling of how Jakkin "sees" the various dragons: "Heart Breaker, one of Heart's Blood's clutchmates, had a similar rainbow signal, but with the colors faded, drifting off around the edges. As he passed S'Blood's stall, the big brown fighter gave off sharp, jagged images. His body worked in the Pit in that same jagged way, with little fluidity in his motions ... Heart Worm, the best brood hen in the nursery, had a signal that was a series of yellow globes" indicating her perpetually sunny temperament. In the heat of battle, S'Blood's sendings are so primal, "a hurricane of yellow-and-red flashings across an ultrabright landscape," that Jakkin loses mental control over him.

The link with other dragons stops, though, at what Yolen calls the "landscape level." Jakkin's sensitivity to dragons allows him to reach into their minds and see their generalized sendings. However, it's only from his red dragon, with whom he actually has shared blood, that the deeper-level exchange of specific images and focused meaning occurs. Yolen shows us facets of Heart's Blood's complex personality through her link with the boy. The dragon's sendings literally show what she feels or thinks or observes, with no disguise or deception – all dragons simply show what is literally true. Although Jakkin's attitude toward the girl Akki ping-pongs all over the map, Heart's Blood consistently sends the image of a "golden silhouette," telling us this character is pure of motive and loved by the dragon as part of her human family.

Yolen's powers of description are at their best in expressing the trust between the linked pair. Thus, when Jakkin expresses his love for the dragon, her response to him is a mental fiery show of rainbows experienced as "a cascade, a waterfall, a sunburst of color." When she opens her mind completely to him, Yolen effectively uses the analogy of a cavern:

"... it was as if he were walking down a glowing path into a cavern where colors dripped like large hanging crystals from a roof of the deepest purple. Rainbow puddles were on the cavern floor and multicolored fish leapt up from the water, singing. There had been a resonant thrumming, a humming that filled the air and then filled him." (DB, 242)

Unlike her human counterpart, Heart's Blood has no inner conflict over the ethical issues of Pit dragon fighting. Staring directly into the dragon's fathomless black eyes before they enter the Pit for her first fight, Jakkin sees her courage and complete trust in him depicted as a sending in which "two colors, a primary red and a primary blue, met in the middle" to form a bridge between them. She understands what he wants her to do and has no hesitation.

As Heart's Blood grows from feisty curious dragonling into serious mature fighter, she develops more subtle shadings of personality, displaying blood lust and fury as easily as sadness and comforting concern, tinges of jealousy as well as all-encompassing love and a desire to protect to the point of self-sacrifice. Her anger sends as "bleeding rainbows ... arcs of red across a maroon-and-black landscape," while her comforting mode takes the imagery of soft grey clouds that "seemed to weep pink-grey tears." We also discover that her feelings can be hurt; when Jakkin's thoughts suggest the girl Akki is more important to him than his dragon, her sleeping thoughts invade his mind as "a soft grey sending laced with black." At his denial, "the grey landscape broke into pieces, like storm clouds," indicating the dragon can easily see the lie behind his cloaking reassurance.

For all her intimidating power and focused dedication to her role as a fighter, Heart's Blood has a very distinct sense of humor. The evidence comes out in tricks she plays on Jakkin, pretending, for example, to be helplessly pinned in a training maneuver only to knock him off his feet the instant his guard lowers. ("He could feel its laughter in his head, great churning waves of blue and green.")

Not only do the dragons laugh in their minds, they are sentient to the point of playing jokes on their human companions and sharing the mirth among themselves. Having learned the concept of "splat" from Jakkin when one of them nearly knocked him off a cliff ledge (although Jakkin's sarcasm was not color-translatable), the dragons quickly turn it into their own brand of humor. Whenever anything falls, the dragons send the image of a red bubble bursting with the sound "*splat!*"

In fact, a good bit of humor infects the books, although the overall trilogy encompasses a tale with serious themes. The major dragon character dies, but her offspring survive with hope for a better future. At the same time we are grieving over the loss of Heart's Blood we're laughing at the antics of her hatchings. In another example, as Jakkin prepares for a daring underwater escape involving Akki, the abused dragon Auricle, and her tiny hatchling, their mental dialogue turns comical for a few seconds. This relieves tension for a few heartbeats and adds shading to Auricle's personality. Having never been allowed to fly, her response to the idea of flying free is "*?????*" until Jakkin sends her an image of a male dragon circling high over a flying female dragon; then her response changes to "*!!!!!*"

The escape through a flooded tunnel with people who can't swim, out into a swiftly flowing river, and over a waterfall with dragons that don't know how to fly is especially harrowing. Yolen piles one danger on another to the point that when all the dragons play a practical joke on the frenzied humans, it's a great tension breaker and moment of relief. It further confirms our suspicion that dragons have a wicked sense of humor. Sending Jakkin and Akki the image of the tiny hatchling tumbling helplessly down the waterfall, the dragons reveal it has landed unharmed at the bottom of the falls: "A splash of chuckles ran through Jakkin's head. '*No splat, no splat, no splat.*'"

Early in *Heart's Blood*, the second novel of the series, Yolen has Jakkin imprint the five hatchlings of Heart's Blood's first laying by pricking his finger and offering it for each dragonling to taste. ("Jakkin was rewarded with a tiny, cool rainbow of light blues and greys across the blank landscape.

It was a sending like – yet not like – Heart's Blood's.") This is an important plot point, for these hatchlings will be needed to carry on the new dragon/human relationship upon the death of their mother at the end of this second book.

Still linked to Jakkin after the death of their mother, the five hatchlings have their own distinct personalities. In addition to the unique color signatures that were apparent when they were first imprinted ("Jakkin could already tell them apart because their minds were startlingly different"), their individual voices can now be heard in the minds of both Jakkin and Akki after their "rebirth" experience. The first time Jakkin hears this sound, he realizes it's a language completely alien, yet now comprehensible to him. To indicate the dragons' telepathic speech, Yolen employs the familiar formula of italics; the syntax is primitive – subject/verb, subject/verb/object – which gives the sense of a foreign tongue squeezed down into the English translations perceived by Jakkin and Akki.

Through these added attributes, Yolen infuses the character of the young dragons with humor and affection, curiosity and concern. The two largest, male Sssargon and female Sssasha, are mutes, but their mental speech is distinctive. The most intelligent of the five is Sssasha, whose verbal sendings are better formed than Sssargon's. She even mimics the honorific style that Jakkin uses as a dragon master. Her sending, "*I am thy heart, Jakkin*," clearly shows that she understands his need for encouragement and support as he plots a desperate rescue plan. He also realizes in that moment that she will help to fill the void left by the death of Heart's Blood.

Sssargon is very self-involved and keeps up a running commentary to no one in particular on everything he does ("*Sssargon stays. Sssargon needs scratching. Sssargon hungers. Sssargon wants—*"). The humans and other dragons tease him and look on his self-importance ("*Brave Sssargon. Sssargon eats.*") as a source of continual amusement. In the end, though, he *is* the bravest, completing a death-defying aerial maneuver to get Auricle safely over the falls.

Yolen uses the color-coded sendings to help describe the various other types of dragons in the series. A so-called beauty dragon, neutered early to stunt its growth and make it placid, sends Jakkin a signature that is "a soft violet glow, not a landscape but a warm pastel feeling." Ironically, the dragon's name is Libertas, *freedom*. This is ironic because, as a pet, she represents the epitome of domesticated, manipulated, declawed, non-threatening dragonkind. In contrast, the feral dragons are all about survival in the rawest terms. Encountering one in the mountains, Jakkin finds his mind filled with a "pulsing, angry purple slime." Territorial and confrontational, their instinct is to attack. Jakkin finds it difficult to deflect the feral dragon from this single-minded pursuit since he can't touch its personality with his mind the way he can domesticated, human-bred dragons.

Another type of captive, the cave dragon Auricle encountered in the third book, sends only in monochrome shadings that emphasize the sad, debased condition of the dragons kept underground. However, when Jakkin explains to her in a graphic sending of the gory fate waiting for her and her hatchling, she suddenly answers him in kind, with a vivid flash of color. Yolen knows how to pace the excitement of the story, building up the risk as well as the potential for reward. As Jakkin and Akki (and everyone reading the story at this point) cheer Auricle's newfound desire for freedom, the red dragon fire unexpectedly sparks in her black eyes.

Yolen's use of imagery, particularly in simile and metaphor, reveal her skill as poet. Most dragon-centered fiction makes use of similes based on dragon imagery, and Yolen is particularly good at it, creating highly visual images with an economy of verbiage. A pool of water rising unexpectedly out of the desert haze shimmers "like dragon scales in the sun," and Austar's double moons "cast shadows like blood scores across the sand." A government senator is described as "hard as dragon bone" beneath the façade of his cultured manners. The touch of Jakkin's lover Akki is "as hot as dragon's blood burning his cheeks."

The most pervading imagery throughout the books is the color red and its connection to blood. It's the most desirable dragon color in the fighting dragon genealogies, indicating heightened power and intensity of fighting spirit. It also becomes the metaphor in Yolen's rites of passage story for life and death and rebirth. As Heart's Blood matures, her ruddy color deepens, described in an image that is both arresting and prophetic because it also describes her death: "This yearling dragon was a beautiful dull red ... the deep red of life's blood spilled upon the sand." As imagery of life, "a riot of reds" fills the dragon's sending while she lays her first clutch of eggs. She sends "scarlet, carnation, crimson, and rose; fiery gems strung on a strand of thought. For each egg, another ruby-colored jewel."

Yolen's Pit Dragon series charts the coming-of-age journeys of both human and dragon protagonists. We also follow the shape of the archetypal hero's quest – leaving the safety of home, going though trial by fire, and surviving to bring a boon or gift back to society. At the close of *A Sending of Dragons*, the third book of the series, Yolen puts this idea into Jakkin's mouth. He realizes the enormity of what he has lived through: surviving in the wilderness after the death of his bonded dragon and surviving a brutal enslavement under the yoke of cavemen who have somehow retained the knowledge of metalworking from their more civilized ancestors. "These were the gifts – metal and the knowledge of the change through sheltering in the dragon's bloody birth chamber – that he and Akki had wanted to bring back to the daylit world."

Yolen's aim in writing these dragon tales is further explained in her book on fantasy and fairy tales, *Touch Magic*, in which she states, "There seems to be no end to dragons," by which she means the trials and experiences that change a person from a child into an adult. This kind of story opens a new and different world to the reader, but in addition "the reader's own real world is opened to him or her in the process of exploring the fantasy world of the story."

St. George Revisited

One of my favorite dragons inhabits a short story Yolen wrote for a 1986 collection titled *Dragons and Dreams*. He's a clever old fellow, full of wisdom and gentle patience for those who have no patience with fantasy. He also keeps the spark of magic alive and passes it on to his dragon grandchildren. In the tale, Grandfather Dragon explains how Thanksgiving came to be. However, the Thanksgiving that he and his family are preparing to celebrate is not the one you and I know, but a commemoration of a legendary event in dragon history. Yolen cleverly parcels out the tale gradually, just as bedtime stories are told to children, so that readers' expectations are continually surprised as the tale progresses.

The legendary event, told to the young dragon grandchildren over several sessions, is the bargain made between mankind and dragonkind after the Dragon Wars have decimated the dragons down to a single remaining pair: that each species should go its own way and never bother the other henceforward, each never setting foot or wing in the territory belonging to the other ever again. The deal is sealed by the Great-Grandfather of All Dragons and his mate, and a human they had once fostered as a youth. His name is Georgi, and he's risen a bit in the world since they last saw him. He's now a knight with an army of men tagging along behind him up to the dragon's lair. This is Yolen's version (or inversion) of the St. George vs. the dragon myth.

She's not the first to address the story from the dragon's point of view or from a point of sympathy for the dragon. Scottish turn-of-the century writer Kenneth Grahame introduced the idea in "The Reluctant Dragon," included in his collection *Dream Days* in 1898, and later in the 1938 novel *The Reluctant Dragon*. In Grahame's story, a boy finds a dragon living in a cave near his village and discovers that it's really harmless and amiable. The dragon even invites him in for tea. Convincing the terrified villagers and the resident St. George of the dragon's good nature is the crux of the plot, which concludes with a mock battle that satisfies everyone. British children's writer Edith Nesbit tackled the same theme in her 1899 story "The Last of the Dragons," in which a princess and her hero prince decide with the peace-loving dragon not to go along with the traditional dragonslayer/rescue of the maiden ritual.

We also have Gordon R. Dickson's 1976 novel, *The Dragon and the George*, in which an experiment gone wrong sends a human couple into a world where dragons rule and humans are called "georges." As discussed in Chapter 4, the dragonslayer motif is further warped with great hilarity by fantasy humorist Terry Pratchett in *Guards! Guards!* The dragon is challenged by a trumped up and totally incompetent hero-knight who doesn't last very long. It takes an amorous and determined little swamp dragon to turn things around, once we realize the marauding dragon is a she. Patricia Wrede and

Robert Asprin have created popular YA fantasies with people-friendly dragons that provide both comic relief and magical help when needed. All of which reminds me of Anne McCaffrey's tantalizing question that launched the Pern sagas: what if the dragons were the good guys?

Yolen's inversion of the St. George story clearly assumes the dragons are good guys. Her rendition of the myth is less overtly funny than those mentioned above, but it's not quite serious either. It has the tone and voice of the world folktale with its stylized repetitions and sense of wonder. Particularly, it's the voice of Yolen's elderly dragon as taleteller and the varying reactions of his young listeners that endear her version of the St. George myth to me. Let me backtrack a bit to explain why.

In her 1981 non-fiction classic, *Touch Magic: Fantasy, Faerie & Folklore in the Literature of Childhood*, Yolen champions the preservation of traditional folk and fairy tales and legends as a desirable part of the childhood experience. Rather than excluding the vast body of fantasy and mythic literature from what children read or have read to them, we should encourage such exposure. Rather than censoring children's literature to the point of removing dragons and other magical creatures, thus robbing the tales of the metaphors for the unknown and the unknowable, we should embrace them. Yolen argues that "metaphor and her sisters – poetry and story – are as natural to humans as breathing." The richly layered meanings in the stories of myth, legend, and folktale as well as modern fantasy help us "explain ourselves to ourselves." In other words, they give us ways of explaining why things are the way they are, of coping with the mysteries of life and death, of adding wonder and possibility into our ordinary, mundane lives.

Her story of how the dragon Thanksgiving came to be is a charming and thought-provoking demonstration of these concepts. It's also an effective example of taking the violent, bloodthirsty tale of danger and death that is the basis of the St. George myth and turning it inside-out, so that it carries instead a message of peaceful coexistence and mutual understanding. The premise of Yolen's reworking is that the last two dragons on earth abduct a shepherd boy named Georgi and teach him their language and lore, so that he can take their "message of peace" back to the world of men.

The wisdom of their actions is rewarded when the knight Georgi returns years later to confirm the bargain offered by the Great-Grandfather of All Dragons. In a note of irony, Grandfather Dragon the storyteller adds that in later years men believed the great St. George had single-handedly rid the world of dragons, but in truth no blood was spilled or life threatened. There is a bittersweet edge to the bargain as well, for although the dragons were never again killed and persecuted by men, it was because men ceased to believe in them. They had become creatures of fantasy. "You are no longer real to us," proclaims George the knight to the Great-Grandfather of All Dragons and his mate.

Thus, on the literal level, we have learned why the dragons celebrate Thanksgiving: men no longer persecute them. The metaphorical content of this seemingly simple tale is more complex. Mother Dragon speaks for the literal-mindedness of those for whom myth and legend hold no value. Dragons, she reminds Grandfather and her children, have no imagination and see things only as they are. Grandfather Dragon represents a different voice, the one that would preserve the old stories and tales, both for their excitement and for their embedded truths. Their debate over what to tell or not tell the dragon children is revealing:

> "You have a gift for making up stories, which is another way of saying you lie. Sometimes I think you are more Man than dragon."
>
> "I tell the truth," growled the old dragon. "This is dragon history." Huffily, he cleaned his front claws.
>
> "It is true that the word *history* contains the word *story*," said Mother Dragon. "But that is the only thing I will admit." (HTBD, 21)

As is often the case, the spark of wonder generated by the old storyteller is caught and cherished by at least one of the listeners. Sskarma, more thoughtful that her playful younger siblings and more imaginative than her literal-minded brother Sskar (who wants no part of this fantasy stuff and flies off with Mother Dragon to catch a deer for their Thanksgiving feast), receives the gift of story. As the rest of the family goes off to gather chestnuts to roast on the Thanksgiving fire, she stays behind to contemplate the wondrous tale of Georgi the dragon-boy who once lived with the Great-Grandfather of All Dragons and made peace with the oldest and wisest of creatures on earth.

Almost reverently, she repeats his name the way the dragons pronounce it, and then attempts something more daring. "'Ssgggi,' she said. Then she said it three more times. The fourth time she said it, it came out 'Georgi.' 'Georgi,' she said a fifth time. This time it sounded right." Yolen has cleverly turned the tables once again – instead of fantasy lovers desiring dragons with a great desire, her little dragon is swept away by the tale of a hero of men.

In Conclusion

Jane Yolen's love of myth and folktale traditions infuses all her fiction and poetry, in particular her works that include dragons. From the gentle humor of Grandfather Dragon and his insistence on telling the legend of Thanksgiving in spite of Mother Dragon's disapproval, to the realistic depiction of the fighting Pit dragons and their life and death struggles, Yolen is a masterful stylist and storyteller.

To give Jane Yolen the final say here, allow me to quote the passage from her chapter on the power of storytelling, whose final two imperative sentences have become a mantra of sorts, appearing occasionally acknowledged and sometimes unattributed in magazine articles, book reviews, fantasy Web sites, and e-mail ID signatures: "They are the most potent kind of magic, these tales, for they catch a glimpse of the soul beneath the skin. *Touch magic. Pass it on.*"

Notes

DB – *Dragon's Blood*
HB – *Heart's Blood*
HTBD – *Here There Be Dragons*

1. The slow-motion unfolding of the dragon's death throes reminds me of the masterful way in which McCaffrey combines terror, sorrow, and graphic violence during the sudden lion attack on Golanth. In both scenes, the writers have effectively put the reader into the emotional core of the event, where an act that takes only minutes or seconds seems to last forever.

2. This question of how graphic or realistic the monsters should be in fiction read mainly by children and young adults (generally ages 10 to 16) raises the problematic issue of censorship. Ursula Le Guin is widely quoted as having made the wry observation that if you eliminate the dragon from fiction read by younger audiences (because it is satanic and too frightening), you must also eliminate St. George, who exists solely to battle and vanquish the dragon, the medieval Christian embodiment of Satan. My own feeling is that censors of this type don't give readers (young or old) nearly enough credit for being able to discern the difference between myth and reality, between metaphor and fact. The vivid physicality of Jane Yolen's dragons (and for that matter, the tournament dragons in J. K. Rowling's *Harry Potter and the Goblet of Fire*) is just fine by me.

Chapter 7

Terry Goodkind
Graphic and Gripping

"I'VE ALWAYS said fantasy is sort of 'stealth philosophy' ... Fantasy allows you bend the world and the situation to more clearly focus on the moral aspects of what's happening. In fantasy you can distill life down to the essence of your story."

In his book *Characters and Viewpoint*, Orson Scott Card states that a minor character typically "does one or two things in the story and then disappears" after creating an interesting plot twist, for example, or facilitating (or hindering) the main character's progress in some way. Sometimes minor characters are created with such precision and enthusiasm that they stick in the memory long after their appearance and use in the story has ended. Such is Terry Goodkind's dragon Scarlet, who appears mainly in the first book, *Wizard's First Rule*, and makes a cameo appearance in the second, *Stone of Tears*.

Terry Goodkind's fiction is not for sissies. It's also not for children and has been described by critics as "raw," "gritty," "brassy," "complex epic fantasy that crackles with vigor," "excessively graphic," "riveting," with a heavy dose of "grotesque scenes of war and human destruction." It's also saturated with the author's Ayn Rand-based philosophy of objectivism.[1] As such, Goodkind's major characters, Richard and his wife Kahlan, espouse the message of individualism and the nobility of those who rise above daunting obstacles, whether through their own wits and skills or an occasional reliance on magic.

In Goodkind's world, magic is just another tool used by villains and heroes alike, and magical creatures such as dragons are more memorable for their human-like personalities than their supernatural abilities. "Like all power," the wizard Zedd explains, "it [magic] simply exists. It's the user who determines what use it will be put to." This piece of lore is demonstrated in Scarlet's magical ability to breathe fire. She uses it equally to crisp her enemies and gently warm her egg in the coolness of her nesting cave.

Goodkind explains in a recent interview that his writing is based on strong emotions that produce "stories of human struggle, of love and devotion, of people whose lives have been torn apart by appalling circumstances." He empathizes so strongly with all his characters that they become imprinted in readers' minds as they live and breathe and bleed all over the pages of his novels. This is true whether they are major players or minor participants who appear with brief "flashbulb" intensity, to use Card's analogy for the effect a minor character should have.

Goodkind's fiction has some impressive examples of how to create a pithy minor character in a few broad brushstrokes; in Scarlet's case, the fact that she is a dragon is almost beside the point. It's her engaging personality – intimidating, snarky, suspicious, impetuous, funny, enthusiastic, and ultimately caring – that endears her to readers. Of course, she does dragony things such as flying riders around and flaming her enemies, and has magical powers that allow her to breathe fire and become invisible to her enemies, but those abilities do not define her personality. What's most important is the friendship she forges with the main character, Richard Cypher.

What makes a minor character essential, especially if that character is non-human? In terms of story construction, the character needs to perform a specific plot task or to embody a specific symbolic message – the challenge is how does the writer pull that off without it becoming a wooden plot device with no real life in it? In Goodkind's case, the answer is that you get beneath the skin to see how this character thinks and what motivates her, especially in terms of the humans with whom she must interact. She is simultaneously an alien creature uninterested their petty wars and contests of power and a hostage caught between the opposing wills of the deranged wizard Darken Rahl and Richard, the legendary Seeker of Truth. She obeys the former out of coercion, but befriends the latter out of respect.

As Goodkind has said in numerous interviews, he is more interested in human psychological dramas than the fantastical settings in which they take place. Goodkind's driving force is answering how the human mind responds to mental and physical trauma, how characters deal with these challenges and emerge with honor. That said, it's interesting that a couple of his best-remembered and most-loved characters are non-human, specifically Scarlet the dragon and Gratch the gar. Internet fan polls ranking their most favorite non-human characters in his Sword of Truth series always rank Scarlet at or near the top.

What this shows is that readers are responding to Scarlet's personality, which has a very distinctive flavor and depth, even in her limited role in the story. In Goodkind's terms, he's not interested in dragons per se, but in how this particular dragon reacts and behaves within the challenges of the events. He's especially concerned with what she represents on the level of metaphor and symbol. The didactic nature of Goodkind's writing is never far below the surface of his novels, and he uses metaphor and symbolism liberally to get his points across. "The story exists on different levels, and this is by deliberate intent on my part," he emphasizes in a letter to fans posted on his web site, www.terrygoodkind.com.

Symbolism and analogy are painted with deliberately broad brushstrokes, an apt analogy for Goodkind's style in that he is also a professional artist who uses his painter's ability to create particularly visual prose. In an interview with James Frenkel, the author's editor at Tor, Goodkind has said that "artistic ability helps me to describe in an accurate way what I'm seeing, what is really there. I think it helps me bring texture and life to my writing." Scarlet's glossy red scales, intense yellow eyes, and bright flames are a vivid splash of color in an otherwise barren landscape, which is both internal and external. Red as a choice of dragon color has special significance, as it does in other fantasy fiction (for example, in Jane Yolen's *Heart's Blood*, the greatest fighters are dark red dragons, whose fierce temperament is genetically linked to scale color).

Depending on the dragon's role, red can evoke various emotions in the reader. The primary association with red is blood, which can have both good and bad connotations: anger and aggression; danger and loss; agitation; a warning or prohibition; the biblical devil, and so forth on the negative end. On the other hand, red also indicates vitality, life's blood, and the flush of excitement. Fantasy authors draw upon these associations, and readers of fantasy understand that shorthand. For that reason, much dragon artwork on fantasy book covers depicts Western-style red dragons in postures of threat with jaws gaping and claws flexed (see the example on the cover of this book), and *Wizard's First Rule* is no exception.[2]

What does red mean in the context of *Wizard's First Rule* and *Stone of Tears*? Scarlet provides a flash of color, literally and emotionally, that is a brief relief from the dreary darkness that has surrounded the main character for many pages. But she also provides a visceral link to that environment from which Richard has just emerged. In particular, red is connected with the dreaded Mord Sith, torturers who have enslaved Richard by control of his own magical power. Their blood-red leather uniforms give gory testament to their profession, but as readers discover, they are also an enslaved group, created against their will by Darken Rahl. When Richard physically confronts Scarlet and learns how Darken Rahl controls her by holding her egg hostage, all these associations come flooding back to the reader.

Although Jane Yolen and Terry Goodkind are galaxies apart in both style and content, their red dragons have something else in common besides their color – both represent and embody an intelligent non-human creature enslaved for selfish purposes by uncaring men. Dragons bred and raised for entertainment as pit fighters are contrasted with the feral free-ranging mountain dragons in Yolen's series, whereas in Goodkind's world, Scarlet, a free "feral" dragon is forced to subject herself as a domesticated beast of burden to the whims of Darken Rahl in order to protect her single egg. That she agrees to become Richard's friend and ally after the abuse she and her offspring have received at Darken Rahl's hands is a testament to the strength of both their characters. Both serve as a symbol of freedom. They both also provide the analogy of life appearing out of the midst of death. Heart's Blood's body births a new race of humans, and Scarlet lays a new dragon egg even though she's disabled by a sorceress's magic.

Goodkind doesn't describe his prominent characters in explicit physical detail, in order, he says, to leave some room for readers to fill in their own impressions and images, thus personalizing their experience of the character. The same is true of Scarlet. His descriptions of her are basic, but much information is given about her personality through dialogue and interactions with the main character Richard and his friends. To see how he accomplishes this, let's look at his creation of Scarlet in more detail.

First Impressions

Information about Scarlet is parceled out gradually, beginning with the opening scene of *Wizard's First Rule*. Goodkind allows his main POV character, Richard Cypher (later Rahl), to see her right at the start of the book, but only as a fleeting impression.

> "... a dark shadow swept over the ground, leaping across limbs and leaves. There was a rushing, whistling sound in the air overhead. The size of the shadow was frightening ... Richard peered up, searching through the gaps in the canopy of green and gold, trying to see the shadow's source. For an instant, he saw something big. Big, and red." (WFR, 4)

He has brought these two characters together just four pages into the book, foreshadowing the fact that Richard is the human with whom the dragon will bond near the climax of the tale. But Richard's first experience of Scarlet is as a dimly glimpsed image of fear. All along, we are given the impression that she's evil, wicked, and dangerous – a magical beast that hunts humans and serves the twisted wizard Darken Rahl of the ensorcelled land D'Hara. Only toward the end, when she meets Richard face to face, is her true nature displayed.

Although Goodkind uses the fantasy setting for his human dramas, world building for its own sake is anathema to him. Thus, readers are given no dragon history or background other than what others say about them in passing. Scarlet lays two precious eggs, one in the first book and another in the second, so we assume there are male dragons about, but they are immaterial to the story. What's of importance to Goodkind is that Richard gains an unexpected ally who initially is an enemy. They must both go through a period of grudging trust, balanced only on a slim promise of honor to uphold a bargain of mutual benefit. As events unfold, the fulfilled bargain opens the way to loyalty and eventually to love at the conclusion of the first novel, which sets up Scarlet's willingness to come to Richard's rescue in the second book.

Our first impression of Scarlet is a shape of menace, in a color that signals danger. When a wound on Richard's hand acquired just before the sighting oozes blood, he makes the mental connection with the proper alarm: "It was red and throbbed painfully. He remembered the thing in the sky." Goodkind is setting us up to expect the worst from this mystery creature that any seasoned fantasy reader will already have guessed is a dragon.

Further evidence of this assumption about the dragon comes from various sources that provide both rumor and fact. The credibility of those who offer information as well as their private agendas give the author an effective way to skew reader's expectations, as we'll see when we look at what others say about dragons in general, and Scarlet in particular.

A sense of danger comes from country folk who spread stories of "beasts from the sky" that leave half-eaten corpses lying in the fields. Alert readers also don't miss Richard's comment that assassins cornering him and the fugitive woman Kahlan on a mountain trail seemed to have "dropped in out of the sky," an allusion to possible riders on dragonback. Further in the same episode, Richard's explanation to Kahlan of his personal feelings about magic perfectly summarizes the dual nature of his future relationship with both Kahlan, who has inherited magic of her own, and Scarlet, a magical beast of the wild:

> "I was always fascinated by it; it sounded exciting. But now I know there is magic to fear. But I would guess it's like people: some you stay clear of and some you are fortunate to know." (WFR, 69)

How this plays out is easy to see. Much later in the book, Richard is warned by a D'Haran soldier to take the left-hand path into the hills that will help him *stay clear* of the dragon rumored to inhabit the area. In defiance of that advice, Richard chooses the path that takes him directly to her; thus, he will end up *fortunate* to have her for an ally and friend. But until we reach that point, all evidence seems to imply that the dragon is an enemy, as Richard's thoughts about Kahlan hint during the long and dangerous trip into the magic-ridden Midlands: "He would slay a dragon, if there were such a thing, just to see that smile."

Others who give us a somewhat differing image of Scarlet are the power-mad wizard Darken Rahl and his sycophant Dimmen Nass. When Goodkind shifts focus in the story from Richard's travels to the adversaries awaiting him in D'Hara, readers learn details that suddenly explain that long-ago opening scene where the dragon made her first shadowy appearance above the treetops. Goodkind packs a surprising amount of information about the dragon into a very brief exchange between Rahl and Nass as they make plans for acquiring the third box of Orden, an object of magic that could destroy the world. From the wizard's command to Nass ("tell the dragon I want her") we learn she's female, and that she serves him somehow. Nass's reluctance to carry out this command gives us a little more information: the dragon serves unwillingly, and she eats humans. Rahl's response reveals that he's using her through coercion ("... she will not eat you. She knows what I will do if she stretches my patience.").

So far, she still fits the prototype of the ferocious Western dragon, but the suggestion that she has some rational thought process beyond that of a feral beast begins to add shadings to her character. Rahl's brief comment hints that he has a control over her that isn't magical; rather, it's psychological, which is the way he prefers to wield power over others. Much is revealed about his character as well in this scene. For example, unlike his lieutenant, he has no fear of the dragon and assumes his control over her is beyond question: "She is to come when I ask, and wait until I am ready." It's hardly surprising that the D'Haran guard warns Richard to avoid "Master Rahl's dragon" in the hills because of her nasty temper.

Further impressions about her come from the Mud People, a tribe of primitives who refer to her as a monster that carries Rahl into their village on an errand of terror and death. The tale they tell Richard continues to paint for the reader the picture of a creature of evil: *"The red demon came from the sky, carrying a man. He wanted you."* We are not told if the sorcerer's rampage wherein fire kills women and children includes dragon's fire, but everything we've gleaned about her so far leads readers to believe she could have added her flame to the assault on the village (*"Our hands could not touch him. Many of those who tried were killed by magic fire."*). Whatever the hold Darken Rahl exercises over Scarlet, we realize it's powerful enough to make her serve him as an ally, to facilitate his bloodlust and desecration of a defenseless village.

It's from Kahlan, the mysterious Mother Confessor, that we get some actual dragonlore and a bit of their history. Since she's a source that can be trusted – we know already that the main character Richard loves and trusts her – we can accept what she says as accurate. Goodkind weaves these details into a conversation between Kahlan and Richard, initiated by his question, "There are dragons in the Midlands?" Since Richard is from Westland, where no magic exists, his ignorance of the species is addressed by Kahlan, who is surprised he thinks they are only legends and not real. From her we learn the following:

- Dragons are magical – that's how they flame and fly.
- Gray dragons are small and shy, and can be kept as pets.
- Green dragons are bigger, bad tempered, stupid, and, for those reasons, dangerous; basically, they're brutes that can't be reasoned with.
- Red dragons are the largest, most aggressive, and most intelligent, making them a formidable enemy or ally. One can communicate and perhaps negotiate with them.
- Red dragons are extremely independent and would rather die than become the slave of human, in whose affairs they have little interest.

It's this last piece of dragonlore that's most pertinent to the plot development and is the clue to Scarlet's personality. Kahlan's stated fact of their intelligence and independence accomplishes two things: it emphasizes the importance of whatever it is that gives Darken Rahl power over the dragon, and will underscore the uniqueness of Scarlet's commitment to Richard as the story nears its climax. The fact that she would willingly help him beyond their bargain demonstrates that she considers him an honorable individual worthy of her loyalty.

Appearances Can Be Deceiving

No one knows how to write unrelenting misery better than Terry Goodkind. Thus, it's a source of some relief to readers that when Richard leaves the torment of Darken Rahl's fortress-city, the next scene that develops is his meeting with Scarlet, which includes considerable sly humor. It also takes place out in the wide open spaces of a rock-strewn hill country, giving readers both a mental breath of fresh air and visual relief from the claustrophobic oppression of the previous chapters.

Goodkind builds suspense through Richard's POV by delaying the visual reality of the dragon and instead giving us a graphic auditory experience of the dragon's sudden attack and her ensuing devouring of Richard's horse. We hear the unexpected attack (flame erupts out of nowhere in a "deafening roar"), but we don't see the actual dragon. Richard crouches behind a boulder, listening in shock as the dragon eats his horse piece by piece. Goodkind relishes this kind of description, establishing through onomatopoeia – especially with words that have sharp and explosive sounds – the event taking place. The horse *screams*, flesh *rips*, bones *break* and *snap*, talons *rasp* over the rocks.

Physically, when we finally meet the dragon face to bloody snout, she's an imposing sight in the standard Western dragon mold. Goodkind's plain muscular prose isn't adorned with lyrical imagery or poetic similes to give you a sense of his dragon (Scarlet is just *big* and *red*). He simply tells you specifically what the main POV character sees: her eyes are yellow, her scales are glossy bright red, her head and tail are adorned with black-tipped spikes. Her size is "immense," gauged by the fact that her head, on a "long, thick neck," is taller than Richard. Her wings reveal rippling muscles across her back. Her long muzzle contains teeth like razors, and smoke gusts from her nostrils. She gives Richard a terrifying bloodstained grin when she discovers his hiding place – a proper villainous dragon in all respects.

What happens next, however, belies this gruesome exterior and comes as a total surprise. The dragon addresses him directly in a distinctly female, slightly coy voice dripping with cheeky attitude. "What have we here," she says, "A tasty treat?" By now the reader will have realized that Goodkind's characterizations are rendered best through dialogue and action, and Scarlet in particular has her own quirky voice. Because the dragon is a magical creature, there is no telepathy involved; she speaks directly to him in perfect English, as does Smaug to Bilbo. There's no need to explain how this is possible, and no need to use italics or other print devices to indicate communication. Thus, the author has free range in creating the voice of his dragon, and she's got a definitely coy, teasing style that is by turns amused, annoyed, curious, and dismissive.

Unlike some of the other authors we've looked at, Goodkind leaves the actual sound of the dragon's voice much to the imagination of the reader. Rather than liken it through simile and metaphor to something else with which we might make a connection (for example, the metallic sound imagery used effectively by Le Guin), we are told simply that the volume of Scarlet's roar is loud enough to shake rocks loose from the surrounding cliffs and her speaking voice is identifiably female. Just how "womanly" he intends is something Goodkind would rather have readers fill in from their own imagination. Whether she sounds like a sexy Jessica Rabbit-type cartoon or a raspy barely humanoid creature from the Twilight Zone is up to the reader.

Scarlet's speech patterns reveal character more clearly than does the sound of her voice. She uses colloquial phrases such as "I must admit," "only too glad," and "some friends you have" that inject sarcastic humor and instantly give her approachability, in spite of her frightening physical presence. Her teasing exchange as she toys with her prey is irony personified: "Oh, please, brave man, don't slay me with your magic sword!" She uses gestures that fit this type of speech, putting a claw to her scaly chest while she feigns indignation or licking Richard with her forked tongue from crotch to throat in a move that is both overtly sexual and coquettish. Her laughter is accomplished with her entire body by throwing her head back, puffing smoke, and rumbling to the point where it shakes the ground. She loves a sardonic joke and most of her humor is of the gallows variety, which she displays by telling Richard that she will be glad to help him, but only after she's eaten him.

The threat to eat him becomes a running joke through both books in which she appears. At first, it's a realistic threat, which fits Kahlan's definition of red dragons. Once Richard manages to sweet-talk himself out of imminent danger, it becomes a threat to make certain he keeps his promise to rescue Scarlet's egg from Darken Rahl's gars. For example, the dragon warns Richard not to let the gars kill him because she wants the pleasure of eating him when he gets back with the egg – a riff on the old "if you die, I'll kill you" joke.

Fulfillment of his promise, at great risk and physical injury to himself, however, elevates Richard to the status of honorable ally in the dragon's mind, such that subsequent references to eating him become a private joke shared between two companions who care deeply about each other. Declaring how much he has missed her when Scarlet arrives to his rescue at the end of *The Stone of Tears*, the dragon quips, "Well, I've already eaten. I guess I must instead give you a ride in the sky to work up an appetite. Then I will eat you." Richard's reaction is to laugh with affection rather than cower from fear.

Goodkind appears to have an amused affection for Scarlet, because nearly all her scenes incorporate touches of dragon humor, a couple of which are good examples of how to do deadpan comedy on paper. One of the best such moments comes when Richard plays straight man to Scarlet's grim comedienne at the entrance to a long dark tunnel through which Richard must squeeze in order to steal back Scarlet's egg. He worries about rumors of something dangerous in the cave. Scarlet gives him a look, shoves her head in the entrance, blasts an enormous flame into the darkness, and delivers the punch line: "Now there's nothing in the cave. Go get my egg."

The exchange in which Richard cajoles his way out of being crisped on the spot is laced with subtle humor. Like most traditional dragons, Scarlet is susceptible to flattery, and it's this fact that saves Richard's life when he first encounters her. Realizing that brute force won't save him, he does the very thing standard dragonlore warns against – he tries to talk the dragon into a bargain. Normally, a dragon's voice casts a powerful spell of deception, weighting the odds heavily in the dragon's favor. But what Richard has going for him is that he's the Seeker, which means he carries the magic of a truth-teller. When he tells Scarlet that she's the most magnificent creature he's ever seen, even though she plans to dine on him, it's stated with such utter lack of guile or dishonesty that it stops the dragon in her tracks. Given that her only experience of humans is their treachery and coldness, the expression of such naked honesty in such a dire situation causes her to doubt her original assessment of the situation:

> Scarlet's head floated closer. "Why would you say such things to me?"
> "Because I believe in the truth. I think you do too." (WFR, 728)

We can tell that the tide begins to turn in Richard's favor once they have exchanged names. Unlike most dragons, Scarlet doesn't hide her name with a riddle, or refuse to tell it. She's proud of who and what she is, and it's that fact that Richard can use to convince her to throw in her luck with him instead of the sorcerer who holds her egg hostage. That Richard is able to guess this fact about the egg cements the deal for Scarlet, convincing her that this human is out of the ordinary and might indeed be worthy.

At Richard's mention of the egg, Goodkind shifts Scarlet's tone of voice and speech pattern, demonstrating her quick temper others have alluded to. Her chattiness instantly turns to fury and her teasing banter to short imperative yelps as she roars flames into the sky, demanding "Where!" and "Tell me where it is!" Goodkind injects a touch of grim humor as well, having Scarlet angrily accuse Richard of being flippant, when in fact she's done the same thing to him throughout the past several pages of dialogue.

There is another important shift in this passage of dialogue, and that occurs with Scarlet's admission that flying humans around is humiliating for her. Their conversation begins with Scarlet in the position of control and confidence, shown by her flippant remarks regarding Richard's status as a puny human whose offer of help is beyond ludicrous to the mighty dragon. She also gives him the false impression that she can choose which human, himself or Darken Rahl, to throw in her lot with. As Kahlan has speculated earlier, the reader knows this isn't so. Her boast that she'll just eat Richard because Master Rahl offers her more opportunity is an empty boast and we know it. The point where she admits what she really feels about her service to Darken Rahl – humiliation and enslavement – marks the shift in her relationship with Richard toward something more interesting than just predator and prey.

A Question of Trust

The question of honor is one of the ubiquitous themes of Goodkind's novels and a defining characteristic of his major character, Richard Cypher. It's important for Richard to discover the many ways in which honor can be tested, and Scarlet provides him with a larger-than-life opportunity. The bargain he strikes with the dragon – he will steal her egg back from Darken Rahl in return for six days of flying Richard over the countryside – gives each something they desperately want and which the other can efficiently provide. The bargain seems rational and fair, as long as neither proves false. When Scarlet agrees to the bargain with the words, "On your honor, on mine," she has essentially sworn an oath, not to be broken under any conditions.

As the Seeker, Richard sees past her exterior to the creature's emotions and basic motivations. He isn't afraid to treat her with respect; he sees it as a reasonable course of action instead of something totally unthinkable or foolhardy. In response, she honors her side of the bargain, even though she could just as easily fly off into the clouds and never return once the egg is in her talons. Instead, she does the honorable thing, although she grumbles about it continually and keeps making snide comments about the fact Richard can't stay out of trouble and needs watching.

We recognize this as one of her personality traits: to mask her real feelings of affection with surface toughness. She's like those people who turn compliments into jokes and deflect praise by making light of something serious, or who avoid sentimentality with gruff posturing. "I made a bargain, that is all," she says when Richard is effusive in his praise of the honor of dragons, deeming it greater than that of most humans he's encountered.

Basking in newfound freedom after Darken Rahl's defeat, he recounts the part played by his loyal friend, the "brave and noble dragon, Scarlet," which praise is met by derision from the dragon herself.

In this matter, though, her actions speak louder than words. She demonstrates her trust in Richard through her willingness to carry all his friends on her back to her aerie to see her new hatchling. She continues this pattern when presented to the Mud People as Richard's honored friend instead of the "red demon" they feared in the past. She states her true feelings to him privately ("If they are your friends, Richard Cypher, they are my friends"), while keeping up the pretense of threat by publicly assessing the meager meal she could make of the village. It's clear that she feels compelled to uphold the reputation of red dragons as the most dangerous and feared of the species, although she has made an exception for this particular human and those he calls friends.

> "Friend! Red dragons are friends to no people! We are feared by all!"
> "You're my friend," Richard smiled. "I'm a person."
> Scarlet snorted a puff of smoke at him. "Paah. I will eat you yet."
> Richard's grin widened. (ST, 66)

As I've pointed out earlier, in writing fiction with a fantasy setting that has alien (non-human) characters, a human point of reference is needed when these characters impact the story. In Scarlet's case, Goodkind gives her certain very human traits that make her more accessible and endear her to readers who have a soft spot for family. Scarlet exhibits a parental exuberance regarding her offspring that human readers can relate to: she wants to show them off to her closest friend. She comes to get Richard when her rescued egg hatches, oblivious of the great battle that has just been won against Darken Rahl. Soldiers and citizens scatter as she drops out of the sky, fearing the worst, but her only intent is to brag to her human friend about the excellence of her precocious red dragonet.

She behaves the same way when she responds to Richard's call for help in *The Stone of Tears*. After parentally scolding him for being in trouble again, she remarks of her hatchling, "Gregory is not so little anymore. He misses you, and would like to see you." It reminds us with amusement of the urge parents have to share their children's photos with old friends, even though more pressing matters might need attention.

Regarding Richard's own family, Scarlet expresses genuine sympathy for him when she learns his brother whom she helped him find has betrayed him. Having just rescued him from a pack of ravening hounds, she berates him for his inability to stay out of trouble, but immediately drops that attitude when she perceives the heartbreak he feels at his brother's treachery. She has just demonstrated for him that she is more worthy of trust and has greater loyalty to him than his own sibling.

An even more concrete demonstration of this loyalty comes in the form of a talisman. She does something surprising for a red dragon: she breaks off a back tooth and gives it to him to carry. Thus, she gives him a physical token of her loyalty by which he can call her if he's in need of help. The symbol of a tooth as a tracking device occurs early in *Wizard's First Rule*, when the tooth of a mysterious beast guarding a book of spells becomes the means by which Darken Rahl can find Richard as long as he carries it. Scarlet's tooth is used in much the same way, but with positive effect. She feels his call and comes, no matter what the reason, although she jokes about it once she arrives. She comes, even though she is carrying an egg that's ready to be laid, and is willing to risk injury for his sake, flying him down into the courtyard of Rahl's palace and sustaining magic lightning strikes in one of her wings. The ultimate expression of her relationship to Richard the Seeker is simply stated to his mentor, the wizard Zedd, who questions seeing a red dragon with a rider: "I would fly this one to the underworld and back."

The final scene in which Scarlet appears, near the end of *The Stone of Tears*, has strong symbolic content. Richard hurries to check on Scarlet who lies wounded from a sorceress's lightning bolt and discovers the dragon guarding a newly laid egg. Some critics have complained about this scene, saying that Scarlet's explanation for her slow recovery from the attack (she has just produced an egg) is completely out of left field and adds nothing to the story at its climax. However, I find this scene fairly typical of Goodkind in that it directly injects a blatant piece of symbolism that comments on the story just completed.

Lying wounded on the ground, yet cradling an egg in her talons, Scarlet embodies the story's message of new life in the midst of death. She gently breathes fire over the egg, combining additional symbolic content through a single image: the fire that she uses to kill also warms the newly developing dragonet. "Tenderly, she stroked her talons over it. As Richard watched, he thought about the beauty of life, and how happy he was that others could continue to have it," now that Darken Rahl has been sent to the underworld and all his twisted magic with him. Some readers may appreciate a subtler symbolic way of getting the message across, but that is not Terry Goodkind's style. As he states matter-of-factly on an Internet chat, "Symbolism, to be effective, must be legible. If I write something symbolic and no one gets it, then it's pointless."

Flight or Fright

Every author who writes about dragons has his or her own way of describing dragonflight. McCaffrey and Pratchett seem to have a hang-glider approach, where dragons drop off high places, open their huge wings, and sail out onto the air currents. Le Guin's dragons, awkward on the ground, crouch from a terrestrial surface and then spring into the air, lumbering upward with beating wings until they achieve flight altitude, where they are in their true element – much like bionic jumbo jets. Smaug launches off the mountaintop like a rocket, with the roar of his approach growing louder as he streaks across the sky, ultimately circling and strafing Lake-town in great swooping runs reminiscent of a B-25 bomber.

Even Terry Goodkind has his pure fantasy moments, when the idea of riding a dragon is a thrill unto itself. Appropriately, most of his dragonflight descriptions suggest the sensation not of hang gliding, but of heart-in-the-mouth sky diving. A trip on Scarlet's muscular back is not for the faint of heart, because the red dragon careens through the sky, banking and diving sharply, heedless of the puny humans clinging to her neck spikes. Such a flight might appeal to thrill-seekers and joy riders, but anyone with fear of flying is going to have a hard time of it.

Pity poor Kahlan, whose main reactions to riding the dragon are fighting nausea and keeping her eyes tightly shut. It's not hard for readers

TERRY GOODKIND

to empathize with her, as wind rips at her body, "snapping the loose ends" of her clothing with a "tugging" sensation that might well convince a fearful rider they are about to fall off. Goodkind gives an effective description of the more alarming aspects of being airborne:

> "[Kahlan] opened her eyes just a little, peeking through narrow, squinting slits. As she suspected, the world was tilted at a crazy angle. Her head spun sickeningly. Why did the dragon have to tip over whenever it made a turn? ... Scarlet's huge, leathery wings caught the air and pulled them into a tight spiral. As the red dragon plummeted earthward, the knot of Kahlan's stomach felt as if it were coming up in her throat." (ST, 63)

I suspect, though, that Goodkind himself is in the camp that would relish the thrills and chills of a mighty dragon in full flight. Consider this passage where his usually earthbound prose spreads its own wings:

> "In the distance, the red wings spread wide as the dragon plunged into a dive ... From the corner of his eye, he watched the dragon plummet straight down. At the last instant the dragon pulled out of the dive. Her long neck stretched out. Wings spread wide, she shot toward them at incredible speed, skimming along just above the ground ... Scarlet swept up with a roar ... Immense wings beat to slow the dragon's speed." (ST, 939)

When Richard thanks Scarlet for teaching him the joy and privilege of flying, you have no doubt he speaks for the author as well.

In Conclusion

In looking back over the events in which Scarlet plays a part, we see that she moves from unwilling participant in the activities of a power-mad sorcerer to tentative partnership with another human. Eventually, their relationship moves from mere partnership for mutual benefit to joyful friendship with Richard and the humans who follow him. Although Scarlet is a minor player who appears only in the first two books, her personality undergoes an interesting transformation over the course of her interaction

191

with Richard the Seeker. His inherited role as Seeker – a touchstone for ultimate truth in the world – brings about change in the dragon's attitude toward humans.

In showing this change, Goodkind humanizes Scarlet the vicious dragon into something more. She has bridged the gap between alien and human, so that readers who may have been attracted first to her "otherness" and bestial power now feel concern for her in the same way they would the human characters. Goodkind has accomplished this through connection to her emotions: disgust at the wizard Rahl, a mother's concern for her offspring, grudging respect for Richard as he delivers on their bargain, and joy in their shared friendship and sense of honor. In a website letter to his fans, Goodkind says, "I simply want everyone to understand that writing these books is an intense emotional experience for me. I feel the emotions along with my characters as I tell their story." It's clear that he identified with Scarlet's feelings and motivations, making her a compelling and convincing character as well as a classic embodiment of dragonflesh.

Oddly enough, in reading a recent article by Tolkien scholar John Garth who speculated about Tolkien's lasting popularity, I was reminded of Goodkind's appeal as well. I certainly have no intention of comparing Goodkind's style to Tolkien's, but the intent of the stories as expressed by Garth holds true for both writers: "In [Tolkien's] story of marvels, the most marvellous thing is the human spirit, often foolish and vain but also tenacious and generous to the point of self-sacrifice. The spirit is tested in a world not so different from our own, in which each element of fantasy relates to reality as if part of a huge symbolist tapestry." Likewise, Scarlet the dragon's part in Goodkind's tapestry enriches it and demonstrates the author's complete understanding of his characters, both human and non-human.

In an interview for Amazon.com, he explains what attracts him to his characters: "Overcoming their greatest fears to achieve what is important to them, whether it's loving someone, or loyalty to someone, or accomplishment of a goal or a cause. To me, the most noble thing about writing is touching the essence of the human spirit." I believe that goes for his dragon, too.

Notes

ST – *Stone of Tears*
WFR – *Wizard's First Rule*

1. To understand the philosophical underpinnings of Goodkind's Sword of Truth series, you'll need to delve into Ayn Rand's classic volumes on objectivism and rational thinking, both fiction and nonfiction. A good place to start is the book that first caught Goodkind's attention, *Anthem*, although *The Romantic Manifesto* would also give some insights into the passions that drive Goodkind's fiction. Of Rand's own fiction, two perennial bestsellers offer the best experience of her philosophy in action: *Atlas Shrugged* and *The Fountainhead* (which begins with one of the more curious and intriguing first paragraphs in modern fiction – the single sentence, "Howard Roark laughed.") In her 1968 introduction to the 25th anniversary edition, Rand wrote, "This is one of the cardinal reasons of *The Fountainhead*'s lasting appeal: it is a confirmation of the spirit of youth, proclaiming man's glory, showing how much is possible. It does not matter that only a few in each generation will grasp and achieve the full reality of man's proper stature – and that the rest will betray it. It is those few that move the world and give life its meaning – and it is those few that I have always sought to address." Richard Cypher, anyone?

2. Interestingly, Goodkind hated the fact that Scarlet was the most prominent feature on his first novel's cover and managed to have the cover changed for later reprints. His dislike of the cover stemmed from the fact that the dragon (and by association, magic) is not the focus of the book, but the cover indicates otherwise. To potential buyers browsing a bookstore shelf, that particular image (a rampant red dragon) broadcasts FANTASY and ADVENTURE. Goodkind has avowed that he would much rather broadcast NOVEL OF IDEAS through the cover art, something he has sought to effect in the marketing of later novels in the series.

Chapter 8

J. K. Rowling
Fantastic Beasts of the Wizarding World

INTERVIEWER: "Could Harry have a pet dragon?"
Rowling: "You can't domesticate a dragon, whatever Hagrid thinks. That's simply impossible. So, no. He's got more sense."

The world of boy wizard Harry Potter, as conceived by author J. K. Rowling, has fascinated readers of widely divergent demographics through five large volumes, with two more planned to complete the series (at the time of this writing). What captivates both young readers and adults in equal numbers is the "what if" factor, the stuff that most children have dreamed about. What if I had magical powers? What if there really was such a thing as a school for wizards? What if dragons are real, but we just can't see them?

Rowling's Harry Potter novels bring that "what if" realm to life with such cleverness and outright glee that they are hard to resist. With considerable storytelling skill, Rowling overlays the "wizarding world" of magic on top of the ordinary non-magical (Muggle) world of present-day Britain. Humans with magical skills rub shoulders with those not so gifted. However, in accordance with laws enacted by the governing body of the wizarding world, this magical realm is kept invisible even though it exists side by side with that of ordinary folk.

This setup gives Rowling great opportunities for both humorous and frightening encounters when those worlds collide, which they inevitably do with unpredictable results. Harry and his companions continually have to shift between the world of magic and the ordinary world, attending Hogwarts School of Witchcraft and Wizardry much of the year and spending summers amongst Muggles. This means that readers also take part in the roller coaster ride between the fantastic and the ordinary that constitutes each new Potter adventure. As you might expect, a zoo-full of imaginary (to Muggles, anyway) and mythical beasts inhabit this wizarding world, including at least ten types of dragons.

While not necessarily evil, Rowling's dragons are clearly menacing, feral beasts, even when raised and controlled by highly trained wizards. Her dragons are not allies or friends, and definitely not pets; hence Rowling's answer to the interviewer quoted at the beginning of this chapter. She goes on to say that they are the most dangerous beasts in the wizarding world and that "you don't want to mess with a dragon, obviously." They're also a protected – and concealed – species, but more on this concept in a moment.

Critics of Rowling's Harry Potter series have accused her of borrowing from every fantasy source available, with the claim that her tale of a boy wizard attending an academy of magic isn't very new. Parallels have been drawn with Jane Yolen's *Wizard's Hall*, Ursula Le Guin's School for Wizards on Roke Island in the Earthsea series, and even the Harper Hall books of Anne McCaffrey. As easy as it is to make such comparisons, they also point to one of the series' major strengths. The mythic motifs are familiar, like tried and true companions with whom readers of fantasy expect to travel on the journey into the author's world. The themes of coming of age, the sorcerer's apprentice (i.e., the use and abuse of power), loyalty, and bravery are world wide and age old. What is compelling for Harry Potter's legions of devotees is *how* Rowling manipulates these universal, ubiquitous materials. The fact is that Rowling is one darned good storyteller.

But what of her dragons? While they easily fit the standard Western dragon model, and particularly those from European fairytale sources, she sprinkles her own clever pixie dust over them to make them unique to Harry's world. Rowling creates the field of Magizoology, which gives a curious twist to the idea of endangered species and protected habitats, especially as applied to dragons. While quite magical – they breathe fire with no help from science or bioengineering – they are also flesh and blood, and thus must be concealed from non-magical humans in order to preserve the illusion that they aren't real.

"But there aren't wild dragons in *Britain?*" said Harry.

"Of course there are," said Ron. "Common Welsh Green and Hebridean Blacks. The Ministry of Magic has a job hushing them up, I can tell you. Our kind have to keep putting spells on Muggles who've spotted them, to make them forget." (SS, 231)

Like most skillful fantasy writers, Rowling puts a good deal of work into setting up the background myths and history of her invented world, and that includes dragonlore. Dragon references and imagery are sprinkled through the books, from the motto for Hogwarts (*Draco Dormiens Nunquam Titillandus* – "Never tickle a sleeping dragon") to the name of Harry's chief adversary at school, young Draco Malfoy. Draco, as most bestiaries and dragon sourcebooks will tell you, is the Latin version of the Greek term *draconta*, a type of monstrous serpent.[1] Fittingly, Draco Malfoy is a member of Slytherin House (one of the four Houses into which the student body of Hogwarts is sorted), whose emblem is a large coiled serpent on a green field.

Because much of the action in Harry Potter's world takes place at an academy with a large (and somewhat intimidating) library, references to books about magic and wizardry abound. Among the titles at Hogwarts that refer to dragons, we find these wickedly funny entries: *Dragon Breeding for Pleasure and Profit; Dragon-cultivation for House and Court; From Egg to Inferno, A Dragon Keeper's Guide; Dragon Species of Great Britain and Ireland; Men Who Love Dragons Too Much; The Monster Book of Monsters*; and most importantly, *Fantastic Beasts & Where to Find Them*, a required textbook for Hogwarts students.

Regarding this last book, Rowling has done something very clever. Not only has she invented an important document containing lore that explains and hints at much of her world's history, a trick that many fantasy writers use, but she has actually written and published the reference book itself. Under the alias of Newt Scamander, Rowling created *Fantastic Beasts & Where to Find Them*, a slim paperback with simulated claw marks and "Property of" tag on the cover, and scrawled student graffiti throughout its rather dry and stuffy entries. The text covers Magizoology and the history of Muggle awareness of magic, as well as an A to Z encyclopedia of the fantastic beasts themselves. This is where we find out about dragons and their different breeds.

The book's lengthy entry for "Dragon" is quite humorous, and its breed categories (Antipodean Opaleye, Chinese Fireball, Common Welsh Green, Hebridean Black, Hungarian Horntail, Norwegian Ridgeback, Peruvian Vipertooth, Romanian Longhorn, Swedish Short-Snout, and Ukrainian Ironbelly) are as fanciful as Lady Ramkin's swamp dragon breed lines in Pratchett's *Guards! Guards!* Her recital of the pedigree lineages with monikers like Gayheart Talonthrust of Ankh or Moonpenny Duchess Marchpaine is similarly smirk-inducing. Also like Pratchett, Rowling employs her dragons for both comic and dramatic effect. For example, her tournament dragons are feral and dangerous (like the *Draco nobilis* of Discworld), and the hatchling Norbert's interaction with the dragon-besotted Hagrid is laced with sardonic humor (as is the swamp dragon Errol's relationship to his owner, Capt. Vimes).

But Rowling's dragons have their own imprint that's different from the dragons we've discussed in previous chapters. Though physically similar to Smaug from *The Hobbit*, Rowling's magical dragons don't speak or telepath their thoughts. They seem excitable and unpredictable, and when riled attempt to incinerate the puny humans around them, but only in a strictly animal way. They are "beasts" as opposed to "beings," where the defining characteristics (according to Hogwarts scholar Newt Scamander) are self-aware intelligence, human conscience, and ability to speak in a human language, i.e., "any creature that has sufficient intelligence to understand the laws of the magical community."

The strongest dragon connection between Rowling and Tolkien isn't with Smaug – it occurs through the half-giant Hagrid, Hogwart's game-keeper and teacher of a course on the care of magical beasts. Hagrid is the total embodiment of Tolkien's famous statement with which I began this book: he desires dragons with a great desire, to the point that he throws all caution out the window in pursuit of them, getting himself into all kinds of trouble. Harry's pal Ron observes that "... you can't tame dragons, it's dangerous," and he mentions how his wizard brother Charlie, a trained dragon-handler, has burns aplenty to show for his chosen profession. From this example of what others say about dragons, readers are alerted that Hagrid's dragon fascination will likely come to grief.

Dragons are a prominent presence in only two of the Potter books to date, so you will not find much character building in Rowling's dragons. The real question, then, is what is their plot significance? Most importantly, they are the means by which the student champions (and vicariously, the readers) confront stark fear and work their way through it successfully. Later in this chapter I'll have more to say about the types of dragons with which the champions must do battle, and the way each chooses to meet that challenge. Dragons also provide some grim amusement of the type the *New York Times Book Review* calls "Rowling's punning, one-eyebrow-cocked sense of humor," seen mostly in Hagrid's encounter with Norbert.

It's safe to say that J. K. Rowling's dragons are a work in progress, because her Harry Potter series is still two books away from completion. She has planted some tantalizing dragon seeds, however, which might pay off significantly in those final two volumes. With that in mind, let's have a look at what she's created so far.

Baby Norbert

In Scamander's *Fantastic Beasts & Where to Find Them*, in the section on dragon breeds, the entry name "Norwegian Ridgeback" has been crossed out (by Harry, we assume) and "Baby Norbert" written in the margin. From *Harry Potter and the Sorcerer's Stone* we know that Norbert is the name Hagrid gives to an illegal hatchling of this rather unmanageable breed. Scamander's category descriptions give us a good summary of what Hagrid is in for when he undertakes to hatch and raise such a beast: "exceptionally aggressive," "known to attack most kinds of large land mammal," and "young develop fire-breathing abilities earlier than other breeds (at between one and three months)," should be warning enough to any would-be dragon tamer. But Hagrid is in a state of denial where dragon danger is concerned, to the peril of all.

As Scamander's book implies, Norbert is a Norwegian Ridgeback. Like the Hungarian Horntail, which Harry confronts in the Triwizard Tournament, Ridgebacks are large black, lizardlike creatures with yellow eyes and bronze horns. Distinct to the Ridgeback, however, is a row of threatening jet-black spikes along its spine. As intimidating as this information is, Rowling's sly humor infuses the passage with clever observations such as this: "Exceptionally aggressive to its own kind, the Ridgeback is nowadays one of the rarer dragon breeds" – an excellent example of deadpan humor on paper.

Although I wouldn't call Rowling a fantasy humorist of the type that Pratchett clearly is, the episodes with Norbert provide rollicking examples of her comedic touch, at Hagrid's expense. However, unlike Pratchett's swamp dragons or Yolen's beauty dragons or Le Guin's *harrekki*, you can't make pets of Rowling's dragons; in fact, it's illegal to do so in the wizarding world. This doesn't stop Hagrid, of course, from following his heart's desire to obtain one (under the influence of some powerful pub brew, as well). Scamander's textbook notes that "dragon eggs are defined as Class A Non-Tradeable Goods," so naturally Hagrid has one, since he is routinely running afoul of the authorities.

Readers first encounter Norbert as an egg – "In the very heart of the fire, underneath the kettle, was a huge, black egg." – but that state doesn't last long. Rowling creates a wonderful chapter titled "Norbert the Norwegian Ridgeback" that sets up Hagrid's penchant for adopting magical creatures he can barely control (heedless of both his and the students' safety) and gives her an opportunity to create a memorable picture of live dragons as they coexist in the wizarding world and twenty-first century England. Hagrid's excitement is contagious. His simple note, "It's hatching," is enough to make even the studious Hermione consider skipping class to watch the event. As Ron puts it, "Hermione, how many times in our lives are we going to see a dragon hatching?" Like Harry, who previously hadn't thought dragon were real, readers watch with vicarious amazement as deep cracks begin to run across the shell.

In *Harry Potter: Perspectives on a Literary Phenomenon*, Roni Natov mentions the way in which mythic images and realistic details are blended in Rowling's depiction of Norbert. We can see this at work in the hatching sequence, which combines slapstick funny business with mythic overtones and realistic details. Hagrid's complete denial of the dangers inherent in the situation continuously collides with the warnings coming from Harry, Ron, and Hermione. For example, as Hagrid cheerily stokes the fire around the egg, Hermione points out that he lives in a wooden house. This is doubly funny if you've read the entry in *Fantastic Beasts* because Hagrid proudly identifies the egg as that of a rare Norwegian Ridgeback, a dragon Scamander tells us acquires its flame-breathing ability much sooner than other breeds, greatly increasing the fire-casualty risk.

When the egg splits open with "a scraping noise," we're treated to a feast of visual and auditory detail: the dragon "flops" onto the tabletop, and its "skinny" jet-colored body is dwarfed by "spiny" oversized wings. By the shape and description of its head we can tell it fits the standardized image of the typical Western dragon: its snout is long with "wide nostrils" for, we assume, flame spouting, and it has horn buds over its "bulging" orange eyes. Sparks fly out of its snout when it sneezes, confirming its precocious fire-breathing abilities.

A colorful writer, Rowling makes good use of simile to give a specific visual impression as the hatchling emerges: "Harry thought it looked like a crumpled black umbrella." This single image conveys the sense of the Ridgeback's angular, membranous wings folded and bent along its much smaller slender body, along with the ideas of sharpness and ungainliness. The metaphor of "baby" is carried to its extreme when Hagrid tries to explain away the wreckage the growing dragon has created inside the gamekeeper's hut, claiming that it's "only a baby, after all." With her typical acerbic humor, Rowling as narrator comments that "The baby banged its tail on the wall, making the windows rattle."

Using the comedic technique of contrast, Rowling punctuates the end of the scene with action in which the dragon repeatedly contradicts the assertions of love and nobility that Hagrid in his besotted state ascribes to it. It has just been described as a crumpled umbrella that snorts sparks, yet Hagrid croons "Isn't he beautiful?" When he attempts to pet its head, it snaps at him and bares sharp little fangs (which, in typical dragon fashion, turn out to be poisonous), behavior that Hagrid doggedly interprets as recognizing "his mommy." Within a week or two, the dragon has tripled its length, smoke continuously curls out of its snout like an ominously sleeping volcano, and it's consuming large amounts of brandy, chicken blood, and dead rats. Hardly a baby.

There is a particular word that best describes Norbert as Hagrid sees him. It's known to every *otaku* (anime fanatic) and that word is *kawaii*. It translates roughly as too cute to be true. Norbert (in Hagrid's eyes) is so *kawaii* he can do no wrong. The contrast between Hagrid's desire for dragons and the reality of trying to tame one is brought home through his and Ron's reactions to Norbert's behavior. Hagrid claims, "He really knows me now, watch, Norbert! Norbert! Where's Mommy?" and sings it lullabies at night. In contrast, Ron brandishes his bloody hand where the dragon has bitten him during a feeding with said dead rats: "I tell you, that dragon's the most horrible animal I've ever met, but the way Hagrid goes on about it, you'd think it was a fluffy little bunny rabbit." Much like a teething puppy run amok, Norbert bites his benefactor on the leg and attacks his foot hard enough to draw tears to the gamekeeper's eyes, but Hagrid excuses everything: "Aargh! It's all right, he only got my boot – jus' playin'" is his typical response.

The main question is this – what is Norbert's function in the story? One literary critic has suggested that Norbert is Harry's alter ego.[2] This seems a bit far-fetched to me, mostly because Norbert reveals more to us about Hagrid than Harry. We know, for example, that magical creatures, and dragons in particular, are Hagrid's weakness. We also know that Hagrid can't keep a secret. Put those two elements together, and he becomes an easy dupe for someone wanting to know how to get past the guardian to the sorcerer's stone. Tempting Hagrid into an illegal transaction to acquire a dragon's egg not only sets the stone's theft in motion, it also sets him up for future trouble from Harry's enemies such as Draco Malfoy. While Hagrid is too trusting to realize the implications of his seeming stroke of luck from a stranger in a pub, Harry can see it for what it is:

> "Don't you think it's a bit odd," said Harry, scrambling up the grassy slope, "that what Hagrid wants more than anything else is a dragon, and a stranger turns up who just happens to have an egg in his pocket? How many people wander around with dragon eggs if it's against wizard law?" (SS, 265)

In addition to the major function of giving the enemy the secret of how to put the Cerberus-like guardian to sleep, the Norbert episode serves a secondary purpose. Rowling is well-known for her meticulous plot structure, carefully planting seeds and events that pay off later in important ways. As she stated in an interview for Amazon.com, the most important ingredients of her books are "humor, strong characters, and a watertight plot." Draco Malfoy's discovery of Hagrid's hidden dragon gives him an important piece of information that can be used to get Hagrid and anyone connected with Norbert in great trouble (including Harry and his friends, as well as Charlie Weasley and the wizards who take the hatchling away by stealth).

The fact that the ploy backfires this time (it's Malfoy who gets in trouble, not Harry or Hagrid) creates a reversal that provides motivation for the first of many instances in which Malfoy seeks revenge on Hagrid and his associates. According to Newt Scamander, dragons are not allies – they are adversaries. On a symbolic level, not all dragons in Rowling's stories are lizard-like beasts – some are human characters who serve that role as well. This fact is underscored by the fact that *Draco* Malfoy is an enemy, not an ally.[3] By the time readers have reached the fifth book, *Harry Potter and the Order of the Phoenix*, no one should be surprised that Draco reports Hagrid in the worst way possible to the Hogwarts High Inquisitor, Dolores Umbridge, getting him sacked and putting his supporters in jeopardy. It's a good example of Rowling's careful long-range plotting that pays off time and again over the course of the books.

Dragons of the Triwizard Tournament

The episode with Norbert also has a long-range impact on the Triwizard Tournament that takes place in book four, *Harry Potter and The Goblet of Fire*. Having been deprived of owning a dragon, Hagrid is so excited over the tournament dragons being corralled not far from his hut near the forest that he can't keep them a secret. Thus, Hagrid gives Harry an unfair advantage by revealing the first challenge of the tournament – trial by dragon. Dr. Tina Hanlon of Ferrum College comments that "Hagrid's indiscretion and love of dragons again provide comedy in this suspenseful episode." In addition to the element of comedy, Hagrid's dragon obsession moves the plot along. Knowing about them ahead of time gives Harry the chance to make some important decisions that affect how the tournament unfolds.

The Triwizard Tournament, a 700-year-old competition between the three largest wizarding academies of Europe (Hogwarts, Beauxbatons, and Durmstrang) pits the most talented student champion from each school in three magical tasks. Prize money is involved, but of more importance is bragging rights for the next five years until the tournament rotates to the next host school. Readers discover along with the stunned and excited Hogwarts students just how outlandish these three tasks can be.

Rowling has great fun setting up the concept of the tournament, and much gallows humor ensues as tournament preparations unfold. For example, Headmaster Dumbledore reveals matter-of-factly that the tournament has been discontinued for the past several centuries because of the mounting death toll. His assurance that the faculty has "worked hard over the summer to ensure that this time, no champion will find himself or herself in mortal danger" adds to the growing anticipation of what lies ahead, which pays off as soon as Hagrid spills the beans about dragons being the first task.

Rowling's tournament dragons fit the mold of chaos dragon – an obstacle or barrier to be overcome, as well as the raw power of unbridled nature. These dragons are not your allies or best friends; they are the opposite. Even the wizards who try to control them do so at their own peril. The dragons' innate magic is so strong it takes a group of wizards using collective magic to stun one into a stupor. When Harry learns that dragons will be the first test of the tournament, the set of instructions given to the school champions suddenly has much more meaning: "The first task is designed to test your daring ... Courage in the face of the unknown is an important quality in a wizard ... The Champions will face the first challenge armed only with their wands."

With *The Goblet of Fire*, Rowling's tone shifts to a darker register, in which facing one's deepest fears becomes the purpose of the tournament but also the larger theme of the book. The fact that Dumbledore admits the tournament tests are difficult and dangerous sets this tone, which carries through to the devastating cliff-hanger ending. Reviewer Robert McCrum of Britain's *The Guardian* says, "When dark references to previous tournaments establish that this is a contest in which the participants can lose their lives, we realise that the stakes are getting dangerously high." Mysteriously selected as an additional fourth champion in the contest, Harry is yanked from the sidelines into the thick of the competition. Building on Harry's own disbelief at being added to the roster of champions, Rowling creates fear and apprehension in the story by alluding to the first task in terms that foreshadow what's to come. She describes how the "fear of what was facing him" starts to sink in, using a simile suggestive of the coming dragon encounter: "The first task was drawing steadily nearer: he felt as though it were crouching ahead of him like some horrific monster, barring his path."

Vaguely reminiscent of Jane Yolen's pit dragon contests, the dragon task involves confronting a winged, flame-breathing dragon inside a fortified ring. In Rowling's competition, the dragons are all female, with a clutch of eggs to protect. The object of the task is to snatch a golden-marked egg from the pile and emerge from the ring alive. The breed of dragon that each champion selects to face (by random drawing) reveals something about the personal test each will face. Lovely Fleur Delacourt, champion from the French team, draws a Welsh Green; Cedric Diggory the Hogwarts champion draws a Swedish Short-Snout; the surly Durmstrang champion Victor Krum draws a Chinese Fireball; and Harry, the unexpected fourth champion, is left with the last – and worst – dragon, the Hungarian Horntail as his adversary.

Readers are given a first-hand look at these creatures described in Scamander's textbook as Hagrid gives Harry and Madame Maxime of the

Beauxbatons team a sneak peak at them, sequestered on the edge of the forest. The first piece of description we get is auditory – "then came a deafening, ear-splitting roar" – followed by Harry's shocked reaction: "... his mouth fell open. *Dragons*." The scene of thirty or so wizards struggling to control four dangerously riled dragons is some of Rowling's best descriptive writing, with sensory details and vivid action that brings the scene alive.

> "Four fully grown, enormous, vicious-looking dragons were rearing onto their hind legs inside an enclosure fenced with thick planks of wood, roaring and snorting – torrents of fire were shooting into the dark sky from their open, fanged mouths, fifty feet above the ground on their outstretched necks."

Although familiarity with the dragon breeds listed in *Fantastic Beasts* isn't requisite to enjoy the spectacle; those who have read the textbook will quickly recognize the Common Green, Short-Snout, Fireball, and Horntail at the center of the melee. The black Horntail lives up to its book annotation by appearing to be the most vicious and threatening of the four, mesmerizing Harry with its yellow catlike eyes and "yowling, screeching scream." We have a great sense of its size and weight as the shouted spell "Stupefy!" momentarily brings it to the ground: "Several tons of sinewy, scaly-black dragon hit the ground with a thud" that makes nearby trees quiver.

It's easy to be reminded of the basilisk from classical legend as Harry stares at its half-closed eye, a "strip of gleaming yellow beneath its wrinkled black eyelid." Charlie Weasley's comments on the beast ("I don't envy the one who gets the Horntail. Vicious thing. Its back end's as dangerous as its front…") immediately tip us off as to which Harry will draw. Looking at its tail, "Harry saw long, bronze-colored spikes protruding along it every few inches." As savvy readers, we know this will be exactly what Harry ends up dodging in his dragon confrontation.

Rowling is particularly good at creating the sense of fear and foreboding that Harry and the other three champions go through in the moments leading up to the first match. Fleur Delacour's trembling and Victor Krum's grim resignation give us a range of emotions people can experience in terrifying situations, but it's through Harry that we experience fully the terror of waiting. Looking at Cedric's green-tinged face, Harry starts to feel sick himself. Through his point of view, we feel all the bodily sensations of fear as the minutes tick by and horrible sounds from the ring outside filter back, much like Yolen's hero Jakkin who listens to the terrifying dragon fights going on while he waits beneath the pit for his turn. This is something every reader can relate to – waiting for something you dread to happen. Anyone who has sat in a medical waiting room or stood in the wings before a performance or listened in terror to something you can't see off in the dark can imagine Harry's torment. The dragon represents the terrible unknown that can devour us if we let it.

"It was worse than Harry could ever have imagined, sitting there and listening … Horrible pictures formed in Harry's mind as he heard: "Oooh, narrow miss there, very narrow ..." (GF, 352)

The Hungarian Horntail performs the same function for Harry that the medieval dragon performed for St. George – testing a hero's mettle and allowing him to pass from initiation into a position of strength and victory. Facing the dragon serves an important function for young (and older) readers as well – by using one's head, by staying calm and drawing on knowledge as well as courage, one can come safely through the most terrifying events and even experience triumph. Innocence gives way to experience and knowledge as the hero comes of age.

Rowling injects more dragonlore into the story by having Harry enlist Hermione in helping him learn everything he can about dragons in the few days before the tournament. Scouring the library for books on dragons uncovers such daunting passages as *"Dragons are extremely difficult to slay, owing to the ancient magic that imbues their thick hides, which none but the most powerful spells can penetrate,"* forcing him to think outside the box, so to speak. Instead of applying spells to the dragon directly, he comes up with a clever workaround: a basic Summoning spell that brings his high-speed broomstick into the ring where he can treat the snatching of the gold egg much like a game of Quidditch, at which he excels. Rowling's hero shows that brains are as valuable as brawn in this contest, and raw courage is perhaps the most important ingredient of all.

Readers' emotions peak and plummet along with the contestants as the action in the ring ranges from the comic to the tragic. All four champions manage to grab the golden egg and escape, but from the viewpoint of the enraged mother dragons, it's the same dilemma posed by Yolen's pit dragon fights: are the dragons being harmed or exploited unfairly? Fleur's non-violent approach, putting her dragon into a sleeping trance, has the desired effect, but an unexpected comic result that it starts snoring great jets of flame, making egg retrieval hazardous. From the dragon-lover's point of view, Victor Krum's tactic of blinding his dragon with a spell aimed at its eye is just cruel, especially when the agonized dragon tramples some of her eggs. We are told that "they took marks off for that, he wasn't supposed to do any damage to them," but it's still an unhappy outcome for the dragon.

The dragon trials episode also brings up issues of trust and betrayal, of doing the right thing rather than the selfish thing. Harry knows he has an unfair advantage because of Hagrid's tip-off, but he also realizes that Madame Maxime will probably tell the same information to her Beauxbatons champion and the Durmstrang coach lurking at the forest periphery will surely alert his own champion. That leaves the original Hogwarts champion, Cedric Diggory, as the only one left in the dark. Harry can keep quiet about what he's seen, or he can tell Cedric about the dragons even though it might expose Hagrid and himself to the accusation of cheating.

Here Rowling models through Harry the only decent thing to do, which is to put everyone on an equal footing. The fact that it *is* the right thing to do is emphasized by what the Defense Against the Dark Arts teacher, Mad-Eye Moody, says to Harry after he warns Cedric – "That was a very decent thing you just did, Potter." Although he acknowledges that cheating has always gone on during tournaments where the stakes are so high, taking the higher ground proves that Harry is the true champion.

In Conclusion
As a writer of inventive fantasy fiction, Rowling creates books that are "brimming with imagination, humor, and suspense," skillfully manipulating

complicated plotlines and "balancing humor, malevolence, school-day tedium, and shocking revelations with the aplomb of a circus performer," according to a *School Library Journal* reviewer. One of Rowling's acknowledged strengths is her knowledge of myth and legend, a result, she says, of her focus on Classical Studies in college. She has obviously studied her literary dragonlore well, as many of the sources discussed in my Dragonology chapters have resonance in the background magic and fantastical creatures of the Potter stories.

At the time of this writing, J. K. Rowling's dragons may undergo further development if the seeds planted in these early books of the Harry Potter series sprout down the line. Will Norbert reappear as a fully grown dragon? If so, will Hagrid get into more difficulties on his behalf? Charlie Weasley, who rescued Norbert, has entered the books twice as a dragon-tamer wizard – will he have yet another part to play? These are speculations that only time and two more Potter novels will prove true or false.

What can be said with certainty is that Rowling's dragons in *The Sorcerer's Stone* and *The Goblet of Fire* contain all the fearsomeness of traditional dragons as encountered in classical Western legends and European bestiaries. Her dragons aren't reasoning or enlightened creatures you can converse with or go for a ride on – they are scary wild beasts. In Rowling's Amazon.com interview, she admits to her enjoyment of the "scariness" element in fiction ("I never set out to make people scared, but it does seem to creep in along the way."). This tendency is part of what gives Rowling her unique voice – a smart yet beguiling blend of terror and smirk, of the darkly comic and the deadly serious. As a result, her dragon episodes are some of the tastiest treats in the wizarding world.

Notes

GF – *Harry Potter and the Goblet of Fire*
SS – *Harry Potter and the Sorcerer's Stone*

1. For example, in Carol Rose's thorough compendium titled *Giants, Monsters & Dragons: An Encyclopedia of Folklore, Legend, and Myth*, we read that the *draco* of classical Greece and Rome was "a vast serpent with wings resembling those of a bat, possibly breathing fire from its flickering tongue." Medieval bestiaries modified the

concept of the Draco into a huge crested serpent that lay in ambush coiled around trees like a python or lurking "in caves and subterranean places of India and Ethiopia" and was the Christian symbol of evil.

2. You can find this argument in Elizabeth D. Schafer's book, *Exploring Harry Potter*, Beacham's Sourcebooks for Teaching Young Adult Fiction. The book contains background material and teaching guides for the first three books in the Harry Potter series, including a section "Magical Animals and Creatures." On page 68 is the quotation in question: "The dragon Norbert is Harry's alter ego, acting toward his foster parent like Harry wishes he could act toward the Dursleys, literally biting the hand that feeds him. Norbert is sent to safety in a crate much like toddler Harry was exiled in a bundle of blankets."

3. Nancy Jentsch discusses the relationship between Draco Malfoy's name and dragons in one of the essays in a volume title, *The Ivory Tower and Harry Potter: Perspectives on a Literary Phenomenon*, edited by Lana Whited.

Part Two:

BACKGROUND

Chapter 9

Dragonology 101
Ancient Near East to Classical Era

WHAT IS a dragon? What does it look like, and how does it behave? I imagine that as soon as you read the word "dragon," a specific image came into your mind's eye. Ask most people to describe a dragon and you will likely get a description of a creature similar to the one on the cover of this book: a larger-than-life heavy-legged reptilian body with serpentine neck, sharp talons, spiny wings, and scaly hide (red is preferred, with its connotation of flame). Its head is long and wedge-shaped, with slanting eyes, a fearsome mouth full of teeth, and nostrils exhaling gusts of fire and smoke. The posture is aggressive, usually aimed at some puny humanoid crouching in its shadow.

If your inclination is more oriental, your mental dragon likely is long and slender, snakelike and undulating, and probably without wings. Its movement is more graceful and perhaps playful than menacing. It has a horse-like face with bulging round eyes, flowing whiskers on the muzzle, and horns between its ears. Its color might be red, but yellow or gold is more likely. Its four short legs will have feet with three to five prominently displayed claws, depending on its royal rank.

These are universal images of a creature that never lived, yet it has prowled around in the world's mythologies and folklores for thousands of years. It's one of our oldest archetypes, whether slain by gods and heroes (Western dragons) or revered as the source of life and good fortune (Eastern dragons). The earliest dragons began to show up in both text and art in civilizations of the Ancient Near East (ANE, also called Mesopotamia) and the Far East, mostly China proper. For example, from ancient Babylon there is the famous Ishtar Gate that displays a composite creature we might call dragonesque. Or there's the *Epic of Creation* with its vivid description of the hero-god Marduk's victory over the monstrous sea-goddess Tiamat. Illustrations of Tiamat from Babylonian art show an imaginative combination of reptile and animal parts.

Ideas about what makes a dragon varied widely among early civilizations, and dragonlore comes from both the written word and visual art. This fact can be very useful to the writer of fantasy, because the presence of dragons has become a virtual requirement of fantasy literature today. The attributes of the beast we call "dragon" are quite standardized in current fantasy fiction, but knowing where these standards come from and the traditions that spawned them allows the writer to create dragons with more invention and conviction.

So, how does one begin to write fiction about dragons? Every writer's process is individual, yet there are some obvious commonalities. The process involves research in both academic and popular sources, reading widely in the fantasy genre itself, and finally taking flight on one's own. Writing well requires talent, but it also takes skill in the craft, and one of the most important skills is the ability to do research, which brings us to the subject of Dragonology.

The Basics

Dragonlore from myths and legends around the world is grist for the mill of the writer. If dragonkind are to be included in the cast of characters, the author needs a highly specific mental image of the beast, as well as an understanding of its nature in order to make it fly off the pages and into the reader's imagination. It must be more than just furniture, so to speak. Some writers are better at it than others, and some are especially good at it. In this book, I've shared with you the dragon creations of seven such authors whose works run the gamut from gentle to humorous to awe-inspiring to the truly terrifying. Where did their ideas come from?

The dragon has been around so long that it has provided comparative mythologists, philologists, archeologists, visual artists, and fiction writers with enough material to fill entire careers. There are many books and articles about dragons, both scholarly and popular, so my aim in this chapter is not to provide a thorough source study of dragons from the dawn of civilization to the present century. That has been done quite thoroughly by a number of researchers and dragonologists listed in Chapter 11, "The Dragon Hunter's Toolkit."

This chapter is intended to give you a sense of dragonlore from the point of view of writers who have done their research and discovered the dragon's wide diversity as a creature of myth and folklore. I'll be dipping into dragon terminology, attributes from the animal kingdom, and symbolism in legends and tales. Of most importance to the discussion in Part I is how these sources have given inspiration to writers of modern fantasy fiction – that is, how the dragons of the past have given today's fiction writers a vast treasure horde that can be mined for ideas. As we take a closer look at these ancient dragons, you may be reminded from time to time of dragons in modern fantasies you've read. By looking at where dragons began, you'll have a better picture of how knowledgeable the best fantasy authors are on dragons and how seamlessly they have blended that knowledge into their stories.

Unearthing Middle Eastern Dragons

No one really knows beyond doubt when and where the first dragon came into being.[1] In fact, a search for its origins will lead to the much-argued but ultimately unanswerable question facing most dragonologists: was there one point of origin, or did the concept of "dragon" develop independently in civilizations around the world?

From a book written by Professor Qiguang Zhao[2] you can read that a 6,000-year-old dragon statue was found during the 1987 Yellow River dam project in China, but as Zhao points out, this shouldn't be taken as evidence of the "birthplace of the world dragon."

For my purpose here, it's a useless argument, but I *am* interested in the various forms, both visual and textual, through which dragonlike creatures have morphed. We might argue that dragons come from worship of serpents, but I'll narrow my discussion of serpents to only those with a direct influence on dragon development. As mentioned before, exposure to myth and folklore fuels the creative imagination, and that's what we're really looking for here.

Ancient Sumeria and Babylon are certainly early enough locations for us to start poking around in. From Sumeria we have the epic battle between Anzu and Ninurta, one of the very first examples of the dragonslayer archetype (that is, if you accept Anzu as a dragon). Maybe we should refer to creatures like Anzu as "proto-dragons," *proto-* meaning first in time or the very beginnings of a series. Anzu is depicted as a lion-headed eagle and is referred to in some translations as a "storm bird" with great wings and a beak like a saw.

As a formidable creature, Anzu is entrusted with the job of guarding the inner sanctum where the Tablets of Destinies are kept. Here is one of the first examples of the guarding motif connected with dragons, and the dragons we know today are still guarding the entrances to treasure hoards and magical objects of great power. When Anzu steals the tablets in order to have ultimate power over the earth, it's up to a hero such as Ninurta to recover them and reestablish order. Anzu is generally considered one of the early so-called "chaos dragons" representing the world before order was imposed on it. Chaos dragons still hold great potential for writers today – just read Terry Pratchett or Melanie Rawn and you'll see.

In a Babylonian tablet listing the Seven Evil Spirits, there is vague mention of a creature often translated as "dragon" but nothing else is known about what it looks like. It does, however, continue to stack the deck against Western proto-dragons as the embodiment of wickedness: "... Workers of evil are they, they lift up the head to evil, every day to evil, destruction to work." If you've seen the film *Reign of Fire*, you'll see that this ancient archetype is still in use.

From Babylonia, we find numerous well-known images of dragonlike beasts on tablets, cylinder seals, and temple carvings. In these earliest "dragons," familiar animal parts were combined to form exotic creatures that did not exist in real life. For example, Assyrian temple art from around 885-860 BCE (before common era) gives us a creature with a human head, eagle's wings, bull's body, and lion's paws. The beast from the Ishtar Gate (sixth century BCE) is a blend of lion's body and forelegs, eagle's legs on the hindquarters, single horn on its long snout, and a forked tongue. The horned serpent is a snake stretched along the ground, with a lionlike head, neck, and forepaws at the front of the body. These are early concepts of dragons, but not yet the creature we know today.

The Greeks would later name such creatures *drákon,* and the label has stuck, so to speak, although the actual beast continued to undergo interesting changes and variations before settling into the typical Western dragon familiar to the St. Georges of the world. Jonathan Evans explains the situation in his entry on dragons in *Mythical and Fabulous Creatures: A Sourcebook and Research Guide,* a type of source book most dragon writers would be familiar with. He explains that "the origin of *drákon* ... is associated with eyesight." A lot of mileage has been claimed from this connection by imaginative authors – dragons are far-sighted, have psychic sight, can tell when humans are lying, can turn their enemies to stone with their gaze, and so on – you know the drill.

Let's go back to Tiamat for a moment. She appears in the opening lines of the *Epic of Creation* as the mother goddess from whom a pantheon of gods emerges. Although she is most often mentioned as the evil monster slain by Marduk, you'll discover that initially she shows maternal protection and indulgence toward her unruly offspring. Only later does she become the angry monster bent on war and destruction, which demonstrates that even on clay tablets thousands of years old, there is character development.

Tiamat has several traits we associate with modern dragons. She attempts to put a dragonspell on her adversary through cunning words and flattery. As the epic tells us, Marduk doesn't succumb to her voice, and in a terrible hand-to-hand struggle, Tiamat is killed by an arrow that pierces her belly, setting a model for many subsequent dragonslayers.

Egyptian mythology has a number of composite demons and beasts, especially of the underworld variety. Among such creatures you'll find Set (" a water-devil"), Apep (" a gigantic snake-like reptile"), and the griffons that draw Osiris' war chariot.

Apep (also called Apophis), the main adversary of the sun god Ra, has familiar dragonlike qualities. Egyptian tomb paintings reveal an undulating serpent of immense length rising out of the waves to confront Ra in his sun boat. In her introduction to *The Ultimate Dragon*, Tanith Lee describes Apep as "the subterranean dragon [who] battles with the sun deity, Ra, by night, in an attempt to destroy the return of the day – and is always overcome." What did the ancient Egyptians think, one wonders, during the occasional solar eclipse when Apep appeared to have swallowed Ra in broad daylight?

At some point in Egyptian mythology, Apep became blended with Set, Osiris' evil brother, who according to myth tore himself from his mother's womb. In a larger context, Set came to represent the concept of wickedness itself, as the perpetual adversary of Osiris, his opposite. In myths predating the Osiris cycle, Set (as the brother of Horus the Elder) was banished to the desert where, by association, he later took form as a monster of the dry lifeless zone. He's not exactly a dragon, but is depicted as a composite beast with four legs, a forked tail, sharp snout, and animal ears – not too far away from our standardized image.

Worth noting is the emblem of the cobra-head (*uraeus*) with widespread hood affixed prominently on the front of the pharaoh's crown, interesting because of its two dragon attributes. It appears anywhere the element of protection is needed – in tomb paintings, papyrus texts, and personal adornment – fostering the idea of the dragon as a guardian.

Like Set, the *uraeus* is not exactly a dragon, but it gives us one of the earliest references to a trait nearly every dragon of fantasy fiction possesses: the ability to breathe a stream of fire. This evidence shows that the idea of fire issuing from a monster's mouth, whether in protection or aggression, is as old as the desert hills, and the physics invented to explain this phenomenon are as varied as the authors discussed in the first part of this book.

Before we leave Egypt, I want to take a moment to mention the universal symbol called the *ouroboros*, a Greek term meaning "tail-eating snake." The earliest evidence of this emblem is from the cult of Isis in Egypt, where the all-in-one serpent encircled the disc of the sun. We don't know for certain that the idea originated in Egypt, but the ouroboros emblem and its general meaning of eternity, oneness, renewal, and sacred, secret knowledge has somehow cross-pollinated into nearly every mythology around the globe. Besides Egypt, Greece, and the Near East, the ouroboros image has been found in Asia, North and South America, India, Australia, New Zealand, as well as the Christianized Northern societies who depicted the serpent as a dragon with wings.

Speaking of Christian societies, all dragonologists know that both the Hebrew Bible (Old Testament) and the Christian Bible (New Testament) contain proto-dragons. The most notable examples are Leviathan and Rahab, plus a couple of unnamed monsters (red, with horns) later equated with an old serpent named Satan. Following the tradition established from earlier ANE texts, these monsters initially represented chaos subjugated by order (and, one assumes, civilization). Like Egyptian Set, who eventually becomes the root of all evil, the New Testament dragons described by John in his Revelation morph into *the* Devil, i.e., the serpent who tempted Eve in the garden of Eden.

The demonization of dragons in Western religion and myth continues. As Professor Zhao says, "Even though the dragon becomes increasingly recognizable in time, and even becomes an ensign in some cultures, the Western dragon is better defined by its meaning than by its shape." Its shape may vary, but so far, its nature is consistently evil or destructive.

Let's go hunting for biblical dragons. First, we have the apocryphal tale of "Bel and the Dragon." In the tale, Daniel demonstrates to King Cyrus of Persia that the idol representing Bel cannot be divine because it doesn't really eat the food set out for it (the priests and their relatives secretly consume the offerings each night). Cyrus then challenges Daniel to disprove the divinity of a live dragon also revered by the Babylonians. "You cannot deny that this is a living god; so worship him," commands the king.[3]

Daniel feeds it a poisonous mixture of "pitch, fat, and hair" (a fair witch's brew!), after which the dragon "burst open" and died. From a Christian perspective, the evil false god was rebuked and destroyed by the righteous Daniel. From a pagan perspective, the king's followers were upset by the death of the dragon, which they considered a victim of deception and treachery. Both scenarios are useful to creators of fantasy fiction, depending on whether the dragon is to be painted as an object of sympathy or villainy.

Moving to the Old Testament proper, we have the dragons Rahab and Leviathan. In Job (26:12-13), Bildad the Shuhite mentions sea serpents as agents of chaos and evil: "By his power he stilled the Sea; by his understanding he struck down Rahab / By his wind the heavens were made fair; his hand pierced the fleeing serpent." Isaiah 51:9-11 refers to this same passage in which the plea for God's intervention asks, "Was it not you who cut Rahab in pieces, who pierced the dragon?" We aren't given a physical description of Rahab, but the symbolism in this story is more than clear – the chosen one overwhelms the ancient terror of chaos and creates the world from its remains.

Going back to the book of Job, we find Leviathan mentioned in verses 3:8-9 as the great primordial sea serpent who threatens all humanity. Evil is conceived of here in cosmic terms, an approach also used by John in his New Testament "Revelation" imagery. More about John in a moment.

This sentiment is echoed in Isaiah 27:1, where the results of God's judgment of the wicked are described in terms of the chaos dragon: "On that day the Lord with his cruel and great and strong sword will punish Leviathan the fleeing serpent, Leviathan the twisting serpent and he will kill the dragon that is in the sea."

The longest Leviathan passage in the Old Testament is found in Chapter 41 of Job, the gist of which is that no matter how omnipotent the great sea serpent seems on the earthly plane, it is but a trifle to God – again, the forces of supreme light are superior to the dark waters of chaos. Warning is given about the creature's trickery through its voice (the "dragonspell" of modern dragons), where "supplications" and "soft words" contain empty promises. Verses 5-8 contain images that appear centuries later in tales of St. George subduing a dragon and leading it around with the rescued maiden's belt.

We're told that Leviathan is of tremendous size and "leaves a shining wake behind it." It has huge scales like "shields in rows" and a tough impenetrable hide. The fire-breathing trait is clearly described in verses 19-21: "From its mouth go flaming torches; sparks of fire leap out. / Out of its nostrils comes smoke, as from a boiling pot and burning rushes. / Its breath kindles coals, and a flame comes out of its mouth." Most important, it has no fear and considers itself omnipotent – "It surveys everything that is lofty; it is king over all that are proud." Sounds like a dragon to me.

For a really rousing description of a biblical dragon, however, you must go to the Revelation of John in the New Testament. Chapter 12 begins with the "great red dragon" that has seven heads and ten horns, and whose girth is such that "his tail swept down a third of the stars of heaven and threw them to the earth." After a terrific battle in heaven with the Archangel Michael and his forces, the dragon is defeated and thrown down to earth along with his supporters. John links this proto-dragon with the serpent of the garden of Eden, whose aliases include "the Devil and Satan, the deceiver of the whole world."

When this dragon makes its last stand at the shore, John describes yet another beast emerging from the waters. It also has seven heads and ten horns, and follows the typical composite for evil beasts: body like a leopard, feet like a bear, and mouth like a lion. Another composite occurs in Revelation 9:16-19, where John describes a creature greatly like the Greek *chimaera* (she-goat): "... the heads of the horses were like lions' heads, and fire and smoke and sulfur came out of their mouths ... their tails are like serpents, having heads; and with them they inflict harm."

Following this, John describes a third beast, this time an earth monster that has two horns and "spoke like a dragon," which to dragonologists indicates some form of the dragonspell. In Chapter 20 of the Revelation, the dragon is once again fused with the New Testament Devil and the serpent from the garden. The angel "seized the dragon, that ancient serpent, who is the Devil and Satan, and bound him for a thousand years ..." Whatever the interpretation, the visual imagery has inspired many a writer. Plus, there's no way around it – the biblical dragon is just plain evil.

Creatures of Classical Mythology

In chasing dragons, how do we make the leap from the sands of the Ancient Near East to European Greece and Rome? Even before Homeric times, the vast sponge of Greek mythology was soaking up imports and influences from the faraway lands of Egypt, Babylonia, Crete, and the area around Palestine.

Homer and Hesiod (8th century BCE) are two of the earliest sources for Greek mythology and its fabulous beasts. In Book 6 of *The Iliad*, we hear the tale of Bellerophontes, who slew the Chimaera, a composite proto-dragon that is "lion-fronted and snake behind, a goat in the middle, and snorting out the breath of the terrible flame of bright fire." A marvelous Etruscan bronze statue of the Chimaera in the Archaeological Museum in Florence shows a thin, sinewy quadruped with spiny arched back, huge taloned paws, snarling lion's head surrounded by a feather-like mane, and curving lion's tail terminating in a fanged serpent's head. Exactly the sort of creature an inventive writer such as J. K. Rowling could draw inspiration from.

Homer offers up some grotesque creatures with dragonesque attributes in *The Odyssey*. In a scene from Book 4 when Telémakhos questions King Meneláos about the fate of Odysseus, the king describes his encounter with the sea-god Proteus. When Meneláos and his men attempt to trap the god, Proteus shape-shifts into a sinuous beast, varyingly translated as "serpent" or "dragon."

More familiar, perhaps, is the creature Skylla, encountered in Book 12 of *The Odyssey*. Circe tells Odysseus what to expect when his ship encounters the monster. She's huge and lives in a den of rocks washed by the sea, has twelve legs like tentacles, has six heads on serpentine necks, and the heads have rows of serrated fangs and "gullets of black death." And here's the clincher: she's the embodiment of "eternal evil itself—horror, and pain, and chaos." Yet another example of the evil Western dragon.

One of the earliest sources for several well-known Greek dragons is Hesiod's *Theogony*. First is the monster Typhoeus, offspring of Gaia and Tartaros. Examples from Greek art depict Typhoeus (also called Typhon, not to be confused with the Typhon birthed by Hera) as having a man's body from the waist up and a double-tailed serpent below the waist. Vase paintings show Typhoeus with coiled serpents for legs and huge scaled and feathered wings that obscure the sun. Hesiod's description of this creature offers different dragonesque characteristics.

"... up from his shoulders there grew a hundred snake heads, those
of a dreaded dragon,
    and the heads licked with dark tongues,
    and from the eyes on
    the inhuman heads fire glittered
    from under the eyelids ..." (lines 24-7)

Further in the description, we find that Typhoeus' voice has a supernatural power, at times persuasive and at times terrifying. The dragonspell
cast through its voice has an ancient pedigree, as you can see. Zeus, in fact,
realizes that he must defeat Typhoeus immediately in order to remain
supreme. The battle between them matches Zeus' thunderbolts with
Typhoeus' flaming breath, so that the seas boiled and "earth melted in the
flash of the blazing fire."

Another monster appearing in the *Theogony* is Echidna, dreadful offspring of Kallirhoë and Chrysaör (who sprang from the blood of the
Medusa). Hesiod describes Echidna as an "unmanageable monster" living
in a cave. Like Typhoeus, she is part human, part dragon-serpent. Her head
and torso are that of a beautiful nymph, yet the lower half of her body is a
"monstrous snake, terrible, enormous and squirming and voracious."
Hesiod tells us that "grisly Echidna" is both ageless and deathless, and
mother to the "grisly-minded Hydra," whose offspring is Chimaera. The
Hydra is described as having nine heads and a serpentine body, living in a
cave from which she would emerge to ravage the countryside. Like many
dragons, both her breath and blood were poisonous; after Herakles killed
her with fire, he used her blood as a poisonous tincture for his arrowhead
and spear tips.

Hesiod gives his own description of the Chimaera, which echoes that
of Homer, with a few additions:

"Hydra bore the Chimaira, who snorted raging fire,
    a beast great and terrible,
    and strong and swift-footed.
    Her heads were three: one was that of a glare-eyed lion,

one of a goat, and the third of a snake,
a powerful dragon." (lines 318-324)

Elsewhere it's said that she spit flames and raging storm winds, as the embodiment of violent weather.

Several of Hesiod's proto-dragons are mentioned in connection with the hero Herakles, when he performs his Twelve Labors. First is the Hydra of Lerna, which he dispatches with his sword. Also mentioned in passing is the "youngest of the deadly snakes, that one who at the gloomy great hidden limits of the Earth guards the all-golden apples" whose fate is described vividly in the *Argonautika*, which we'll get to presently.

Another poem of Hesiod, *The Shield of Herakles*, describes terrifying snakelike monsters embossed on the great shield created by Hephaistos. Their heads were "dreaded, indescribable" and twelve in number. In the heat of battle they would become animated, and their markings "could be seen, bluish upon the backs, but at the jaws darkening."

We also find proto-dragons lurking among a collection of poems known as the Homeric Hymns, dated anywhere from the 8th to the 4th century BCE. Of interest to us is the *Hymn to Pythian Apollo*, which contains the story of how Apollo laid out the foundations for his temple, but in the process had to remove a pesky dragon guarding a nearby spring. With a well-aimed arrow, he killed the "bloated, great she-dragon, a fierce monster wont to do great mischief to men upon earth." In some accounts, the beast is called Python, a "dragoness." Like other examples of the dragonslaying motif, Apollo's swift arrow finds the unprotected mark so that the beast "lay drawing great gasps for breath and rolling about that place."

This motif of a construction site impinging on a nearby spring guarded by a dragon that must be killed appears in two other myths: the founding of Thebes by Kadmos, and the exploits of Jason the Argonaut. These two stories dovetail into each other, and the artifacts that tie them together are dragon's teeth.

Our story of Kadmos begins when, on the advice of the Delphic Oracle, he divines where to establish a new city (Thebes). Kadmos' men are killed by a dragon guarding the nearby Spring of Ares. Kadmos in turn slays the dragon and is guided by Athene to pull its teeth. She keeps some of the teeth and gives him the remainder to sow in the earth. From the teeth arise armed warriors, the Spartoi (Sown Men), who threaten Kadmos until he tosses a stone among them, causing them to fight each other. The five who survive pledge to serve Kadmos and establish the aristocracy of the Thebans. From here, we can follow the tale in two directions, (1) down the road to where Kadmos' descendant Oedipus kills his father and then delivers Thebes from the proto-dragon Sphinx, or (2) we can find out where the rest of those dragon's teeth ended up.

From Etruscan seals and statues from Sparta and Athens, the Sphinx, offspring of Echidna, appears as a typical composite monster, having a female head and breasts, a lion's body, and eagle's wings. Of more interest, perhaps, is her penchant for riddling, a time-honored tradition of dragonkind. Perched on a nearby mountaintop, she guards the entrance to Thebes, demanding that all travelers take part in her battle of wits. The price of losing is death. Oedipus, wily descendant of Kadmos, is clever enough to answer her famous riddle: "What is the animal that has four feet in the morning, two at midday, and three in the evening?" The answer, of course, is Man, who crawls as a baby, then walks as a man, then needs a cane as a senior citizen.

Those dragon's teeth extracted by Kadmos lead us to a very old myth involving a young hero (Jason), a perilous quest (stealing the golden fleece from its dragon guardian), and a princess (Medea, daughter of the King of Kolchis). The guardian dragon and sown warrior motifs from the Kadmos myth are interpolated into the tasks set before Jason by Medea's father, who hopes Jason will die in the attempt. He doesn't, of course, because he has divine and magical help. Specifically, Medea enchants the dragon once they confront the beast in the forest (in some accounts she kills the beast; in others, she puts it to sleep).

The great poet Pindar gives a rendition of the same tale in his Fourth Pythian Ode, where the fleece is protected by a dragon guardian "which, in length and breadth, exceeded a fifty-oared ship wrought by iron-nailing blows." The same core story can be found as the myth of Diomedes (Jason) and Pelias, where the tasks set for Diomedes include plowing a furrow with fire-breathing bulls and wresting a treasure from a sea-dragon.

Euripides makes use of the story to craft his play *Medea*. When Jason abandons her for another woman, Medea retorts, "I saved you ... when you were sent to master the fire-breathing bulls with the yoke and to sow the field of death. I killed the dragon which, ever unsleeping, guarded the all-golden fleece, encircling it with many folding coils ..." Here the dragon is both guardian and an obstacle to be overcome, a motif many later writers from the Beowulf poet to Tolkien have used. The end of the play signifies the evil and depravity into which Medea has fallen – she and the children she murdered appear above the palace roof in a chariot drawn by dragons.

For a more thorough retelling of the Golden Fleece tale, we shift to 3rd century BCE Alexandria and the *Argonautika* of Apollonios. To his credit, Apollonios doesn't try to explain away or sneer at the magic and the fabulous beasts as later Hellenic and Roman authors tended to do. Before the Argonauts set sail on the Fleece quest, the old soothsayer Phineus tells them what they can expect: "... then you'll see ... the shady grove of Ares, where the Fleece is, spread out on the top of an oak tree, watched by a serpent, a fearful creature to look at, ever gazing round, on guard, nor by day or night does sweet sleep close his fierce eyes." The refugee Argos also warns the crew that "it's no easy matter to lay hands on the Fleece—so monstrous a serpent, deathless and sleepless, coils guard about it."

As in earlier versions, the task of sowing dragon's teeth with fire-breathing bulls is set. In explaining how Aiëtés acquired the teeth, Apollonios recounts in detail how after Kadmos slays the creatures, Athene "dashed from the dragon's jaws" its teeth and gave half to the king as a gift and the other half to the dragonslayer.

When Jason and Medea approach the dragon guarding the fleece, it hisses at them so loudly that people on neighboring islands hear it with terror. Slowly its vast coils with "their protective armor of hard dry scales" undulate toward the two thieves, but Medea forces it into a stupor with the magic of her gaze and chanted charms. She then smears a sleeping potion into its eyes even as its huge jaws still attempt to devour her and her companion. Her dragon-charming is successful, and in a wonderfully evocative passage Apollonios describes how its "jaw dropped where it lay, in one last spasm, and far behind it those endless coils lay stretched out, through the dense trunks of the forest."

There are other dragons mentioned in *Argonautika*. Herakles' victory over Ládon, the monster guarding the golden apples of the Hesperides, is given as a flashback when Jason and his sunburned crew arrive at the spring of the Hesperides. They're amazed at the sight of the "old chthonian serpent" stretched out dead under the apple tree: "only the tip of his tail was still twitching, from his head down the whole length of his dark spine he lay lifeless" from Herakles' poisoned arrows.

The Roman poet Virgil refers to this guardian of the golden apples in his epic poem the *Aeneid*. In Book IV, the heartbroken Dido, contemplating suicide, mentions the beast guarding Zeus' apples in the garden of the Hesperides. Also in the *Aeneid*, two great sea-monsters appear at the precise moment the Trojan priest Laocoön and his twin sons speak against bringing the great wooden horse inside the city. In Virgil's account, all three men are killed by these serpent-dragons sent by Apollo to prevent the Trojans from burning the wooden horse. Virgil's description of the beasts and their attack gives us some great dragon imagery:

> ... Coiling, uncoiling, they swam abreast for shore,
> Their underbellies showing as their crests
> Reared red as blood above the swell; behind
> They glided with great undulating backs...
> ... and we could see
> Their burning eyes, fiery and suffused with blood,
> Their tongues a-flicker out of hissing maws ...
> They whipped their back-scales, and their heads towered,
> While with both hands he fought to break the knots,
> Drenched in slime, his head-bands black with venom." (II, 282-300)

In *The Library*, Apollodorus adds a few more details to some of the monsters we've met so far. Regarding the hydra, he says that of its nine heads (Ovid later expands the hydra's heads to a hundred), the middle one was immortal. He describes the Hesperides treasure-guardian Ladon this way:

"... an immortal dragon with a hundred heads, offspring of Typhon and Echidna, which spoke with many and divers sorts of voices." So here's yet another mention of the power of the voice in connection with dragon-serpents.

Apollodorus' *The Library* contains a bare-bones version of the Perseus and Andromeda myth, wherein the citizens of Philistia demanded that King Cepheus offer his daughter to a marauding sea-serpent sent to punish his vain wife. Chained to the rocky coast in nothing but a display of jewels, Andromeda barely escapes being devoured by the sea monster when Perseus, wearing his winged sandals, swoops down on the monster and beheads it with the same sickle that enabled him to cut off the gorgon Medusa's head.

In a fancier (and thus more exciting) version of the dragonslayer tale, the Roman poet Ovid gives us a blow-by-blow description of the battle between Perseus and the monster in Book IV of his *Metamorphoses*. We learn that the monster is large enough to cause a huge wake across the ocean like a galley as it approaches its prey on the rocks. Hovering overhead, Perseus fools the beast when it sees his shadow across the water's surface. Unlike Apollodorus' account in which Perseus beheaded the sea-dragon with one blow, Ovid's retelling has Perseus stabbing the beast multiple times, so that it rears high above the waves and then crashes down in a dive, in a frenzy to get at its attacker. Eventually he spills enough of its "purple blood" to kill it.

> "On his swift wings
> Perseus eludes the snapping fangs and strikes
> The parts exposed and plunges his curved sword
> Between its ribs and in its back, all rough
> With barnacles, and where its tapering tail
> Ends in a fish. The beast belched purple blood,
> Sea spume and blood together." (IV, 726-32)

Ovid's *Metamorphoses* contains other dragons, some we've encountered and some not. Ovid's tale of Cadmus' soldiers (remember Kadmos?) being eaten by the guardian of the Spring of Ares goes into great detail about the monster's appearance. He tells us the beast has a gold crest, fiery eyes, three rows of teeth, a triple-forked tongue, scales like armor, and its huge venom-filled body rears up as tall as the trees, not unlike modern writer Terry Goodkind's dragon Scarlet. When Cadmus' iron-tipped javelin pierces its spine, Ovid's florid depiction of its death throes runs on for 35 lines in grim detail as the beast foams at the mouth and is finally impaled on a tree trunk. With its dying breath, the serpent speaks aloud a curse of doom on Cadmus, as he stands horror-struck.

In Ovid's tale of Achelous and Hercules, we find a river god who shape-shifts to a serpentine dragon-form. Losing to Hercules in combat, Achelous tells how he "changed to a long smooth snake" with a horrid flickering tongue; but Hercules mocks him, saying he is not nearly as horrid as the hydra, who at least had more than one head. The hero is not impressed by a creature that's "just skulking in a shape you've begged and borrowed." Achelous is often depicted in Hellenic art as a man from the chest up with the horns of a bull on his head, and a huge sea-serpent with scales and fins from the waist down.

With Roman scholar Pliny the Elder we come to an interesting stage in dragon development – elaborate bestiaries and encyclopedias of the so-called natural world. Such compendiums existed before the Romans (Aristotle even wrote a peculiar little tome called *The History of Animals* in which he asserts that dragons eat bitter lettuce).

In Pliny's *Natural History*, you can find wide-ranging pronouncements on dragonkind, such as this famous elephant/dragon reference: "... so enormous a size as easily to envelop the elephant with its folds and encircle with its coils. The contest is equally fatal to both; the elephant, vanquished, falls to the earth and by its weight crushes the dragon which is entwined about it." Book VIII includes sections on medicines derived from dragons, and serpents, and Book XXIX establishes the differences among the varieties of lizards, snakes, and dragonlike creatures. Elsewhere, Pliny seems to combine both serpentine and dragonesque attributes under the single term *draco*.

He wasn't above including some fantastic tales into the mix, including a boy saved by his pet dragon, and African crested dragons floating along on the waves entwined in a knot. Other related beasts discussed in Pliny are the leucrota, yale, manticore, unicorn, catoblepas, and basilisk. When you read the Harry Potter fantasy series, you'll have no doubt which classical authors J. K. Rowling studied.

Classical bestiaries illustrate both a popular and scientific attempt to catalog exotic creatures reported from around the world, contributing to the greater lore of the evolving dragon. In addition to those already mentioned, you'll find the phoenix and griffon (see Herodotus, *The History*); crocotta and other exotics (look in Ctsesias' *Indica*); serpent lore including the amphisbaena, jaculus, scytale, seps, and dipsa (Lucan's *Pharsalia*). You can also plunder around in the works of travel writer Pausanias, fabulists Aelian and Phaedrus, the sophist Philostratus, and 3rd century Roman geographer and linguist Solinus.[4] Bestiaries and encyclopedias of the natural world continued in popularity into the post-classical and medieval world, further honing the physical manifestation of the Western dragon that we recognize today.

Although actual belief in the physical existence of fabulous creatures was well on the wane by the time of the Roman encyclopedists, the imagery and symbolism of the dragon remained popular. For evidence, we find the red dragon of Rome as an emblem of powerful protection and guardianship in the heraldry of the army, particularly on standards carried by the emperor's Auxiliary Guard, particularly in Britain. William Crampton of the British Flag Institute wrote, "Dragons in one form or another were used all round the Roman Empire, including Britain, and it is thought that such a standard was in use by the Romanised Britons who were left to fend for themselves from about 400 AD onwards. Thus the standard came to be associated with the Celtic heroes Uther Pendragon and Arthur," but that's another story.

In all these appearances of early dragons, we have the pattern of the conquering hero overcoming creatures of chaos and darkness. In other words, Western dragons are bad business, and it's the duty of the enlightened warrior to slay them.

Water Deities of the Far East

Bidding farewell to the classical world, we'll now follow the dragon tracks eastward. In addition to China, this section includes evidence from Japan and Korea. Dragons of Eastern descent have taken a somewhat different path from their Western cousins, emphasizing their power as beneficial rain gods or denizens of pools and springs that facilitate agriculture and nurture all life. Although you'll find some destructive Chinese dragons in folktales and fables of the common people, the dragon of formal, classical Chinese mythology is all-wise and beneficent.

In the beginning, according to Chinese cosmogony, was chaos, out of which was formed a cosmic egg, from which was hatched Pan-Gu, the first man. With him came the Four Most Fortunate Beasts: the phoenix, the unicorn, the turtle, and the dragon. Upon his death, Pan-gu's body became the geophysical features of the earth, and the four Beasts remained to support and aid the emerging gods and goddesses in the birthing of the world with its population of mortals. From the dragon came nine offspring, associated with battle and argument, but also with music, literature, strength, risk-taking, water, and peace. As you can see, dragons are looked upon as allies rather than the embodiment of evil.

This transition from western to eastern thinking regarding dragons requires a reassessment of visual image and symbolic meaning. Specifically, the Western dragon has, from its earliest roots, been tied to the idea of negative, destructive, chaotic qualities, while its actual shape is subject to a wide variety of change. Conversely, the nature of the Eastern dragon traditionally ranges from all-benevolent to capricious trickster and even bringer of bad luck, yet its physical form varies little from the sinuous four-legged creature seen on tapestries, temples, paintings, and statuary from as early as 5,500 BCE.

The difference between the dragons of East and West is not all-encompassing, of course. Several Roman fables tell of Western dragons that are kind and protective of humans, just as there are examples of destructive Eastern dragons from Chinese folk literature. Although there are dragonslayers from both East and West, the larger pattern of difference remains valid. In the Western mythologies, the great sea monsters typically represent chaos and something to be vanquished; the Eastern water-god dragons are revered for their life-sustaining attributes. Fantasy fiction writers have made use of both models and have even combined them in interesting ways.

We don't need elaborate bestiaries to show us what the Eastern dragon looks like – its basic shape was set in the earliest records of Chinese culture and has not wavered greatly through the centuries. There are stylized variances depending on individual artists' renderings, but the imagery is predictable: long slender serpentine scaly body, horse-shaped head with sharp teeth, horns, beard or flowing whiskers, prominent eyes, no wings although the dragon easily sails through the skies, four legs with a specific number of clawed toes (five reserved for the emperor, four for lesser nobility, and three for all others). The royal dragon color is yellow or gold. Some carry a magical pearl that can grant wishes or bestow good luck; it can be embedded in their foreheads, lodged under their whiskery chins, or held between their sharp teeth or claws. In the larger cosmology, the pearl represents the sun and thus the symbol of light and life. The dragon serves as either a guardian of human life or a link to the gods who oversee human existence.

Like their Western counterparts, oriental dragons are guardians of inland water bodies such as rivers, springs, and wells, and demand human sacrifice for various reasons. Unlike their Western cousins, however, they are assumed to be the bringers of life-giving rain to cities and farms. When storms or floods occurred, people assumed it was because they had committed some wrong; thus, prayers to the merciful dragon gods could bring relief. Of course, the reverse would be true as well – in times of drought, storm dragons were urged to visit the region with rain.

The Eastern dragon is also a fascinating composite that became solidified early in its history, incorporating the antlers of the deer, the mane of the horse, and the claws of the eagle. In some cases, it has vestigial wings on its shoulders. It can also breathe water or fire. Across the broad spectrum of visual art in China, the dragon is everywhere, and its general form is predictable. Any good book of Oriental art will give you plenty of beautiful, elegant dragons begging to leap off the page and into the writer's imagination. Eastern art is full of fluid, soaring images of the four dragons of the heavens, the waters, the earth, and the underworld.

These four mythical dragon types – Celestial (guardian of the heavens), Divine (deity of wind and rain), Earth (deity of earthbound waterways), and Underworld (guardian of hidden wealth) – come from the Confucian and Taoist sources. In contrast, the Dragon Kings of folk religion and local narratives are much more humanized and can be helpful, a bit of a trickster, or downright dangerous.

Eastern tradition dictates that the dragon has nine specific "resemblances" or features from other creatures: a head like a camel, horns like a deer, eyes like a hare, ears like a bull, a neck like an iguana, a belly like a frog, scales like a carp, paws like a tiger, and claws like an eagle. It flashes rows of sharp teeth along its jaws, and a forked tongue. It sports long tendril whiskers like a catfish.

A beautiful example of this creature can be seen in Chinese architectural screen walls. Three "nine-dragon" screen walls dating from the Ming dynasty (1368-1644) display glorious flying (but wingless) dragons in intricate color tile mosaics. All the dragons are in the "curly" style, with slender scaly serpentine bodies coiling and recoiling in graceful "S" curves, from which four short legs (two near the front of the body and two near the tail) display five imperial claws.

Their head shapes are not the sloping triangular wedge shape we have come to recognize in modern dragon faces; rather, they resemble a more boxy horsey/crocodilian mix, with squared jaws full of sharp teeth. Their round eyes are large and protruding. Long slender horns grow out of the brow crest and slope back over the head, and beards with long trailing "feelers" on their muzzles. Each body has a spiny ridge running down the backbone from head to tail. In bright colors of gold and blue, they undulate among waves or clouds.

The Chinese dragon manifests its power of life in the form of the seasons, bestowing rain, the sun's warmth, wind from the seas, and soil from the earth. In other words, the dragon is a force of nature. As the symbol of divine protection and vigilance, it's the supreme being among all creatures, with the ability to live in the seas, fly to the heavens, or lie coiled on the land in the form of mountains. As a divine mythical animal, the Chinese dragon can ward off evil spirits, protect the innocent, and serve as a charm or talisman of safety. It's the ultimate symbol of good fortune.

As I mentioned earlier, oriental dragons aren't completely beneficent. Eastern dragons can be vain in spite of their divine wisdom. They can become insulted when a ruler doesn't follow their advice, or when people don't honor their importance. To show their displeasure, they may thrash about, breathing black clouds that bring storms and floods; or they might fall in to a sulk and withhold rain, causing drought conditions. Small dragons can do minor mischief with water, such as making roofs leak or causing rice to be sticky.

The best sources for the personality and nature of Chinese dragons are myths, folktales and fables, but especially the "wisdom" documents such as the *I Ching*. Here we find examples of benevolent nature deities, the more capricious Dragon Kings, and some downright bad news local dragons. Above them sits the exalted cosmological dragon that commands the highest respect as a symbol of the *yang* or male essence, power, and self-worth.

With that description in mind, consider the tale "Li Ching and the Rain God," from the early 9th century CE, as translated by Moss Roberts.[5] Here we encounter the dragon in its semi-divine aspect. The military hero Li Ching becomes lost in the mountains and discovers a castle that turns out to be the home of a dragon. "Li Ching was astonished and awed, for the dragon, dwelling in the deep and rising into the clouds, governs the cycle of rainfall over the earth." In the dragon's absence, Li Ching undertakes the duty of sending rain to the province below. He bungles the job and floods the village, and so must beat a hasty retreat from the castle to avoid the dragon-god's wrath. The mistress of the castle wryly remarks at his departure, "You are but a man from the world of mortals, who knows nothing of the movements of cloud and rain." Then the entire castle disappears as if it had never existed.

In other myths we encounter Fêng Po, the god of the wind who is a shape-shifter, a talent many modern dragons enjoy. As a human, Fêng Po is a bearded old man dressed in a yellow cape and colorful cap. As a dragon, he is sometimes stirs up gales and damaging storms. On occasion, he has been depicted as a fearsome composite creature with a horned bird's head and a stag's body with the tail of a serpent.

The Sea-Dragon Kings, the lords of the four seas, star in some appealing dragon stories that betray their human-like foibles. In "The Foolish Dragon," the deep-sea dragon's wife is ill and has a craving to eat a monkey's heart. To oblige her, the sea-dragon goes in search of a monkey. He cleverly cajoles one to ride on his back out to sea, but when he dives, the monkey panics and asks what he's up to. Foolishly, the dragon tells him the truth. The clever monkey, of course, tells the dragon that he left his heart in a tree on land and they must go back for it. Of course, the monkey does not return and the sea-dragon goes empty-handed.

For those dragons of evil intent, there are plenty of Chinese dragonslayers. "The Spiritual Alligator," a tale of dragonslayer Hsü Chên-chün, is one such example. A bit of a shaman and magician, Hsü is able to recognize that the son-in-law of Kiangsi Province's Chief Magistrate is actually a shape-shifting dragon. He further learns that this dragon is the cause of the many floods the area has endured. An open challenge causes the dragon to shift to the shape of a yellow ox and run back to his house, where he appears again as a young man. Hsü pursues him and calls out, "Dragon, how dare you hide yourself there under a borrowed form?" The son-in-law shifts back into his dragon form, only to meet death at the weapons of Hsü Chên-chün's spirit warriors. In that moment, the house in which the dragon had been living sinks under the ground and disappears. Hsü Chên-chün is then taken up into heaven with all his family.

Another famous dragonslayer is Lü Tung-pin, one of the Eight Immortals, who travels across the land with a magic sword slaying dragons that prey upon the populace. One important point should be made here about the act of slaying dragons in Chinese folk literature. Higher myth teaches dogma, but folktales provide entertainment. Thus, dragons in Chinese tales from the common people can behave badly and can be slain, unlike the benevolent dragon-gods of mythology who bring rain to farmers and good luck in general. A Chinese folktale dragon can be either a villain or a hero.

In fact, in the tale of "Short-Tailed Old Li," one dragon slays another. In a reversal of typical Western color symbolism, the evil dragon that inhabits the river and sends devastating floods over the land is white, and the good dragon, Short-Tailed Old Li, is black. Working together with a clever villager, Old Li outsmarts the white dragon in mortal combat, ridding the river and villagers of the menace.

For evidence of the dragon as an object of reverence and divination, we turn to the Book of Changes, or *I Ching*. The annotations use the dragon as symbol, and interpretations are based on the various aspects of its nature. For example, the general meaning for the annotation "Hidden dragon. Do not act." is that the dynamic, creative force of the dragon (expressed as energy in thunderstorms that renew the earth) is hidden. Thus, one should not "expend one's powers prematurely in an attempt to obtain by force something for which the time is not yet ripe."

Much of the preceding dragonlore is to be found in several pivotal Chinese encyclopedia/bestiary collections. The first is the *Shanhai Jing* ("Classic Wonders of Land and Sea") of Guo Pu (compiled during the Jin dynasty); the second is the medical compendium titled *Pan Tsao Kang Mu*; and the third is the *Yuen Kien Lei Han*, an amazing set of documents in 450 volumes, completed in 1710. Over eighty pages are devoted to the dragon.

Japanese dragons are very similar to their Chinese counterparts, but with some traits of their own. Japanese rain gods were basically sea serpents, which were blended into the Chinese concept of the Dragon Kings, with an added dash of Indian nagas (semi-divine cobra entities). Still the emphasis on the dragon as a sea deity prevails, with the Sea Dragon King or "Luminous Being" holding court at the bottom of the sea near the islands off southern Japan.

Japanese dragons are generally associated with manifestations of vitality and energy, such as thunder and lightning, and sexual kundalini energy. Royall Tyler, prolific translator of Japanese folktales, says, "Perhaps the dragon is best thought of as the energy of the water cycle: rain, river, sea, vapor, and rain again." Royalty and commoners alike were the beneficiaries of dragon energy; thus, Buddhist and imperial Japanese imagery is full of dragons.

Japanese art depicts winged dragons, which rarely occurs in Chinese art; the *hai riu* is shown with the head of a dragon, but with a bird's feathered wings and tail as well as talons. Colors of scales on the curving snakelike body can be violet, yellow, green, red, white, and black; other attributes include a long mustache and wide staring eyes, long horns, scowling brows, a row of dorsal spines, usually three claws per foot (although four and five are possible), and feathers at the joints where its four legs join the body.

All bodies of water in Japan are likely to provide a haven for a Dragon King, and the dragon palace located at the bottom of the sea is a fixture in Japanese folklore. Physically, these Japanese dragons are practically indistinguishable from the Chinese variety, with small details of difference. There are four types of Dragon King in Japanese mythology: Sui-Riu (commands the rain, which can turn red from its blood); Han-Riu (striped with nine different colors); Ka-Riu (brilliant crimson, the image of fire); and Ri-Riu (keen of eyesight).

Japanese folktales are filled with these creatures, and as characters they show a wide range of personality traits. Tales include examples of the bond between dragons and humans, often as marriage partners or friends for life. In the tale called "The Invincible Pair," a monk and a dragon are grabbed by a tengu (winged demon) and stashed in a hole in the rocks of Mt. Hira for later consumption. The monk gives the dragon his last drop of water so that the dragon can shape-shift. Turning into a small child, the dragon wriggles its way out of the hole with the monk clinging to its neck. Once out, the dragon shifts to its serpentine form and flies away, returning the astonished monk safely to his monastery. "Each had saved the other's life – surely the result of a deep karmic bond between them in lives gone by," observes the narrator.

In a tale simply titled "Rain," a monk and a dragon are inseparable friends, and daily the dragon comes to listen to the monk chant sutras. When the dragon willingly sacrifices himself to end a devastating drought so that humans on the land may live, the grief-stricken monk builds a series of temples to his honor, and "all his life the monk chanted the Sutra for the dragon's final enlightenment."

Worship of and reverence for the dragon have an ancient tradition on the Korean peninsula, primarily as a nature deity connected with seasonal rain and clouds. Under Chinese influence, the dragon assumed its role as

caretaker and guardian of human well-being. From this, dragon art flourished from ancient times and appears in many manifestations. Dragons
appeared in tomb murals from the Three Kingdoms period (the earliest
examples of Korean painting) and flourished during the Choson dynasty
when Confucianism was dominant. They appear in both traditional and folk
art as symbols for water and heaven, and their images were painted on
houses, screen walls, tombs, and temples to invoke the dragon's power to
repel evil as well as bring good luck. Its image was also used to control the
weather, particularly rain clouds.

Korean dragons differ from Chinese and Japanese dragons in that the
heads often resemble other animals, such as the cock or wild boar with
upward-protruding tusks. Later dragons take on a more snakelike resemblance. By the 9th century, dragon horns appear more curved, like antlers,
and indicate rank – hornless dragons are considered below their horned
counterparts in power and authority. The feet and claws resemble those of
large raptors. Wide, glaring eyes and open toothy mouths complete the
picture, although later images shorten the snout to an almost dog-like
appearance.

The dragon as sea-god is considered a protector of the Korean nation,
given its geographical configuration as a peninsula surrounded by mostly
open ocean. Dragon worship was tied closely to the support of the emperor,
and the image of the dragon served as a symbol of royal authority, with the
imperial lineage descending from the Divine Sea Dragon. There are four
named Korean dragon-gods: the Fish Dragon, Cock Dragon, Spiritual
Dragon, and Heavenly Dragon.

Indian Influences

The Chinese *lung*, Japanese *ryo*, and Korean *riong* began life as respected,
benevolent water deities. They served as symbols of good luck and could be
petitioned to bring rain or drive away an excess of water caused by flooding.
However, naga-worship (cobra cults) imported through Buddhist mission-
aries from India (who entered China first, then Japan, then Korea) changed
all that.

The notion of evil, destructive demons was melded onto the indigenous dragons, resulting in a new belief system that filled believers with fear; the familiar friendly dragon had been supplanted by demons that lurked in hidden places and stalked their human victims. The Indian "dragon" was named Vritra, a creature not unlike Typhon, Apep, or Set, who represented heedless destruction and challenged the orderly universe. In a strange way, it was the return of the chaos dragon, clothed in Shiva energy.

Vritra, whose name means "to withhold," appears as early as 1000 BCE, in the Indian *Rig Veda* and *Taittiriya Sanhita*. He is mainly known as a cosmic negative force in the form of a giant serpent-dragon. Vritra sucks up the water of life (keeping the rain goddess imprisoned within his coiling clouds), thus preventing the earth from coming into physical manifestation. His dominant characteristics are wanton greed, obstruction, and negative energies. Here's the actual passage from the *Rig Veda,* titled "The Killing of Vritra:"

"With his great weapon, the thunderbolt, Indra killed the shoulderless Vritra, his greatest enemy. Like the trunk of a tree whose branches have been lopped off by an axe, the dragon lies flat upon the ground ..."

"Over him as he lay there like a broken reed the swelling waters flowed for man. Those waters that Vritra had enclosed with his power – the dragon now lay at their feet."

Along with Vritra came the myths of the nagas, snakelike gods of the Vedic pantheon, of which cobras were considered the living incarnation. The nagas live in splendid palaces beneath bodies of water or in caves under the ground. They carry poison, but also the water of life; they control weather, guard treasures; their senses of sight and hearing are acute; they can shape-shift and in human form can intermarry with mortals. They are depicted in art as beautiful richly adorned men and women with a snake's tail instead of legs, often with a seven-cobra canopy arising from their shoulders.

The merging of naga worship with Buddhism is reflected in the teaching that the nagas guarded the Buddha as he sat unmoving on the riverbank, undergoing transformation into his enlightened state. Noted for both their wisdom and quick tempers, the nagas figure in many Hindu and Buddhist legends. The nagas were both loved and feared, for they could be loyal protectors or remorseless, vengeful enemies. Many houses maintained a shrine for the propitiation of the local serpent incarnations of the nagas.

By name, the naga lords of most importance were Ananta (naga king), Kaliya (who battled the young dragonslayer Krishna), Manasa (female fertility goddess), Mudama (snake goddess), and Vasuki (god involved in the "Churning of the Ocean" creation myth). The fourfold division of naga gods has familiar resonance with the previously discussed Chinese mythological dragons: Heavenly (upholding the firmament and guarding the entrance to heaven), Divine (controlling clouds and rain), Earthly (maintaining canals and waterways), and Hidden (guarding treasure).

With the Vedic dragons came the negative role of the deity who brings disaster as well as nourishment. When a drought prevails and crops fail, it's from the spiteful actions of the naga lord/Dragon King. While the spiritual superiority of the original dragon-as-rain-god has slipped, it has acquired a more easily explainable character in human terms. Humans are as quick to be vengeful and commit evil acts as they are to be generous and helpful – why shouldn't their gods be likewise? And that is how, in legend and folktale, the Eastern dragon gradually acquired a fearsome, destructive quality that had not existed before.

Before We Move On

Let's take stock of what we've collected so far in the way of dragonlore. Early Western dragons could look like any number of imposing composites, usually involving four-footed beasts with jaws full of jagged teeth, serpentine or fishlike bodies or tails, and birdlike rather than batlike wings. Generally, their functions were to combat the ruling deity who struggled to impose order (civilization) over chaos. Locally, these creatures guarded water sources or other items of value and demanded sacrifices of one sort or another. Rarely were they helpful or beneficial – they were frequently regarded as evil incarnate.

Migrations into India brought these tales, eventually moving further eastward into China, Korea, and Japan in the form of naga-laced Buddhist teachings. From their influence, the placid, benevolent weather dragon-gods gained greater dimensions, but perhaps less spiritual purity. Outward form was less affected, but the dragon's purpose and motive had changed.

This brief look at the immense body of visual and written material dealing with dragons is just a hint of the vast wealth of ideas that creators of fantasy fiction can draw upon. It's only the tip of the draconic iceberg. Speaking of icebergs, the next chapter (Dragonology 102) heads north into the frozen wastes of Nordic mythology and legend, where we find the likes of Nídhoggr, Fáfnir, and Beowulf's bane.

Notes

1. Ancestral memory regarding dragons is a much-contested topic among dragonologists, and I wouldn't wade into that fray with a ten-foot dragon lance. However, if you're curious to know more, David E. Jones' thought-provoking book, *An Instinct for Dragons*, argues that a possible explanation for global dragonlore and art, documentable as far back as primitive rock paintings, comes from our genetic predator/prey instincts. According to Jones, the three species that consistently would have preyed on primates across the continents were raptors, big cats, and snakes. If you create a composite of those creatures, you get the classic composite dragon.

2. One of the most exhaustive scholarly bibliographies of dragon research can be found in Dr. Qiguang Zhao's slim volume, *A Study of Dragons, East and West*, produced by Temple University's Asian Thought and Culture series. It's especially valuable for its many references to Chinese publications on dragon folklore and art.

3. For all biblical references, I've used the *New Oxford Annotated Bible* (New Revised Standard Version, third edition), which contains the Hebrew Bible and the New Testament (the Gospels, the Letters/Epistles, and the Revelation).

4. For an entertaining 21st century version of the classical bestiary, let me recommend Joseph Nigg's *The Book of Dragons and Other Mythical Beasts*.

5. Moss Roberts' anthology of delightful and little-known folktales, *Chinese Fairy Tales and Fantasies*, is one of my favorite collections. For my taste, Roberts strikes just the right balance between whimsy and the grotesque, the charming and the menacing.

Chapter 10

Dragonology 102
Middle Ages to Modern Times

W HERE DO we look for dragons during the Middle Ages? This is a legitimate question because the basic model for many dragons in modern fiction comes from this period. The label "Middle Ages" usually suggests stereotyped images of castle siege engines, terrible hygiene, and maiden-munching dragons lurking in the hills. It's also a handy timeline marker for separating the ancient classical world of Western history from what happened after the decline of Rome. What this shift has to do with dragons I'll explain in a moment.

The Middle Ages (also called the Dark Ages or medieval world) encompasses a span of nearly a thousand years. The period runs roughly from the fall of Rome to the beginning of the European Renaissance. Superstition ran rampant in some societies while others enjoyed an enlightened approach to life. Dragons served as symbols of great evil as well as good fortune, and a number of bestiary and travel writers claimed to know exactly how these creatures looked and behaved.

Dragon Gods of the Americas

In ancient Mexico, a dramatic feathered composite deity appears in the art of the Olmec people who flourished from around 1250 BCE to 200 CE. This snake-bird, with feathered serpent's body and dragon-shaped head displaying rows of sharp teeth in its gaping jaws, was an early fertility god, but of interest to us is its much later development into the dragon of the Americas: the Plumed Serpent, better known as Quetzalcoatl.

The trail of the fabled Plumed Serpent leads us through the art and myths of Mesoamerica (Mexico and Central America), specifically the cultures of the Mayas, Toltecs, and Aztecs. Contrary to popular belief, this does not include the Incas, a civilization that flourished along the mountainous South American coastline from Chile to Colombia centuries later.

Our knowledge of this unusual dragonlike deity comes from paintings, carvings, and tales made by the people themselves, and from chronicles made by foreign invaders much later. Sad to say, most of the mythology of the Americas was lost during the destruction of these empires by the conquistadors who arrived in the 14th and 15th centuries. A few Aztec illuminated scrolls called *codices* that detailed their gods and rituals have survived, but most were burned as heathen documents by the Spanish conquerors.

Our focus on the great feathered serpent god begins with the culture centered around the city of Teotihuacán in central Mexico. Flourishing about the same time the Vikings were pillaging Ireland, these people revered a wind god often depicted as a flying serpent with a collar of feathers adorning its dragon-shaped head. To the Maya of Guatemala and Yucatán lowlands, this feathered serpent god was called both Gucumatz and Kukulcan. To the Toltecs and later Aztecs, its name is Quetzalcoatl (*quetzal* – a Central American bird with spectacular plumage, and *coatl* – a rattlesnake). In his male wind god avatar, Quetzalcoatl is named Ehecatl.

During the Mayan golden age, from around 200-900 CE, stories involving the feathered serpent god were recorded in sculpture, pottery, and, most importantly, writing. The ingenious Mayan hieroglyphic system combined pictures (logographs) with symbols representing both sound and meaning, which allowed a sophisticated level of communication. These hieroglyphs are the chief means by which we know anything about the Plumed Serpent and its attributes.

Visually, the Plumed Serpent is a wingless snake with a long undulating body that soars through the sky. Instead of scales, its head, back, and tail are covered with feathers. Images from temple carvings show a head of roughly alligator shape with a blunt snout and rows of sharp teeth; a collar of feathers surrounds the head at the neck. These heads appear as decorations on well-preserved buildings such as the Temple of Quetzalcoatl at Teotihuacán, Mexico. At Chichen Itzá, the post-Classic Mayan site in Yucatán, Mexico, innovative architecture incorporates the head and body of the Plumed Serpent into rows of columns fronting such structures as the Temple of the Jaguars and Temple of the Warriors.

Robert Sharer describes elaborate doorways "carved in the form of feathered serpents; the head is on the floor surface, the body is vertical, and the tail runs forward and up to support a wooden lintel. Feathered serpents also appear frequently as ornaments on balustrades, panels, and other architectural elements."[1] The El Castillo temple (also called the Kukulcan pyramid) offers what has been humorously termed the first Mesoamerican motion picture: the zigzag shadow of a giant serpent moves up the steeply pitched stairs as the sun progresses across the sacred plaza.

The color model for the feathered dragon comes from the sacred quetzal of the cloud forests, with its iridescent plumage of green, red, and white. Whether in human or dragon form, Quetzalcoatl is depicted with brilliant plumage, either in a towering headdress or feathers around its head and down its back. One Aztec codex shows the feathered serpent god with turquoise green head, crest, body, and plumed tail, accented by stripes of gold and red underneath and around its muzzle. The skull shape is more like an animal predator than a snake, with slanted eyes, wide fanged jaws ending in a blunt snout – sort of a snake-lion-bird composite beast.

Interestingly, Olmec carvings of the Plumed Serpent bear more than a passing resemblance to some Eastern dragon images. Anthropologist David E. Jones (I mentioned him in Chapter 9) has pointed out its similarity to the Chinese celestial dragon with its undulating body, folded wings, long toothy jaws, and cloudlike decorative elements beneath it.

A major source of information on the Plumed Serpent is the Mayan document called *Popul Vuh* ("council book"), which includes the Mayan creation myth. The original hieroglyphic codex is lost, but it survives as a Spanish translation (made around 1700 by a Dominican priest). From this document and others like it, we know the following about the Plumed Serpent and his variations as Gucumatz, Kukulcan, Quetzalcoatl, and Ehecatl.

A male fertility deity, depicted in both serpent and human form, he's a god of the wind, especially as it blows in advance of the rains. More importantly, however, he is one of two creator gods (the other is Huracan – "Hurricane") who fashion human beings out of maize. Interestingly, he's also the "light" half of a light/dark duality in the Amerindian pantheon. His dark adversary is Tezcatlipoca, the source of discord and destruction in the universe. Quetzalcoatl was also associated with the planet Venus, in its phase as the morning star that leads the sun out of the underworld. Thus, to the Aztecs, the Plumed Serpent is primarily a beneficent deity who brings light, life, and learning into the world.

The Mayan creation myth tells how Hurricane and the Plumed Serpent decided to create beings to populate the world, with the intention that these beings would in turn provide the gods with praise and sacrifice to sustain them. It takes several tries, but they finally get it right – too right. They have to veil the sight of these new humans who see too much of the knowledge possessed by the gods. But Kukulcan does get his required praise and sacrifices, another example of the global motif of maidens being sacrificed to placate the dragon.

In the Aztec creation myth called "The Four Suns" (a "sun" is an age or an era), we find evidence of the feathered serpent's dual nature. His actions seem paradoxical – out of bloodshed and violence, life is created. Like the Chinese celestial dragon, Quetzalcoatl is a creator who brings and sustains life. In this tale, however, he alternately creates and destroys worlds as he struggles with his dark nemesis Tezcatlipoca for supremacy.

Quetzalcoatl destroys the third Sun of his enemy with fire in much the same way a flame-spouting dragon would do. The two gods fighting each other for the domination of creation echo aspects of other chaos dragons in the way that each new world goes through upheaval and elimination as the gods win and lose with each new Sun. According to one version of the story, Sun 5 (our current era) was created from the dismembered body of the sea monster Tlaltecuhtli, mistress of the primordial ocean. Her dismemberment by Quetzalcoatl and Tezcatlipoca in the form of giant serpents has a distant resonance with the fate of Tiamat.

A similarity to the Dragon Kings of China can be seen in the Aztec legend, "The Birth of the Blue Hummingbird." In this myth, retold by Diana Ferguson, Quetzalcoatl is a "cultured god of a cultured people." He lives like the opulent Dragon Kings in their pearl palaces under the sea: "Quetzalcoatl lived in a palace more lavish than fancy can conjure. Indeed, it was not one palace but four, oriented to the four corners of the Earth and adorned with gold, with jade and turquoise, with shells and silver and precious stones."

Surprisingly, there are references to dragons in North America, as well. Native American myths from many tribes – Shawnee, Hopi, Zuni, Huron, Piute, Seneca, and Apache, to name a few – tell of serpent and bird creatures similar to composite dragons from other cultures. In some cases, the creature is a sea serpent or water dragon living in a lake or river, or around the base of a hill; sometimes the beast has more than one head. Algonquin tales tell of the fearful *wendigo*, described in some stories as crocodile-like with feet of a bear. Stories from the Carolinas tell of *uktena*, a winged water serpent with poisonous breath, associated with the Southeast Cherokee and related tribes. Ceramic vessels found at the Moundville site in Alabama show the uktena as a scaled serpent with feathered wings, horns, and dragon's head with forked tongue. Artifacts from a 13th century Oklahoma site are decorated with a hydra-like creature having six horned heads emerging from a serpent's body that ends in a rattlesnake's tail.

Artifacts in the landscape include the serpent mounds of Ohio and other sites, and in particular, the odd rock painting found in the 17th century near Alton, Illinois. A complex composite, this proto-dragon had a bearish face with prominent sharp teeth, a head with mane and beard, branching antlers, scaly body like a fish, and a long barbed tail coiling around its body. Its birdlike elements include wings and raptor feet with long talons; its original colors were red, black, and blue. The creature's discovery by explorers Marquette and Joliet is detailed in the *Journal* of Father Jacques Marquette, 1675. Other travelers along the Mississippi River recounted seeing the image carved and painted on a bluff until its destruction by a developer in 1876. Marquette labeled the creature "piasa" (destroyer), but the Native Americans of the region referred to it as the "stormbird" or "thunderer" and reported it to have been carved by ancient members of the Illinois tribe to commemorate the brave deeds of their Chief Ouatoga.

Australia's Rainbow Serpent

The phenomenon of the rainbow has inspired a snake-shaped sky deity in a number of cultures, and the best-known examples are from Australia. The area known as Arnhem Land contains 6,000-year-old rock art of a deity known to us as the Rainbow Serpent, but the tradition continues among aborigine artists today, who preserve the style and content of the ancient images on rock, bark, and now paper. Visually, the Rainbow Serpent takes the composite form of serpent body, kangaroo head, and crocodile tail, sometimes with reeds and water lilies growing along its back.

Myths of this Australian dragon vary widely, depending on the particular territorial group from which the story is gathered. The main variance is that the creature can have both male and female forms. A 1996 article in *Archaeology in Oceania* provides a good summary of the basic attributes of these deities: "*Yingarna*, the female Rainbow Serpent, is the mother, the original creator being; and the male Rainbow Serpent, *Ngalyod*, is the transformer of the land. They often live in deep waterholes below waterfalls."

Creation of the human race is attributed to Yingarna, seeding the pools and other bodies of water with elements of life; however, the Rainbow Serpent can also send floods as punishment, taking life rather than giving it. The serpent's spirit can also enter into a human, conferring seeming magical powers or causing illness and death. There is a certain ambivalence surrounding the Rainbow Serpent: it appears as both positive and negative, male and female, yin and yang.

Medieval Mayhem in Words and Pictures

Moving on to the dragons of post-Roman Europe, we're back on familiar ground. Over the course of centuries, the beasts of Western biblical and classical literature have sorted themselves out into a more standardized shape with specific symbolic baggage. The wild composites of the Ancient Near East have settled into a four-legged creature with a heavy, saurian body, scaly hide, muscular hindquarters, smaller front legs with dagger-like claws, batlike wings, and a long snaky tail. A serpentine neck topped by a reptilian or lionlike head with horns, catlike eyes, and rows of pointed teeth in open jaws complete the general image. This fire-breathing monster is wicked and dangerous, serving as a symbol for all that's evil in the world, and in particular, the Christian arch-enemy Satan.

To discover what sources contributed to this coalescing image, I've looked at both visual art and written text in the centuries after the fall of Rome and leading up to the High Renaissance around 1500. Religious frescoes and sculpture in Romanesque and Byzantine churches and monasteries give us some clues, but an even better source turns out to be illuminated manuscripts.[2] Lavishly illustrated documents of all sorts from Italy to Ireland (especially transcriptions of the Bible) were a direct means by which the essence of the Western dragon became set in people's imaginations.[3]

In addition to religious works, classical myths transcribed and illustrated for wealthy patrons contained fanciful images of sea serpents and treasure-guarding dragons. Also influential were medieval bestiaries and encyclopedias of the natural world. And finally, as a bridge between the pagan and Christian worlds, we need to consider the geometrically stylized dragon imagery of Viking age art from Scandinavia.

Danish, Swedish, and Norwegian Vikings explored and exploited the waterways and coastlands of several continents from around 792 to 1066. While the pagan Vikings themselves didn't fear the dragon as the root of all evil, their use of its image certainly struck terror into the hearts of unfortunates who saw the dragon-headed prows of longships emerging from coastal mists. In fact, these full-size raiding vessels came to be called dragons. The dragon face that dominates Viking art isn't reptilian; truth be told, it more closely resembles an enraged mastiff, with short jaws and snarling muzzle, as seen on the famous Oseberg burial ship prow. The ferocious intent can't be missed.

References in the Icelandic sagas bear this out. From King Harald's saga, the poet Thjodolf says:

> See where the great longship
> Proudly lies at anchor
> Above the prow, the dragon
> Rears its glowing head ...
> Men will quake with terror
> Before the seventy sea-oars
> Are given deserved respite
> From the labours of the ocean. (*Heimskringla*, "History of Harald Hardrade" 541)

The snarling dragon's head and elongated, full-body winged dragons appear just about any place where decorative elements can be added. We know this from artifacts found in burial sites: buckles, brooches and all types of gold and silver jewelry; axes, swords, scabbards, and helmets; pillars, lintels, and gables of buildings; domestic items such as furniture and sleighs, finely carved ships' timbers, and rune stones great and small. Here, dragon shapes are artistic and elegant, as well as intimidating.

Examples of dragons in Viking art found in Iceland include jewelry artifacts such as 10th century dragon-headed pendants in gilt bronze or silver, where the chain or cord passes through the animal's mouth, and Thor's hammer pendants dating from around 1200 where the dragon's head is the vertical section, complete with toothy jaws and flaring nostrils. Clearly, the pagan Vikings weren't afraid to wear this creature as a talisman of power.

After becoming Christianized, Viking settlers blended the dragon's image with their newfound religion. An example is the carving on a church door from Valthjofsstadur that shows the motif of four intertwined dragons biting their tails –the worm ouroboros again. An interesting Viking addition to dragonlore is the word "worm" (*worm, orm, vurm*) indicating a type of dragon that typically has a long, heavy serpentine shape, no wings, and a preference for fens and marshes. It leaves a stink as it crawls over the land. Worms usually have the ability to breathe fire or poisonous fumes, with totally malicious intent. From modern fiction, Tolkien's Glaurung, a truly wicked worm, comes to mind.

From Sweden, the incised memorial stones of Gotland give us some good examples of dragons. The Sjonhem Stone from the late Viking age, around 1100, incorporates both pagan and Christian elements, with a heart-shaped design created from the dragon's body. The dragon is long and sinuous, with longer snout and more curved neck and body than those found on ships' prows. Here, the dragon's appearance shows the coexist-ence of pagan and Christian ideas rather than the defeat of the evil dragon by Christian saints.

In 8th century England, the dragon as an evil omen appears in the *Anglo-Saxon Chronicle*, a collection of manuscripts (annals or yearly accounts) detailing the history of early medieval England:

"Here terrible portents came about over the land of Northumbria, and miserably frightened the people: these were immense flashes of lightning, and fiery dragons were seen flying in the air ... A great famine immediately followed these signs; and a little after that in the same year on 8 January the raiding of heathen men miserably devastated God's church in Lindisfarne island by looting and slaughter." (Swanton edition, 57)

Manuscripts from the late Middle Ages offered citizens of the 14th and 15th centuries an even more prolific source of dragon art, thanks to the inclusion of art from woodcuts and engravings and the invention of the printing press. Also widespread were "books of hours," collections of devotional verses with a schedule of daily prayers drawn from the Book of Psalms or other similar sources. It's clear that the scribes and illuminators who created these books frequently employed the dragon as a teaching tool, warning against seduction by Satan and his minions.

Bible renditions such as the Utrecht "History Bible" (circa 1430) depict numerous scenes of the Apocalypse with St. John the Evangelist's multi-headed dragons, dragons threatening the Christ, and angels dragging Satan the old dragon away in chains. Illustrations of biblical books of Daniel and Job give us dragons tempting the weak and being subdued by the righteous. The archangel Michael hovers with sword in hand over a cowering dragon of reptilian shape. The dragons are variously red, pale gray/bluish, greenish, or black, usually with spiny bat wings and doglike or crocodilian heads, although some have humanlike or lionlike faces. On a humorous note, some of the small dragons look eerily like Paul Kidby's Discworld illustrations of swamp dragons!

Images of St. George (the Roman Georgius – more on his story shortly) can be found everywhere. Typically, St. George is shown on horseback in armor, spearing a crouching dragon that has a forked tongue, ridges down its back, splayed talons, and blood dripping between its fanged teeth. In many of the paintings, the dragon's head is a cross between lion and crocodile; the wings might be a different color from the body (for example, blue wings, reddish body), with scaly skin and clawed feet.

At this point, it seems a good idea to mention the folktale motif of the dragonslayer as categorized by Stith Thompson in his six-volume 1950s opus, the *Motif-Index of Folk-Literature*. Thompson described a folktale motif as an element "having the power to persist in tradition," and this motif of slaying dragons has certainly persisted from ancient times through to the present. As I've indicated in Chapter 9, the idea of the dragonslayer is as old as the concept of dragons and the need for heroes.

The dragonslayer motif's importance in medieval Christian tales and artwork revolves around the dragon's role as an agent of evil: innocent victims (mostly sacrificial females) are saved from the creature, and heroes who fight it undergo a ritual of passage that tests their worthiness. Because this archetypal "wonder tale" of the dragonslayer (Type 300 in Antti Aarne's 1961 *Types of the Folktale*) employs the dragon as both a physical plot device and a symbol, it has allowed the dragon to take on more importance than just a piece of furniture on the set. The door has been opened for character development.

Look at the first known instance of the dragon recounted as part of St. George's developing legend. As told in *The Golden Legend or Lives of the Saints*, compiled by Jacobus de Voragine, Archbishop of Genoa, 1275, a dragon was terrorizing a village by demanding human sacrifice, and eventually the king's daughter was to be offered. George rides up, impales the dragon with his spear, rescues the princess, and delivers the villagers from a great evil. He leads the dragon into town by the princess' girdle tied around its neck and then promptly beheads it. The grateful townsfolk are thus converted to Christianity. Except for the fact that the dragon was eating villagers on a regular basis, one can almost feel sorry for it, being speared, then led injured and docile into town by the princess's belt, only to lose its head. We'll return to this tale when the writers of epic romance get hold of it during the Renaissance.

Bestiaries, made popular by classical authors, continued their popularity into medieval times, providing semi-scientific, highly imaginative pronouncements on both real and fabulous creatures. Dragons continued to be included as a role model for the dark side. Moral attributes as well as physical characteristics were ascribed to them, inviting their use as symbols in Christian instruction on vices and virtues. Following the lead of biblical authors such as St. John, bestiary writers and illustrators of the Middle Ages gave full rein to their imaginations regarding dragons and their cousins, the serpents.

Dragon expert Jonathan Evans offers a revealing explanation for this equation of the dragon with the arch-fiend of the Christian Bible.[4] Through a series of mistranslations from ancient Hebrew into Greek into Latin, the dragon became associated "as a symbol of pride." A further error in translation turned the Hebrew word for *jackal* into *dragon*, and "this error is the origin of the long tradition, culminating in the medieval bestiaries, in which the dragon appears as an allegorical symbol for the sin of pride and thus for the original author of pride, Satan."

Because most medieval bestiaries draw from two primary sources, what these two encyclopedic works say about dragons has been propagated into many derivative manuscripts through the centuries (which, by the way, is true of modern bestiaries as well[5]). The first source is the *Physiologus* (a 36-chapter treatise from an 11th century CE abbot and poet moralizing on the Christian virtues, or lack thereof, as they apply to all manner of beasts). The second important source is the *Etymologiae* (sometimes called *Origines*) of Isidore of Seville, a Christian bishop who completed the manuscript shortly before his death in 636.

A 12ᵗʰ century Latin manuscript known simply as *A Bestiary* or *The Book of Beasts,* translated by T.H. White in 1954, contains numerous references to dragons in the context of the *Physiologus* and *Etymologiae*.[6] For example, according to *Physiologus*, the breath of the panther (representing Christ) sends the "dragon-devil" running for its hole, where it falls into a stupor and often dies. Also, the dragon is the enemy of the dove, which represents the Holy Ghost, and will eat it if he can, the moral being to beware "lest that Dragon, the serpent of old, should seize you and gobble you up like Judas."

The main entry for "Draco" falls in the section titled Reptiles and Fishes, where the dragon is described as the "biggest of all serpents, in fact of all living things on earth." Its most lethal attribute is its long, serpentine body and tail, not its jaws or poison. It hides in caves, but when it emerges, it flies into the sky, flaming. Its crest is a type of crown, reminding the faithful of its role as "the King of Pride." Illustrations depict a two-legged dragon (wyvern) with folded feathered wings on a stout body with coiling serpent's tail. The head is doglike, with snarling mouth and sharp fangs, not unlike the dragon's heads found on Viking ships' prows.

Which leads us to a discussion of Northern worms. All the while dragons were getting involved in saints' lives in Christian European lore, a distinctly Northern version of the creature was taking shape in Viking and Anglo-Saxon tales. The Old English term *wyrm* (Germanic *wurm*; Old Norse *ormr*) applies to a treasure-guarding, dangerously greedy, man-eating beast inhabiting caves and hillside terrain. These worms are well-armored, but with a vulnerable soft spot or underbelly, have fire-breathing ability, and vary in size from filling a cave lair to encircling hills and mountains ... or even the known world.

As I'm approaching dragonlore predominantly from the fiction writer's point of view, especially regarding visual imagery and plot significance, three worms from Northern literature of the medieval period stand out: the unnamed dragon that kills the hero Beowulf, the dragon Fáfnir slain by the hero Sigurd, and the world-serpent Jörmungand of Norse mythology. All three have cast long shadows across the fiction of everyone from William Morris in the late 1800s to Gene Wolfe in 2004. They are of primary importance, of course, in the fiction of Tolkien and his successors.

As Tolkien pointed out so convincingly in his essay, *Beowulf: The Monsters and the Critics*, the dragon in this much-studied Anglo-Saxon poem stands on its own as a character and can be appreciated as more than just a vehicle for Christian symbolism. I'm squarely in the camp of people like Old English scholar Bruce Mitchell who believe that those "3,182 lines of alliterative verse" are a conscious work of art by a skilled poet. This highly influential dragon model deserves more than a passing glance.

Just consider the wealth of dramatic elements present in Beowulf's third great challenge, the single-handed combat with a marauding dragon. We have a large fire-breathing monster guarding an ancient tomb that contains a rich hoard with a curse on it, a desperate thief who takes a jeweled goblet, the great dragon's wrath and revenge, the old king's vow to call out the dragon from its lair, the gruesome details of the fight, the death of both the hero and the dragon, the ignominious disposal of the great beast – plus plenty of foreshadowing of doom from the curse activated by greed for gold.

The dragon itself is masterfully rendered by the poet. Initially, our expectations of fear are built up through the thief's POV in the presence of the sleeping dragon, much as Tolkien presents our first glimpse of Smaug through Bilbo's eyes. A brief evocative flashback contains the lament of the hoard's last human owner (some of the finest alliterative verse in Old English, echoes of which can be heard in verses of the Rohirrim from Tolkien's *The Lord of the Rings*). This passage reveals how the dragon comes to possess the hoard, but also foreshadows the bitter end that both heroes and dragons can expect from the pursuit of treasure and glory:

> "Then an old harrower of the dark
> happened to find the hoard open,
> the burning one who hunts out barrows,
> the slick-skinned dragon, threatening the night sky
> with streamers of fire. People on the farms
> are in dread of him. He is driven to hunt out

hoards under ground, to guard heathen gold

through age-long vigils, though to little avail." (Heaney, 155)

The poet then gives a fascinating picture of the dragon's fury over the theft of a single cup. It flames the ground where it finds an intruder's footprints, waits in frustration for the wretch to return ("Hot and savage, he kept circling and circling the outside of the mound."), then exhibits mounting rage when no one shows up. Through the dragon's POV we're shown its incredulity that a prowler would have the nerve to come so close while it slept, much less to steal a gold cup from its bed! The dragon's frustration and desire to kill anything in its path is palpable: "So the guardian of the mound, / the hoard-watcher, waited for the gloaming / with fierce impatience; his pent-up fury / at the loss of the vessel made him long to hit back / and lash out in flames." In images of scorched earth and burning homesteads, the poet vividly draws the dragon's vengeance, then lets us sense its satisfaction as it darts back into the tumulus at daybreak, a mighty worm secure in its power to terrify the countryside and defend its turf.

From the description of Beowulf's battle preparations, the fight itself, and his followers' treatment of the bodies (both worm and hero), many essential traits of the Western dragon emerge. Its size is huge (50 feet long), filling the cavern of the barrow with its coils and wings. The monster's charge out of the barrow causes the ground to shake with the weight and power of its body, which is covered in glittering scales hard enough to repel the hero's sword. It can spit sheets of flame over enough distance to roast anyone standing in the cavern's entrance and wreath its body in an aura of fire. In its final attack on the failing Beowulf, its fanged jaws clamp in a death-grip, doubly dangerous because the dragon's breath is also poisonous. And finally, it loathes humans and knows them to be its enemies.

The dragon's death is achieved by discovery of its vulnerable spots: a place under its arm where the sword can enter and its unprotected under-belly. But what's most interesting to me in this scene of the aftermath of the carnage is the poet's remarks about the dragon's death. We expect some bitter words over the death of the king who "bartered" his last breath "to own this fortune," but there is also a seeming lament for the extinguished glory of the worm as well:

> "No longer would his snakefolds
> ply themselves to safeguard hidden gold.
> Hard-edged blades, hammered out
> and keenly filed, had finished him
> so that the sky-roamer lay there rigid,
> brought low beside the treasure-lodge.
>
> Never again would he glitter and glide
> and show himself off in midnight air,
> exulting in his riches: he fell to earth
> through the battle-strength in Beowulf's arm." (Heaney, 191)

From our modern perspective, it's not difficult to feel some sympathy for the hapless dragon as well as the aged king bravely meeting his doom. I like the ring of Seamus Heaney's translation best for this final scene: "The treasure had been won, / bought and paid for by Beowulf's death. / Both had reached the end of the road / through the life they had been lent."

Also in *Beowulf* is the kernel of another dragonslayer story: the digression about the hero Sigemund who was said to have killed a treasure-guarding dragon by running it through with his sword. In an example of dramatic irony, this passage calls to mind Sigemund's son Sigurd (Germanic Siegfried), whose own exploits in dragonslaying win him a cursed treasure that brings on his ruin, as happens to Beowulf.

Sigurd's tale grew in popularity through both its Norse and Germanic versions, better known to us in the *Saga of the Völsungs* and the *Nibelungenlied*. Fáfnir the shape-shifting worm and Sigurd the flawed hero are so vivid that modern artists from Wagner to Tolkien have felt compelled to give their own spin on the characters. In Chapter 2, I've discussed how a great deal of Fáfnir shows up in Tolkien's characterization of Glaurung.

The 13th century prose version of the story given in *The Saga of the Völsungs* is by no means the only Scandinavian source – "The Lay of Fáfnir" in the older *Poetic Edda* spins out the same plotline in more detail and a prose summary appears in the Icelander Snorri Sturlusson's *Prose Edda*. In both versions, the dragon Fáfnir is a shape-shifter. We find out all about him by that oldest of devices, what others say about him in rumor and history. At the mention of Fáfnir's name, Sigurd says he's heard rumors about this worm: "I know the nature of this serpent, and I have heard that no one dare go against him because of his size and ferocity."

Regin, Sigurd's foster father, fills in more clues. The treasure-guarding dragon was once Regin's older brother ("the largest and fiercest of the sons, and he wanted to call everything his own"). But the treasure (including a gold ring) had been cursed by its former owner, Andvari the dwarf. Under the curse, Fáfnir kills his father and takes ownership of the ill-gotten goods, and years of single-minded hoarding turn him into a wicked worm. This becomes Sigurd's challenge: to do Regin's dirty work by killing the monster and recovering the treasure.

Once Sigurd agrees, we learn more about Fáfnir from two sources: Regin and Odin. Saga prose is not without a certain grim humor, which I call Viking deadpan, and you get a sense of it when Regin shows Sigurd the dragon's track to its watering spot. Complaining that Regin has misrepresented the size of the monster, Sigurd observes dryly, "You told me, Regin, that this dragon was no larger than a serpent, but his tracks seem excessively large to me." Regin sets the general plan (a pit in the dragon's path to water where Sigurd can hide and stab upward with his father's reforged sword). Odin refines the plan, explaining that Sigurd should dig several ditches to avoid being covered in the dragon's caustic blood.

Like the *Beowulf* dragon, Fáfnir's great size causes the ground to tremble, and he breathes out poison as he passes over the ditches. Events play out as we expect, but what's unexpected is that the dragon doesn't just roll over and die – instead, it engages the dragonslayer in one of the most famous conversations in literature. The hero must beware the dragon's voice, even in death. Asks Fáfnir:

> "Who are you, or who is your father, or who is your family, you who are so impudent that you dare to bear weapons against me?"

The dragon's voice is by turns outraged, wheedling, insinuating, threatening, and ultimately foreboding as it pronounces the curse that brings Sigurd and everyone close to him to a bitter end. "And that same gold will be your death, as it will be the death of all who possess it." In dying, Fáfnir provides Sigurd with a dubious gift – the blood from the serpent's heart gives Sigurd power to understand the language of birds, from which he learns of Regin's intent to kill him. As with many such tales, the hero reaps rewards at first and his fame as a dragonslayer spreads, but eventually the curse pronounced by the dying dragon will catch up with him.

Around 1200, the anonymous Austrian court poet who penned the *Nibelungenlied* referred to Siegfried's heroic dragonslaying, but omitted the actual event and the dragon's name. Roughly contemporary with the *Saga of the Völsungs*, the Germanic *Nibelungenlied* echoes the Norwegian *Saga of Thedrik*. Both tell of their respective heroes bathing in the slain dragon's blood, which makes their skin thick and impervious to steel except for a vulnerable spot between the shoulder blades, much like the old motif of Achilles' unprotected heel.

From Norse mythology, we find a serpent-dragon worth mentioning. Snorri Sturlusson's *Prose Edda*, completed around 1220, contains several references to Jörmungand, the Midgard serpent ("... the Midgard serpent, which lies encircling all lands, and its length was hardly enough for both its head and its tail to touch the ground"), by which we discover yet another image of the ouroboros.

The Midgard serpent is Thor's greatest opponent. Summarized from accounts in the *Poetic Edda* and elsewhere, this is a rousing story of Thor's ocean expedition to haul the Midgard serpent out of the depths in a test of might. The creature is such a leviathan that once Thor hooks it on his line, his feet go through the ship and brace on the sea floor while he struggles to pull the dragon out of the water. In this struggle, Jörmungand becomes a Scandinavian chaos dragon, marking the boundaries between the known world and the frightening realms beyond it. Jörmungand shares with Fáfnir and the *Beowulf* dragon the trait of spewing poison in its breath.

"And one can claim that a person does not know what a horrible sight is who did not get to see how Thor fixed his eyes on the serpent, and the serpent stared back up at him spitting poison." (*Edda*, 47)

In listing the calamities expected at Ragnarök, the "Völuspá" or "Prophecy of the Seeress" in the *Poetic Edda* predicts the monster's terrifying return at the end of the world. As Snorri Sturlusson's summary explains, "Then the ocean will surge up on to the lands because the Midgard serpent will fly into a giant rage and make its way ashore ... The Midgard serpent will spit so much poison that it will bespatter all the sky and sea, and it will be very terrible." In a dragonslaying episode reminiscent of Beowulf's struggle, Thor kills the Midgard serpent, but dies from its poison.

Leaving Scandinavia behind, we move to Geoffrey of Monmouth's 1138 prose epic, *History of the Kings of Britain,* which contains a dragon story that has become part of the Arthurian tradition. The legend of the white and red dragons that undermine the foundations of usurping British ruler Vortigern's tower is widespread. In this tale, the two dragons are unearthed by the youthful Merlin and engage each other in mortal combat in the air – the red dragon, symbolic of the native Celts, defeats the white dragon, representing the invading Saxons. Hence the heraldic red dragon adopted on the Welsh flag.

A few hundred years later, a very similar theme appears in the Welsh tale of "Lludd and Lleuelys," in the *White Book of Rhydderch.* In this tale, two fighting dragons (one native, the other foreign) are the cause of a terrible recurring scream that disturbs the peace of the Isle of Britain. King Lludd consults his wise brother Lleuelys, the King of France, who devises a most ingenious plan to trap and confine the two dragons. Lludd is told to dig a pit in the exact center of the island kingdom, put a vat of mead covered by a silk cloth down in the pit, and wait for the dragons (shape-shifted into pigs) to fall exhausted into it. When this occurs as predicted, the mead-sated sleeping pigs (dragons) are wrapped up and buried in a stone chest in a secret place. This puts an end to the terrible dragon's scream that had shaken the land, and peace is restored.

From Irish myths and sagas, the "Cattle Raid of Fróech," found in the *Book of Leinster* (c. 1160), contains a deadly swamp dragon. While not specifically a symbol of evil, the creature is used by the parents of Findabair to indirectly bring about the death of her suitor Fróech. Inviting him to swim in the river where the monster lurks, the duplicitous parents assure him, "We know of nothing dangerous in it." The dragon doesn't come immediately, so several delaying tactics are used to keep Fróech in the water. When he is sent back out into the pool to obtain a branch from a rowan tree, the monster finally strikes. Weaponless, Fróech appears certain to be killed and dragged under. Findabair, however, comes to his rescue, tossing a sword to him, with which he lops off the monster's head. Fróech survives the attack, dragging the dragon's head up on shore with him, but must be taken to the land of the fairy-folk to be healed of his wounds.

From High Romance to Folktale Worms

Dragons were a highly popular image and plot device in tales of chivalry involving knights-errant, especially during the time of the Crusades. We have Chrétien de Troyes to thank for the establishment of the medieval romance, a peculiar blend of courtly love and bloodthirsty quests for valor and honor where dragons often appear as obstacles in the path of the quest. But even as the age of chivalry began to wane, dragons continued to serve as Christian symbols of evil and end up on the wrong end of sharp weapons. They could also serve as portents of greatness, as I'll illustrate in a moment.

An interesting choice is presented in Chrétien de Troyes' 12th century chivalric romance *Yvain*. If you were to encounter two dangerous wild beasts in a forest locked in a fight to the death, and got close enough to see that one was a lion and the other a dragon, which would you kill first to ensure your own safety? Following proper crusader etiquette, the choice is obvious to our hero Yvain: "Then he determined that he would take the lion's part, since a venomous and wicked creature deserves only harm: the dragon was venomous and fire lept from its mouth because it was so full of wickedness. Therefore my lord Yvain determined that he would slay it first."

The dragon's description reveals the usual attributes; it breathes flames from a huge gaping mouth ("larger than a cauldron"), and its blood and breath are poisonous. Its size is large enough to subdue a full-grown lion, and its intent is pure evil. Even in death, its sharp teeth remain clenched on the lion's tail. Ensuring that readers feel no pity toward the dragon, Yvain observes regretfully that he will have to sever part of the lion's tail to free it. The lion is so thankful to be saved from the wickedness of the dragon that it becomes a sort of guard dog to Yvain, following him faithfully through the rest of his adventure.

The story motif of St. George defeating a dragon and rescuing a virtuous maiden, so popular in the early Middle Ages, has its Arthurian counterparts in the stories of the knights Tristan and Lancelot. The widespread stories of Sir Tristan and his adulterous love for the lady Iseut often includes a dragonslaying episode that contains an interesting and unusual motif: the dragon's tongue used as proof of the deed. Later Anglo-Norman romance versions of Tristan's story merged his tale with that of Arthur, turning him into one of the dragonslaying Round Table knights.

Now that we've raised the specter of King Arthur, let's talk about dragons in Arthurian romance. The dragon becomes an omen of good fortune in a dream King Arthur has while on a sea voyage to defend his rulership of Britain against the Romans. The most famous account of this tale is in Sir Thomas Malory's *Le Morte D'arthur* (c. 1470), which is the main channel for many earlier Arthurian tales and histories.

"And as the king lay in his cabin in the ship, he fell in a slumbering and dreamed a marvellous dream: him seemed that a dreadful dragon did drown much of his people, and he came flying out of the west, and his head was enamelled with azure, and his shoulders shone as gold, his belly like mails of a marvelous hue, his tail full of tatters, his feet full of fine sable, and his claws like fine gold; and an hideous flame of fire flew out of his mouth, like as the land and water had flamed all of fire. After, him seemed there came out of the orient, a grimly boar all black in a cloud, and his paws as big as a post; he was rugged looking roughly, he was the foulest beast that ever man saw, he roared and romed so hideously that it were marvel to hear. Then the dreadful dragon advanced him and came in the wind like a falcon giving great strokes on the boar ..." (*Le Morte D'arthur*, V, 4).

Arthur's wise man interprets the omens thusly: the dragon stands for Arthur himself; the wing colors are the lands under his rule. The beast's tattered tail represents the Knights of the Round Table. The dragon may be "dreadful," but its use in this context is that of power and victory.

Lancelot is also a dragonslayer. After rescuing a maid from an enchantment that had held her prisoner in a tower, he agrees to deliver the townsfolk from a dragon making its lair in a nearby tomb. Sir Thomas Malory describes the dragon's defeat this way in Book XI of *Le Morte D'arthur*: "So then Sir Launcelot lift up the tomb, and there came out an horrible and a fiendly dragon, spitting fire out of his mouth. Then Sir Launcelot drew his sword and fought with the dragon long, and at the last with great pain Sir Launcelot slew that dragon." Here, the dragon is evil, especially since it has made its heathen lair in a place that should be considered holy.

Into the high Renaissance and Reformation, the theme of St. George battling the dragon began to appear as art for its own sake, from a point of view that was as much aesthetic as religious. By the time 16th century masters such as Raphael, Tintoretto, and Rubens tackled the St. George subject, the archetype is very clearly set, with St. George on horseback, spearing a writhing serpentine beast on the ground. Typically, the dragon in such paintings is reptilian – dull-colored and scaly like a giant salamander or lizard, with toothy doglike snout, winding serpent's tail, clawed feet, and outspread bat wings, displaying all the characteristics we associate with typically Western dragons.

Edmund Spenser's epic poem, the *Faerie Queen*, riffs on the St. George theme with two dragons that serve as symbols in his allegory of the English Reformation. In Book I, Cantos i and ii, a female dragon labeled Error (who represents the false teachings of Catholicism) attacks the Redcrosse knight, coiling her serpent's tail around him. He beheads her, and her young die from drinking her blood (ingesting "wrong knowledge").

The second dragon that keeps the parents of Una (Truth) imprisoned in a tower gives Redcrosse a harder time. The battle Spenser describes is epic, with the dragon first being wounded in a vulnerable spot under a wing and eventually dying from a sword thrust into its open jaws. Spenser's detailed description in Cantos xi and xii is riveting enough to have the lingering effect of standardization for the Western dragon type. Here are some of the dragon's traits and a few modern echoes (you can probably think of more): the dragon's roar is deafening and causes the ground to shake (Goodkind's Scarlet and Yolen's St. George dragons); its size is so vast that it's initially mistaken for a feature of the landscape (both Tolkien's Glaurung and Le Guin's Dragon of Pendor); hovering overhead, its ponderous weight and bloated shape cast a fearsome shadow below (Pratchett's Dragon of Ankh-Morpork); its scales are like plates of armor and make a loud metallic sound as it moves (Le Guin's Kalessin); it displays huge spiny wings of black and red and a long coiling barbed tail sharp as steel (Rowling's Hungarian Horntail).

Other general attributes include a scaly ridge back, gaping jaws filled with "ranks of iron teeth," smoldering eyes that burn like "broad beacons" and "glaring lamps," a bristling head crest, a sulfurous stench to its breath mixed with smoke and fire, razor-sharp claws like scythes, and paws strong enough to snatch both horse and armored rider from the ground and fly away with them. Once the knight's spear point finds the dragon's vulnerable spot under its left wing, its surprise and rage is monumental, of hurricane proportions. It bleeds poisonous black blood, and when Redcrosse hacks off the barbed end of its tail, its pain and rage are of truly epic scale:

> "Hart cannot thinke, what outrage, and what cryes,
> With foule enfouldred smoake and flashing fire,
> The hell-bred beast threw forth unto the skyes,
> That all was coveréd with darknesse dire ..." (Book I, Canto xi)

Spenser creates a lasting mental image of terror as the wounded dragon drops out of the sky onto the knight's upraised shield, clamping its talons around it. The scene is cinematic, with the dragon hanging on, belching smoke and flames, as the knight hacks away at it with his sword. Likewise, its death throes with the sword stuck in its maw make a highly visual scenario: "So downe he fell, and forth his life did breath, / That vanisht into smoke and cloudés swift ... So downe he fell, and like an heapéd mountaine lay." This epic struggle, which runs on for pages, set a standard for dragon battles in gory detail that wasn't really equaled until the fantasy novels of the 20th century.

With the age of chivalry fading and the age of reason lurking in the wings, interest in dragons as real beasts and the embodiment of the biblical Devil waned as well. Renaissance encyclopedias and travelogues such as Edward Topsell's *History of Four-Footed Beasts* and *The Histories of Serpents* (1607-8) demonstrated that the dragon was becoming an object of esoteric curiosity rather than an icon of damnation.

But perhaps even more interesting is the dragon's link with alchemy. Alchemy as a realm of study was both practical and spiritual, although not necessarily Christian, so dragon symbolism in alchemy was quite different from that of the Bible. The alchemical dragon symbolized the duality of earth and spirit and the attempt of spirit to fly out of its earthy bonds. Specifically, the dragon was linked with Mercury (both the physical element and the mythological figure) for its mutable properties. Each stage of the alchemical process was greeted with a change in the color of the base material and association with a different animal. The image of the dragon in the flask is a common illustration in many manuscripts of alchemy.

Writers and artists were also making dramatic use of the dragon without the dire religious connotations it had carried previously. This sea-change in attitude paved the way for the rise of the popular folktale, which eventually began to fill the void left by the dragon's decline as an icon of wickedness and immorality. Collections from many nationalities began to circulate widely. In the dark (and sometimes downright warped) folktales and fairy stories collected by the Brothers Grimm, we've reached a point at which dragons become the seminal fairytale element and not the embodiment of Satan required for biblical instruction.

Modern Themes and Variations

Now that we've reached dragons at the turn of the 20th century, I can only say, so many worms, so little time. There are so many folktales and fairy stories containing dragons in this period that it's beyond the scope of this book to detail them all. A brief sampling from several well-known collections will give you an idea of the draconic themes and motifs that begin to appear in fantasy fiction from here on into the second millennium.

Before we open the book on folktales, I want to mention a 19th century bestiary of sorts that continues to enjoy a certain amount of popularity. Geologist Charles Gould's *Mythical Monsters*, first published in 1886, is still being reprinted under the title *Dragons, Unicorns, and Sea Serpents: A Classic Study of the Evidence for their Existence.* By the late 1800s, naturalists and historians were just beginning to come to grips with the implications of dinosaur bones, and Gould's book attempts to connect ancient beliefs in monsters, especially dragons, with possible fossil evidence.

Gould's overview of classical dragonology covers both east and west, with separate chapters for the dragons of Western tradition, the Chinese dragon, and the Japanese dragon. What's most interesting to me about this book is the variety of illustrations liberally sprinkled throughout the chapters. Some of these images have been seen elsewhere, but it's fascinating to see them all gathered under one roof, so to speak, with documentation on where the image originated. Modern-day bestiaries such as Carol Rose's thorough collection keep these old sources circulating and very much alive.

Old sources infiltrate and combine in curious ways in folktales as well. In the German folktales collected by the Brothers Grimm over a period of years and published in two volumes in the early 1800s, dragons lurk in the forests and hills. They have all the menacing attributes that Western dragons have come to own, but they're also somehow ... folksy. Here's what I mean. "The Two Brothers" combines several dragonslaying motifs: a dragon terrorizes a village by demanding a virgin sacrifice that includes the king's daughter. The hero of the story figures out how to slay the dragon with an enchanted sword and hacks it into pieces. He then cuts out the dragon's tongues from its seven heads for proof of the deed. The evil king's marshal falsely claims credit for the job and demands the king's daughter in marriage; the true dragonslayer appears with the evidence and marries the princess.

Although this story has a Christian setting and the dragon is an agent of evil, it also has a bit of down-to-earth attitude that you might recognize in Tolkien's Smaug or Chrysophylax: the dragon is simply astonished at the nerve of a mere human thinking to outwit it or do it in. In essence, the dragon says, "Fool, what *were* you thinking?!" The dragon in the Grimm tale is dispatched in a desperate battle fought in stages much like that we found in Spenser's *Faerie Queen*, and it eventually meets the same fate.

Scottish writer/editor Andrew Lang's *Red Fairy Book* of 1890 includes a retelling of the *Völsungs* dragonslaying story. Although the dragon gets rather short shrift in this summarized version of the ancient tale of Sigurd's victory over Fáfnir, it still evokes the thrill of fantasy and legend. It certainly made an impression on a young reader by the name of John Ronald Reuel Tolkien, who read it first in Lang's collection and then went on to do marvelous things with dragons and swords. As Tolkien remarked in his famous Andrew Lang lecture (later published as "On Fairy-Stories"), "Fairy-stories were plainly not primarily concerned with possibility, but with desirability. If they awakened *desire*, satisfying it while often whetting it unbearably, they succeeded." And nobody desired dragons more than he did.

In addition to rehashing and reworking old motifs, something else was taking place in these 19th century story collections. Part of that sea-change I mentioned is that dragons are now allowed to be humorous. Take the Russian fairy tale "Ivan-Young of Years, Old of Wisdom," for example. In this episodic tale, the witch Baba-Yaga has a son – a dragon named Zmei Gorinich – who holds three magical objects sought by Ivan, the young hero. When the dragon arrives at Baba-Yaga's hut, he feasts on roast bull and a pail of wine, then wants a little relaxation: "Have no fear, I won't harm anyone, for I'm dying for a game of cards, and a bit of fun." Clearly, this isn't Fáfnir.

Ivan agrees to play, but Zmei sets the stakes of the game: "Let us play, and mind: the winner eats the loser." Obviously, Zmei expects not to lose. But surprise! After three days of card playing, in which the dragon spends his free time flying off around the world and not sleeping, he loses three games in a row. His abject groveling to save his skin is the stuff of comedy, with a dark East European twist: "Zmei Gorinich was very frightened, and he fell on his knees and he cried in pleading tones: 'Don't kill me, Ivan-Young of Years, Old of Wisdom! I shall do you any service you like.'" As soon as Ivan agrees to spare the dragon if he'll give up the three magical objects, the truth comes out. "Zmei Gorinich laughed out with joy, and he set to hugging his guest and his old mother Baba-Yaga. 'You can have them, and welcome!' he cried. 'I can get myself still better ones.'" He even agrees to give Ivan a ride to the next town.

Dragon tales allowing humor became fodder for younger readers in stories such as Kenneth Grahame's "The Reluctant Dragon" (1898). A precursor of many comedic tame dragons, Grahame's peace-loving dragon turns the St. George legend upside down. The dragon is quite civilized and develops a warm friendship with the boy. When St. George gets involved, they discover that he never really bought into all that subduing and killing the dragon stuff. The three of them provide a mock battle in which everyone has a grand time at the end. What is most significant about this gentle tale is the degree to which the dragon has become a character is his own right, on equal footing with the two human protagonists.

In a similar vein is the dragon-oriented fiction of Edith Nesbit. Words such as "madcap," "fun," and "whimsical" describe Nesbit's dragon tales. In 1899, she wrote a series of dragon stories for popular literary magazine *The Strand,* and later collected them into *The Book of Dragons* (1900). Readers of her story "The Dragon Tamers" may find resonances of Tolkien's Chrysophylax, who must play along with his human captors in order to gain freedom, only to become their partner and friend.

In Nesbit's "The Last of the Dragons," we find the same theme that was presented in Grahame's story: a reluctant dragon who'd rather sip tea than eat sacrificial princesses and battle heroic knights. Again, the dragon is as much a fully developed character with its own personality quirks as the humans with whom it interacts. Although it has the physical appearance of a proper Western dragon, all glistening scales, steel talons, spiny wings, and dangerous-looking teeth, it has a heart of mush. When the very modern princess addresses it as "dragon, dear," she touches a nerve. "And then they saw that great tears were coursing down its brazen cheek. 'Whatever's the matter?' said the Prince. 'Nobody,' sobbed the dragon, 'ever called me "dear" before!'"

These early humorous personifications of dragons set a tone and approach that has persisted into modern fantasy fiction with greater and lesser success. Some of the best dragon humor can be found in Terry

Pratchett's *Guards! Guards!* and *The Last Hero* (see Chapter 4 for a detailed analysis of these novels), but for the more whimsical type of treatment akin to Grahame and Nesbit, you can't do better that Patricia Wrede's Enchanted Forest Chronicles series.

Early 20th century Irish writer Lord Dunsany had a rather different take on dragons that also set some precedents. His humor is sharp and satirical, and Pratchett is his direct descendant. Dunsany created several dragons worth mentioning, as much for their changing role in the overall tone of the stories as for their actual description and action in the plot. In "The Hoard of the Gibbelins," a very short tale from Dunsany's 1912 collection, *Tales of Wonder*, a dragon is pressed into service by a knight who threatens him in the usual way (being speared or run-through by a sword). The difference is in attitude; the dragon's cynical agreement to serve as the knight's trusty steed is a source of off-kilter humor.

Here's an example. When challenged by Alderic the knight, the "foul dragon" is canny enough to refrain from flaming and ravening, "for well he knew the fate of those that did these things." Instead, the beast opts to clamp teeth on his pride and allow the knight to saddle him up. The image Dunsany paints of the armored knight galloping away on dragonback is quite comical. As they pass through the towns, with "the dragon snapping at maidens as he went, but being unable to eat them because of the bit in his mouth," images of Chrysophylax galumphing through the streets of Ham are not far from the reader's mind. Alderic spurs on his draconic charger with spear jabs "where he was softest," a mirthful nod to the common knowledge that every dragon has an unprotected spot.

In Dunsany's story "The Fortress Unvanquishable, Save for Sacnoth," we find a highly inventive description of a dragon in metallic terms that's rivaled only by Le Guin's much later creation, Kalessin (see Chapter 5). Tharagavverug's body is hardened steel with an iron underbelly, but his nose is soft lead; thus, the hero is advised to keep the creature at bay by whacking its nose with a stick, which makes it yelp in pain. Reading that passage, I can't help but be reminded of Lady Ramkin telling Vimes to smack the ravening dragon of Ankh-Morpork on the nose to make it stop (see chapter on Pratchett). Tharagavverug is about as maneuverable as a tank, "pondering slowly in his metal mind" which villager to eat as he stomps down to the town for dinner.

Dunsany makes effective use of sound imagery to describe both the dragon's voice and heartbeat: "Then Leothric followed the tracks till he heard the bronze heart of Tharagavverug before him, booming like a bell." During a three-day battle, Leothric wears the dragon out by continually beating its tender nose with a stick, (a mild parody of the three-stage battle fought in Spenser's *Faerie Queen*). The dragon utters a "fearful cry like the sound of a great church bell that had become possessed of a soul that fluttered upward from the tombs at night – an evil soul, giving the bell a voice." At the dragon's death, its voice changes from the metallic gong of bells to the brash sounds of horns.

The metal metaphor is carried further. By smelting down the dragon in the town foundry, blacksmiths fashion the blade Sacnoth from Tharagavverug's enchanted steel spine and set the hilt with one steel eye of the beast. In true Dunsany fashion, this fact comes in handy in a way that's pure fantasy action but with a touch of wry amusement. We're given a great metallic sound image as the dragon Wong Bongerok hauls its lethal barbed tail over the fortress stones, "as when sailors drag the cable of the anchor all rattling down the deck." Even the dragon's name has onomatopoeic qualities. Then the tail goes into action. But the eye of Tharagavverug in the sword hilt sees Wong's scorpion tail rising before it can strike Leothric from behind, and directs the blade broadside, knocking the barbed appendage aside. Basically, it takes a dragon to outwit a dragon.

For my taste, Dunsany's best dragon is the nameless dragon that carries away a proper Victorian lady named Miss Cubbidge. A story in the *Book of Wonder* collection, "Miss Cubbidge and the Dragon of Romance," serves as a perfect metaphor for the shift in consciousness regarding dragons in the modern age. Here, the dragon is purely a creature of magic and high romance, having nothing to do with threatening the lives of saints or enhancing the reputation of knights. In fact, dozing alongside the abducted Miss Cubbidge in the land of Romance, the dragon "never dreamed of any rescuing knight," and none came. This short, short story (three and a half pages) is more a mood piece, an idyll, than a developed story – it's a meditation on Faerie itself and the dragon as its specific manifestation and symbol.

The creature is introduced to us in standard terminology ("a loathsome dragon"), but this is in sharp contrast to the actual beauty of its appearance and nobility of its nature. Its grand entrance into the scene as eighteen-year-old Miss Cubbidge sits primly on the balcony is wonderfully cinematic, from the reader's point of view:

> "She did not notice the roar of the dragon's golden scales, nor distinguish above the manifold lights of London the small, red glare of his eyes. He suddenly lifted his head, a blaze of gold, over the balcony; he did not appear a yellow dragon then, for his glistening scales reflected the beauty that London puts upon her only at evening and night." (*Wonder Tales*, 24)

Dunsany makes it clear that this is not the dragon of St. George; it's a beautiful, elegant, magical dragon straight from the "eternal and ancient lands of Romance." Giving in to the dragon's spell completely, Miss Cubbidge doesn't even consider being rescued, because the Age of Chivalry is long past. If she's alarmed at being swept off the balcony, she doesn't even know "what knight to call on." Instead, she settles happily into the realm where the material world is dreamed by the dragon itself: "... asleep in his marble tank the golden dragon dreamed: and a little way out from the coast all that the dragon dreamed showed faintly in the mist that lay over the sea." What we have is a mystical blending of the benevolent water dragon of the East with the Western realm of Faerie. While centuries rolled by in the ordinary world, "her marble palace passed not away nor the power that there was in the dragon's spell." Clearly, to use Tolkien's famous words, this is a dragon with "the trade-mark *Of Faerie* written plain upon him."

Once *The Hobbit* made Smaug a popular icon of fantasy literature, from 1937 on to the present, the door of opportunity was flung wide open for dragons of fantasy. A flowering of dragonlore began in the 1960s, resulting in part from Tolkien's escalating popularity in the U.S. but also from newly established Science Fiction/Fantasy associations. In 1970-71, British folk-lorist Katharine Briggs published her two-volume collection of folktales containing such intriguing entries as the Dragon of Wantley, the Gurt Vurm of Shervage Wood, the Linton Worm, and the Longwitton Dragon. Early dragon masters such as Jack Vance, Andre Norton, and Anne McCaffrey began crafting new dragons for magazine stories and novels, and the beast has never looked back.

Dragons have invaded fantasy fiction and art today in an unprecedented way. No longer feared, dragons are revered and desired, and even invited in through the front door (see D. J. Conway's *Dancing with Dragons* for a guidebook). Thanks to TSR and the Dungeons & Dragons phenomenon, dragons have hit the media in a huge way. Role-playing fantasy games and the novels based on them, particularly the *Dragonlance* worlds of Tracy Hickman and Margaret Weis, are an industry unto themselves. Once dragons began to take shape on movie screens and TV sets, they were truly launched.

Media Dragons

Western dragons have flown onto our movie screens with a flourish and an interesting range of characterizations. From the truly frightening, bestial creatures in the apocalyptic *Reign of Fire*, to cuddly cutesy critters in such fare as *Pete's Dragon*, they make great drama and exciting eye candy. Some dragon characters have even managed to convey more depth and emotional range than their human cohorts. After all, who could forget a dragon with the voice of Sean Connery? At the time of this book, no one has yet made a live action film of Tolkien's *The Hobbit*, but with the technology available today, there's an eye-popping version of Smaug just waiting to be brought to life.

In case you've been wondering what Eastern dragons have been up to, they're alive and well – and thriving – in Japanese anime. These virtual dragons represent a culmination of dragonlore that's truly eclectic. Eastern and Western attributes are mixed and matched with enthusiastic abandon in styles that range from crude comic book outlines to beautifully detailed works of art.

Since dragon lovers and anime fanatics tend to belong to overlapping circles, I suspect that few people reading this book will be unfamiliar with the concept of anime. However, for those who need a rough guide, here's the quick and dirty version. Japanese animation ("anime") is not your Saturday morning cartoon fest. Designed with different objectives, anime knows no age group or subject matter limitations, and can range from a series as simplistic and childlike as *Dragonball Z* to the sophistication of adult series that routinely deal with such issues as transgender relationships, abandonment, and space piracy. No subject is too mundane or too "out there" for anime – in fact, the stranger the better..

The format can be anything from a popular manga set (graphic novels) that spins off a lengthy TV series to a short original video to feature films such as the incredibly artistic work of Hayao Miyazaki (*Princess Mononoke*, *Spirited Away*). Where dragons are concerned, the range is equally wide. *Spirited Away* showcases a shape-shifting, oriental dragon. In his human form as the boy Haku, he helps the heroine find her parents and escape back to the non-magical world. As the spirit of the river, Haku is the essential Eastern water deity, benevolent and supporting of human life. The visual presentation of Haku is purely Eastern, with long sinuous body, horse-like face, and drooping muzzle whiskers. But in typical anime fashion, his near-death from swallowing a magic talisman is graphic and horrifying as he spits gouts of blood all over himself and scenery.

Western-style, fire-breathing dragons can be found in *Record of Lodoss War*, *Yu-Gi-Oh*, *Yu-Yu-Hakusho*, *Orphen*, and *Vision of Escaflowne*. In this latter series, a dragonslaying ritual makes Van Fanel the new king of Fanelia and confirms his rite of passage as a warrior. The jewel ("energist") he extracts from the dragon's body bonds him with a huge dragon-robot (the mecha Escaflowne) by blood. Cutting his thumb and letting the blood drop into the energist, Van says the ritual words: "I, Van Fanel, new king of Fanelia, by blood pact do bind myself to thee, Escaflowne. Thou sleeping dragon, awake!" Van has become a true dragon lord, proved by the awakening of the mecha-dragon that only responds to the blood of the true king. This vow is not unlike the pact Jakkin makes with Heart's Blood in Jane Yolen's Pit Dragon novels. It's the familiar motif of a magical or otherwordly quality related to dragon's blood.

Sometimes anime dragons are an interesting combination of both Eastern and Western imagery. In *Yu-Yu-Hakusho*, when the demon Hiei unleashes the Dragon of Darkness Flame during the final rounds of the Dark Tournament, it comes as a long undulating shadowy form that darkens the skies. Circling the arena in a whirlpool of light and shadow, it descends with gaping toothy maw and swallows its summoner. Tense moments later, Hiei reappears, engulfed in the dragon's power with a beatific expression of terror and joy on his face. The dragons of anime are to be both feared and loved.

Full Circle

So here we are, in the 21st century, still in awe of dragons. They decorate our walls in posters, ride around on our bodies as T-shirt art, and populate our movie screens and television sets in a rainbow of scaly splendor. But most of all, they live in books.

The descendents of Tiamat and Fáfnir have come a long way. Ever since Anne McCaffrey wondered what it would be like to write about dragons that were "the good guys," writers' ideas about what could be done with them as real characters, with emotional depth and intelligent minds, have expanded in many directions. If you haven't read the chapters in Part I of this book yet, you will understand the strength of this statement when you do.

Like Tolkien and so many others seduced by the Worm, I love the idea of them and the power of Faerie that clings to their hides. I hope you've enjoyed this trek through the wilds of history and myth in search of a creature known by many names the world over. On your next stroll down the fantasy fiction aisle of your favorite bookstore, take an extra look at the vibrant covers with their rampant dragons: you might find dragon gold between those covers.

Notes

1. Everything you could possibly want to know about the rise and fall of Mayan civilization can be found in the amazing (and weighty) volume titled *The Ancient Maya*. The work is now in its fifth edition, which has been expanded and brought up to date by Robert Sharer.

2. By far the best source of information about illuminated manuscripts of the early to late Middle Ages is Christopher De Hamel's *A History of Illuminated*

Manuscripts. Make sure you get the 1997 second edition from Phaidon Press, which is updated and expanded.

3. The National Library of the Netherlands is the mother lode for catalogued images from illuminated manuscripts of medieval Netherlands, Belgium, France, and Italy. A search through their database yields more dragons than you can imagine! You can dig through over 10,000 entries for icon style, subject, place, date range, and artist/workshop style. The Library's Internet searchable database is found at www.kb.nl/kb/manuscripts/index.html.

4. Evan's comprehensive essay on dragon history is found in an indispensable guide to medieval folklore compiled by Carl Lindahl and colleagues, titled *Medieval Folklore: A Guide to Myths, Legends, Tales, Beliefs, and Customs.* No self-respecting dragonologist should leave home without it.

5. Distillations of fabulous beasts from these two works and their immediate descendents are still being made. Several examples are Joseph Nigg's *The Book of Dragons & Other Mythical Beasts*; Carol Rose's handy *Giants, Monsters & Dragons*; *Dragons and Unicorns: A Natural History* by Paul and Karin Johnsgard; and too many others to list.

6. If you're still wondering about the evolution of bestiaries, look on page 233 of White's book and you'll find a "family tree" of bestiary writings from 5th century BCE origins down through the 16th century CE. Also thought-provoking is the "Influence in Literature" chart on p. 263.

Chapter 11

The Dragon Hunter's Toolbox

Where to Start

Any dragonologist worth his or her brimstone will have dipped into the following basic texts: Jacob Grimm's *Teutonic Mythology* (1883), H. C. Dubose's *The Dragon, Image and Demon* (1886), Charles Gould's *Dragons, Unicorns, and Sea Serpents* (1886), John F. Campbell's *The Celtic Dragon Myth* (1911), M. W. de Visser's *The Dragon in China and Japan* (1913), G. Elliot Smith's *The Evolution of the Dragon* (1919), C. G. Child's *The Natural History of the Dragon* (1921), Ernest Ingersoll's *Dragons and Dragonlore* (1928), and Stith Thompson's massive *Motif-Index of Folk-literature* in six volumes (1931-36). Whatever else you may have on your bookshelves, these tomes are essential background material for studying the development of dragon myths and draconic symbology.

Moving into more modern territory, several works are a must-read for getting a handle on current thinking in the field of Dragonology. Academic works include Robert Graves' two-volume *The Greek Myths* (1955), J. E. Fontenrose's *Python, A Study of Delphic Myth and Its Origins* (1959), Katharine Briggs' *A Dictionary of British Folktales in the English Language* in four volumes (1970), Jorge Luis Borges' *The Book of Imaginary Being* (1978), Peter Dickinson's

The Flight of Dragons (1979), Jonathan Evans' entry in *Mythical and Fabulous Creatures* (1988), and Joseph Campbell's *The Power of Myth* (1988).

Evans lists the various names we have called this creature: *drákon* (Greek), *draco* (Latin), *draca* (Old English), *dreki* (Old Norse), *Drache* (German), *draig* (Welsh), and *drauc* (Old Irish). Further, anthropologist David E. Jones offers an amazing range of names across the globe for the same basic avian/feline/serpentine type of composite monster. For example, he cites *lung* (Chinese), *tatsu* (Japanese), *kelekona* or *mo'o* (Hawaiian), *zmaj* (Croatian), *lohikaarme* (Finnish), *unktena* (Cherokee), *unhcegila* (Lakota Sioux), *smok* (Polish), *ejderha* (Turkish), *tarakona* (Maori), *sarkany* (Hungarian), *lindwurm* (German), and *draak* (Dutch).

Treasure troves of modern popular dragonlore include TRS's many gaming manuals and spin-off publications connected to the *Dungeons & Dragons* phenomenon, books with a New Age slant such as D. J. Conway's *Dancing with Dragons*, and quasi-historical beautifully illustrated treatments such as Anne McCaffrey's *A Diversity of Dragons* (1997) and Nigel Suckling's *Year of the Dragon: Legends and Lore* (2002). Film and video have also contributed much to our visual imagery of dragons, as well as bringing their personalities alive. The screen-scorching presence of dragons in films can range from cute and cuddly (*Pete's Dragon, Joy of Dragons, The Flight of Dragons, The Neverending Story*) to fierce and dangerous (*Dragonslayer, Dragonheart, Dungeons & Dragons: the Movie*, and *Reign of Fire*) to the exquisitely rendered dragons of anime in movies such as Hayao Miyazaki's *Spirited Away* or television series such as the *Record of Lodoss War, Orphen, Yu-Gi-Oh, Saiyuki* and *Vision of Escaflowne*.

Dragons Are Alive on the Internet

Dragons have become such a universal image in popular culture that the very best place to go looking for them is on the Internet. Everything from dragon art, history, fiction, appreciation, and literary criticism to places to buy dragon-themed posters, clothing, banners, and art prints flows through the World Wide Web in torrents of bit and bytes.

For example, a random search on dragons and culture yields items such as the following:

Dragons in Ancient China: www.chinapage.com/dragon1.html. Dragons in Chinese architecture and art, with references.

Dragons of the British Isles: www.wyrm.demon.co.uk/ukdracs.htm. List of legends categorized by place.

The Historical Dragon Page: http://members.tripod.com/~gfriebe/drach.htm. Legends, essays on their origin, and artwork.

D.R.A.G.O.N.S.: www.colba.net/~tempest1/dragons.htm. Anatomy and physiology, map of modern sightings, and discussion of dragon legends.

Chinavoc.com: Chinese Dragon Culture: http://www.chinavoc.com/dragon/default.asp. Explores Chinese dragon culture through articles, clipart, pictures, art, and calligraphy characters.

Descendants of the Dragon: www.geocities.com/bernardburn/. The folklore and role of dragons in Chinese and Asian cultures, with large picture gallery.

The Dark Dragon: www.weyr.org/~drakaina/. Dragons in international history, list of dragonslaying saints and ancient great beasts, with links to dragon-related businesses.

The Joys of Visual Dragon Art

Writers aren't the only ones having a blast conjuring up dragons. The work of visual artists who create dragons with pencil, paint, and computer fill calendars, posters, picture books, fantasy book covers, films, video games, and websites. Type "dragon art" into any Internet search engine, and you will find more sites than you can comfortably browse in your lifetime.

To help you narrow the field a bit, here are my personal favorites among dragon artists (or fantasy artists whose art includes dragons):

· Wayne Anderson – I'm awestruck at his illustrations for *Year of the Dragon: Legends and Lore* (2002)

· Ciruelo Cabral – Argentine illustrator who produces beautiful dragons that often find their way onto prints, posters, and calendars.

· Bob Eggleton – You've seen his work everywhere on the covers of fantasy titles by major writers. Also have a look at his own books: *Alien Horizons: The Fantastic Art of Bob Eggleton* (1995), *The Book of Sea Monsters* (1998)

- Greg & Tim Hildebrandt - Their dragons are everywhere, from calendars to posters to book covers, and even on the cover of *this* book!

- John Howe – Visionary artist of calendar and poster fame, catapulted to even greater renown for his art design on director Peter Jackson's *The Lord of the Rings* films. I especially love his oversize illustrations for Anne McCaffrey's coffee-table book, *A Diversity of Dragons* (1997).

- Christiaan Iken – Belgian artist with a fondness for Tolkien; you'll find his vision of Middle-earth on the cover of my book, *Tolkien in the Land of Heroes: Discovering the Human Spirit.*

- Lissanne Lake – A prolific book cover artist, who also specializes in collectable cards for games.

- Todd Lockwood – Where would TSR be without Todd? Too many classic Dragonlance images to even count.

- Peter Pracownik – Best set of Tarot cards I ever owned have his gorgeous dragons on them.

- Geoff Taylor – Great U.K. artist; his dragons are seen on the covers of books by David Eddings and others.

- Ruth Thompson - Ohio native Ruth Thompson's popular fantasy paintings can be found on children's book covers, card games, fantasy games, and magazines for Wizards of the Coast, TSR, Iron Crown Enterprises, Royal Fireworks Press, Dragon Magazine, and much more. Her dragon prints (*Tempest, Storm, Dead of Winter*) feature some of the most beautiful, supple, luminous creatures I've ever seen. If I wanted to *be* a dragon, that's what I'd want to look like!

- J. R. R. Tolkien – A talented artist, Tolkien's watercolors of Smaug and the illustrations for *Roverandom* are a delight.

- Boris Vallejo – The godfather of fantasy art, his dragons rule.

- Michael Whelan – Probably the most prolific fantasy cover artist in the business, his dragons prowl the book covers of most major fantasy writers.

Japanese anime (television series, original videos, and feature films) is a fertile source for dragon art as well as some very cool dragon characters. I should also point out that many of these films and series began life as a manga (graphic novel) series, so the anime dragon art is both static and dynamic.

Here are some examples of old classics and new creations that contain dragons I've enjoyed, either as actual characters or background art:

- *Visions of Escaflowne* (TV series; contains both metaphorical dragons as well as actual fire-breathers)
- *Orphen* (TV series; student magician Azalie turns herself into a dragon and much mayhem ensues)
- *Record of Lodoss War* and *Chronicles of the Heroic Knight* (TV series; fantastically drawn, five elemental dragons serve as thematic backdrops for the warring factions)
- *Saiyuki* (TV series, specifically the character of Hakuryu, a shoulder-sitting dragonet who transforms himself into a jeep at will)
- *Spirited Away* (feature film, specifically the character of Haku in his river dragon form)
- *X* (TV series, thematically important, the metaphorical Dragons of Heaven and the Dragons of Earth battle for the fate of the world)
- *Yu-Gi-Oh* (TV series; most of the characters have at least one dueling card that calls up some type of dragon)
- *Yu-Yu-Hakusho* (TV series; specifically the black Dragon of Darkness Flame that Hiei conjures up during the Dark Tournament)

Additional Reading for the Adventurous

Leonard Baskin and Hosie Baskin, *Book of Dragons* (1987)

Jorge Luis Borges, *The Book of Imaginary Beings* (1978)

Katharine Briggs, *A Dictionary of British Folktales in the English Language,* in four volumes (1970)

Andrew M. Butler, Edward James, and Farah Mendlesohn, editors, *Terry Pratchett: Guilty of Literature* (2000)

John F. Campbell, *The Celtic Dragon Myth* (1911)

Joseph Campbell, *The Masks of God: Occidental Mythology* (1964)

_____. *The Power of Myth* (1988)

Richard Cavendish, *Man, Myth, and Magic* (1983)

C. G. Child, *The Natural History of the Dragon* (1921)

Chinese Literature Press, *Dragon Tales: A Collection of Chinese Stories* (1988)

D. J. Conway, *Dancing with Dragons* (1994)

Stephanie Dalley, ed. and trans. *Myths from Mesopotamia: Creation, the Flood, Gilgamesh, and Others* (2000)

M. Desmond and P. Sheingorn, *Myth, Montage, and Visuality in Late Medieval Manuscript Culture: Christine de Pizan's "Epistre Othea"* (2003)

Peter Dickinson, *The Flight of Dragons* (1979)

Patrick Drazen, *Anime Explosion* (2003)

H. C. Dubose, *The Dragon, Image and Demon* (1886)

M. Eliade, *Cosmos and history; the myth of the eternal return* (1985)

J. E. Fontenrose, *Python, A Study of Delphic Myth and Its Origins* (1959)

Gail Gibbons, *Behold...the Dragons!* (1999)

Charles Gould, *Dragons, Unicorns, and Sea Serpents: A Classic Study of the Evidence for Their Existence* (1886; reprinted 2002)

Robert Graves, *The Greek Myths,* in two volumes (1955)

Jacob Grimm, *Teutonic Mythology* (1883)

Thorkild Jacobsen, *The Harps that Once.... Sumerian Poetry in Translation* (1987)

Joyce Tally Lionarons, *The Medieval Dragon: The Nature of the Beast in Germanic Literature* (1998)

Ruth and Vincent Megaw, *Celtic Art* (2001, revised edition)

Bruce Mitchell, *An Invitation to Old English & Anglo-Saxon England* (2001)

Christine Rauer, *Beowulf and the Dragon: Parallels and Analogues* (2000)

Jacqueline Simpson, *British Dragons* (2001)

G. Elliot Smith, *The Evolution of the Dragon* (1919)

Nigel Suckling, *Year of the Dragon: Legends and Lore* (2002)

R. Campbell Thompson, *The Devils and Evil Spirits of Babylonia,* two volumes, (1904; reprinted 1976)

Stith Thompson, *Motif-Index of Folk-literature,* six volumes (1931-36)

J. R. R. Tolkien, *Beowulf: The Monsters & the Critics and Other Essays* (1983)

M. W. de Visser, *The Dragon in China and Japan* (1913)

I.F. Walther and N. Wolf, *Codices Illustres: The world's most famous illuminated manuscripts 400 to 1600* (2001)

Margaret Weis, Tracy Hickman, and Denise Little (compiler), *Realms of Dragons: The Worlds of Weis and Hickman* (1999)

William Willetts, *Foundations of Chinese Art* (1958)

David A. Wilson, *Dragon Study: Fact and Fantasy* (1986)

David M. Wilson and Ole Klindt-Jensen, *Viking Art* (1980)

Collections of Dragon Tales

John K. Anderson, *Tales of Great Dragons* (1985)

Hosie Baskin, *A Book of Dragons* (1985)

Margaret Clark, *A Treasury of Dragon Stories* (1997)

John Gardner, *Dragon, Dragon and Other Tales* (1975)

Michael Hague, *The Book of Dragons* (1995)

Helen Hoke, *Dragons, Dragons, Dragons* (1972)

Anne McCaffrey, *A Gift of Dragons* (2002)

E. Nesbit, *The Complete Book of Dragons* (1900; reprinted 1972)

Jack Prelutsky, *The Dragons are Singing Tonight* (1993)

Brian Preiss, and others, *The Ultimate Dragon* (1995)

Robert Silverberg, editor, *Legends: Short Novels by the Masters of Modern Fantasy* (1998)

Dorothy G. Spicer, *13 Dragons* (1974)

Katrin Tchana, *The Serpent Slayer and Other Stories of Strong Women* (2000)

Margaret Weis, *A Dragon Lover's Treasury of the Fantastic* (1995)

A Draconic Literary Timeline

If you're a bit left-brained and spatially minded, as I am, you probably have a fondness for charts, maps, and diagrams. It's important to me to be able to visualize relationships between and among topics as well as read text about them. If you're inclined toward lists of this sort, you should definitely have a look in the back of Anne McCaffrey's *A Diversity of Dragons*, which is included in this book's bibliography.

To help you visualize how the various dragon sources discussed in this book line up and overlap, I've arranged them in a timeline that groups the documents of myth and legend as well as icons of fantasy fiction relevant to dragons according to time and place, beginning with ancient Mesopotamia and running up to the launch of the twenty-first century. Additionally, a few cultural milestones are scattered along the timeline to place the source documents in the context of the times in which they were written.

BCE (Before Common Era)
BRONZE AND IRON AGES
2800-2500? Babylonian *Epic of Gilgamesh*
1900-1100? Babylonian/Assyrian *Epic of Creation*
1065? (21st Dynasty) Egyptian *Book of the Dead*
c. 1200-900 *Rig Veda*
c. 1150? (Chou Dynasty) Chinese *I Ching*

THE CLASSICAL WORLD
8th century Homer's *Iliad* and *Odyssey*
8th century Hesiod's *Theogony*
140 Apollodorus' *The Library* (Labors of Hercules and other myths)
500 – 450 CE *Mahabharata* and *Bhagavad-gita*
431 Euripides, *Medea*
3rd century Chinese *Shanhai Jing* (*Classic of Mountains and Seas*)
3rd century Apollonios of Rhodes' *Argonautika*
29-19 Virgil's *Aeneid*

CE (Common Era)
THE POST-CLASSICAL AND MEDIEVAL WORLD
1st century Ovid's *Metamorphoses*
1st century Pliny's *Natural History*
200-900 Mayan golden age
635-36 Isidore of Seville's *Etymologiae (Origines)*
712 Japanese *Kojiki* or *Record of Ancient Things*
750-1000? *Beowulf*
7th – 8th centuries *The Book of Kells* and *The Lindisfarne Gospels*
8th century *The Anglo-Saxon Chronicle*

1022-1035 *Physiologus,* attributed to Abbot Of Monte Cassino

1136 Geoffrey of Monmouth's *History of Britain*

12th century Chrétien de Troyes' Arthurian Romances

12-13th centuries *Poetic Edda*

c. 1235 Snorri Sturlusson's *Lives of the Norse Kings*

c. 1220 Snorri Sturlusson's *Prose Edda*

13th century *Saga of the Völsungs*

13th century *The Nibelungenlied*

1300-1325 *The White Book of Rhydderch,* containing the Mabinogion and other Welsh tales

1325 Aztec capital Tenochtitlán founded

c. 1356 Sir John Mandeville's *Travels*

1400 *Sir Gawain and the Green Knight*

1440 The *Gutenberg Bible* published

c. 1470 Sir Thomas Malory's *Le Morte D'arthur*

THE RENAISSANCE WORLD

1582, Salomon Trismosin's *Splendor Solis*

1590 Spenser's *The Faerie Queene*

1607-8 Edward Topsell's *History of Four-Footed Beasts* and *The Histories of Serpents*

1611 *The Holy Bible,* King James Version

1640 Ulisse Aldrovandi's *Two Books on the History of Serpents and Dragons*

THE REVOLUTIONARY WORLD

1812-15 Jacob and Wilhelm Grimm's *Children's and Household Tales*

1840 Elias Lönnrot, *Kalevala*

1886 Charles Gould, *Mythical Monsters*

1890 Andrew Lang, the *Red Fairy Book*

1898 Kenneth Grahame's "The Reluctant Dragon"

1900 E. Nesbit, *The Book of Dragons*

THE MODERN WORLD

1912, 1916 Lord Dunsany's *The Book of Wonder* and *Tales of Wonder*

1919 Grafton Elliot Smith's *The Evolution of the Dragon*

1926 E.R. Eddison's *The Worm Ouroboros*

1937 J. R. R. Tolkien's *The Hobbit*

1952 C. S. Lewis's *The Voyage of the Dawn Treader*

1954-55 J. R. R. Tolkien's *The Lord of the Rings*

1955-58 Stith Thompson's six-volume *Motif-Index of Folk-Literature*

1961 Antti Aarne's *Types of the Folktale*

1968 Ursula K. Le Guin's *A Wizard of Earthsea*

1969 Anne McCaffrey's *Dragonflight*

1970-71 Katharine Briggs's *A Dictionary of British Folktales in the English Language*

1977 J. R. R. Tolkien's *The Silmarillion* (posthumously published)

1982 Jane Yolen's *Dragon's Blood*

1989 Terry Pratchett's *Guards! Guards!*

1994 Terry Goodkind's *Wizard's First Rule*

1997 J. K. Rowling's *Harry Potter and the Sorcerer's Stone*

Bibliography

Works Cited

Apollodorus. *The Library*, Sir James George Frazer, trans., Cambridge: Harvard University Press, 1921.

Apollonios. *Argonautika*, Peter Green, trans., Berkeley: University of California Press, 1997.

Asprin, Robert. *Another Fine Myth*, Norfolk: The Donning Company, 1978.

Budge, E. A. Wallis. *Legends of the Egyptian Gods: Hieroglyphic Texts and Translations*, London: Kegan Paul, Trench, Trübner & Co. Ltd., 1912; reprint New York: Dover Publications, Inc., 1994.

Buttaci, Salvatore Amico M. Internet interview: Anne McCaffrey, April 22, 2002.

Byock, Jesse L. *The Saga of the Völsungs*, London: Penguin Classics, 1999.

Card, Orson Scott. *Character & Viewpoint*, Cincinnati: Writer's Digest Books, 1988.

_____. *How to Write Science Fiction & Fantasy*, Cincinnati: Writer's Digest Books, 1990.

Carus, Marianne. *Fire and Wings: Dragon Tales from East and West*, Chicago: Cricket Books, 2002.

Coogan, Michael D., ed. *The New Oxford Annotated Bible*, third edition, New York: Oxford University Press, 2001.

Cummins, Elizabeth. *Understanding Ursula K. Le Guin*, Columbia: University of South Carolina Press, 1990.

Dunsany, Lord. *Wonder Tales*, New York: Dover Publications, Inc., 2003.

Euripides. *Medea*, James Morwood, trans., Oxford: Oxford University Press, 1997.

Flewelling, Lynn. Terry Goodkind Interview, *Bangor Daily News*, November, 1995.

Ferguson, Diana. *Tales of the Plumed Serpent: Aztec, Inca and Mayan Myths*, London: Collins & Brown, 2000.

Garth, John. "No More Tolkien Gestures," *The Scotsman*, Dec. 15, 2003.

Goodkind, Terry. *Stone of Tears*, New York: Tor Books, 1995.

_____. *Wizard's First Rule*, New York: Tor Books, 1994.

Green, Deirdre. "Tolkien's Dictionary Poetics: The Influence of the OED's Defining Style on Tolkien's Fiction," *Proceedings of the J. R. R. Tolkien Centenary Conference 1992*, Milton Keynes: The Tolkien Society, 1995.

Hambly, Barbara. *Dragonsbane*, New York: Del Rey, 1985.

_____. *Dragonshadow*, New York: Del Rey, 1999.

Heaney, Seamus. *Beowulf: A New Verse Translation,* New York: W. W. Norton & Company, 2000.

Hesiod. *Theogony,* Richmond Lattimore, trans., Ann Arbor: The University of Michigan Press, 1991.

Hollander, Lee M., trans. *The Poetic Edda,* second edition, revised, Austin: University of Texas Press, 1962.

Homer. *Hymns,* Hugh G. Evelyn-White, trans., London: William Heinemann Ltd., 1914.

_____. *Iliad,* Richmond Lattimore, trans., Chicago: The University of Chicago Press, 1061.

_____. *Odyssey,* Robert Fitzgerald, trans., Garden City, NY: Doubleday & Company, Inc., 1963.

Ingersoll, Ernest. *Dragons and Dragon Lore,* London: Payson & Clarke Ltd., 1928.

Jones, Diana Wynne. *The Tough Guide to Fantasyland,* New York: Daw Books, Inc., 1996.

Jung, C. G. *Modern Man in Search of a Soul,* New York: Harcourt Brace Jovanovich, 1933.

King, Stephen. "Wild About Harry," *The New York Times Book Review,* July 23, 2000.

Preiss, Byron, and others, eds. *The Ultimate Dragon,* New York: Simon & Schuster, Inc., 1995.

Le Guin, Ursula K. *The Farthest Shore,* New York: Simon Pulse, 2001.

_____. *The Language of the Night,* New York: HarperCollins, 1989.

_____. *Lao Tzu: Tao Te Ching: A Book About the Way and the Power of the Way*, Boston: Shambhala, 1998.

_____. *The Other Wind*, New York: Harcourt, Inc., 2001.

_____, *Tales from Earthsea*, New York: Harcourt, Inc., 2001.

_____. *Tehanu*, New York: Simon Pulse, 1990.

_____. *The Tombs of Atuan*, New York: Simon Pulse, 2001.

_____. *A Wizard of Earthsea*, New York: Bantam Books, 1975.

Lindahl, Carl, and others. *Medieval Folklore: A Guide to Myths, Legends, Tales, Beliefs, and Customs*, Oxford: Oxford University Press, 2002.

Mahy, Margaret. "Two Trilogies and a Mystery: Speculations on the Earthsea Stories," *Magpies*, Vol. 17, No. 3, July 2002.

Malory, Thomas. *Morte D'Arthur*, Keith Baines trans., New York: Signet Classics, reissue, 2001.

Martin, George R. R. *A Game of Thrones*, New York: Bantam Books, 1996.

Martin, Philip. *The Writer's Guide to Fantasy Literature: From Dragon's Lair to Hero's Quest*, Waukesha, Wis.: Kalmbach Publishing Co., 2002.

McCaffrey, Anne. *All the Weyrs of Pern*, New York: Del Rey, 1991.

_____. *Dragonsdawn*, New York: Del Rey, 1988.

_____. *Dragondrums*, New York: Del Rey, 1979.

_____. *Dragonflight*, New York: Del Rey, 1968.

_____. *Dragonquest*, New York: Del Rey, 1971.

_____. *The Skies of Pern*, New York: Del Rey, 2001.

_____. *The White Dragon*, New York: Del Rey, 1978.

_____. Interview, AOL: "The Book Report," April 6, 1997.

_____. Interview, *Writers Review* website, 1999.

McCaffrey, Todd J. *Dragonholder*, New York: Del Rey, 1999.

Neilson, Robert. "There Had to Be Dragons in the Title: An Interview with Anne McCaffrey," *Albedo*, Vol. 1, No. 10, 1996.

Nesbit, E. *The Book of Dragons*, New York: Harpers, 1900.

Nye, Jody Lynn, with Anne McCaffrey. *The Dragonlovers Guide to Pern*, New York: Del Rey Books, second edition, 1997.

Pindar. *Odes,* Peter Pindar, trans., Chicago: University of Chicago Press, second edition, May 1976.

_____. 4th Pythian Ode, Steven J. Willett, trans., unpublished, 2001.

Pratchett, Terry. *The Color of Magic*, New York: HarperPaperbacks, 1989.

_____. *Guards! Guards!*, New York: HarperPaperbacks, 1989.

_____. *The Last Hero*, New York: HarperCollins, 2001.

Rand, Ayn. *The Fountainhead*, fiftieth anniversary edition, New York: Signet, 1993.

Rawn, Melanie. *The Star Scroll*, New York: Daw Books, Inc., 1989.

Rishel, Mary Ann. *Writing Humor: Creativity and the Comic Mind*, Detroit: Wayne State University Press, 2002.

Roberts, Robin. *Anne McCaffrey: A Critical Companion*, Westport, CT: Greenwood Press, 1996.

Rose, Carol. *Giants, Monsters & Dragons*, New York: W. W. Norton & Company, 2000.

Rowling, J. K. *Fantastic Beasts & Where to Find Them*, New York: Scholastic, 2001.

_____. *Harry Potter and The Goblet of Fire*, New York: Scholastic, 2000.

_____. *Harry Potter and The Sorcerer's Stone*, New York: Scholastic, 1998.

_____. Interview, Amazon.com, 2000.

_____. Interview, Raincoast Books, March 2001.

Schafer, Elizabeth D. *Exploring Harry Potter*, Beacham's Sourcebooks for Teaching Young Adult Fiction, Osprey, FL: Beacham, 2000.

Sharer, Robert J. *The Ancient Maya*, fifth edition, Stanford: Stanford University Press, 1994.

Shippey, T. A. *The Road to Middle-earth*, second edition, London: Grafton, 1992.

Smith, Stephen J. Metherell. "Terry Pratchett: Carpe Discworld," *Crescent Blues*, Volume 2, Issue 4.1, 1999.

South, Malcolm, ed. *Mythical and Fabulous Creatures: A Source Book and Research Guide*, New York: Peter Bedrick Books, 1987.

Spenser, Edmund. *The Faerie Queene: Book Four*, *The Works of Edmund Spenser Series*, Vol. 4, Edwin Greenlaw ed., New York: Johns Hopkins University Press, 1958.

Spivack, Charlotte. *Ursula K. Le Guin*, Boston: Twayne Publishers, 1984.

Starfire, Xerxes. Internet interview: Anne McCaffrey, *Corridors of Communication*, February 16, 1999.

St. Clair, Gloriana. "Völsunga Saga and Narn: Some Analogies," *Proceedings of the J. R. R. Tolkien Centenary Conference 1992*, Milton Keynes: The Tolkien Society, 1995.

Stern, Jerome. *Making Shapely Fiction*, New York: W. W. Norton & Company, Inc., 1991.

Sturlusson, Snorri. *Heimskringla or Lives of the Norse Kings*, A. H. Smith trans., New York: Dover Publications, Inc., 1990.

_____. *Edda*, Anthony Faulkes trans., London: Everyman, 1987.

Swanton, Michael, trans. *The Anglo-Saxon Chronicle*, New York: Routledge, 1996.

Tacon, Paul S.C., Meredith Wilson, and Christopher Chippindale. "Birth of the Rainbow Serpent in Arnhem Land Rock Art and Oral History," *Archaeology in Oceania* 31 (1996), 103-124.

Thompson, Stith. *Motif-Index of Folk-Literature*, six volumes, Bloomington: Indiana University Press, 1955-58.

Tolkien, J. R. R. *Beowulf and the Critics*, Michael Drout, ed., Tempe: Medieval and Renaissance Studies, 2002.

_____. *Farmer Giles of Ham*, New York: Ballantine Books, 1969.

_____. "The Hoard," in *Beowulf and the Critics*, Michael Drout, ed., Tempe: Medieval and Renaissance Studies, 2002.

_____. *The Hobbit*, revised fourth edition, Boston: Houghton Mifflin Company, 1978.

_____. *The Letters of J.R.R. Tolkien*, Humphrey Carpenter, ed., with the assistance of Christopher Tolkien, Boston: Houghton Mifflin, 1981.

_____. *Roverandum*, Boston: Houghton Mifflin Company, 1998.

_____. *The Silmarillion*, Christopher Tolkien, ed., Boston: Houghton Mifflin Company, 1977.

_____. *Unfinished Tales*, Christopher Tolkien, ed., Boston: Houghton Mifflin Company, 1980.

_____. Interview, BBC Radio, 1965.

Trachtenberg, Martha P. *Anne McCaffrey: Science Fiction Storyteller*, Berkeley Heights, NJ: Enslow Publishers, Inc., 2001.

Troyes, Chrétien de. *Arthurian Romances*, William W. Kibler trans., London: Penguin Books, 1991.

Tyler, Royall. *Japanese Tales*, New York: Pantheon Books, 1987.

Vance, Jack. *The Dragon Masters*, New York: Galaxy Publishing Corp., 1962.

White, Donna R. *Dancing with Dragons: Ursula K. Le Guin and the Critics*, Columbia, SC: Camden House, 1999.

White, T. H. *The Book of Beasts*, New York: G. P. Putnam's Sons, 1954.

Wilhelm, Richard, and Cary F. Baynes, trans. *The I Ching or Book of Changes*, with Foreword by Carl Jung, Princeton: Princeton University Press, 1950.

Witcover, Paul. Interview: Anne McCaffrey, *Del Rey Internet Newsletter*, No. 72, January 1999.

Wolfe, Gene. *The Knight*, New York: Tor Books, 2004.

Yolen, Jane. *Dragon's Blood*, New York: Delacorte Press, 1982.

BIBLIOGRAPHY

_____. *Heart's Blood*, New York: Delacorte Press, 1984.

_____. "Here Be Dragons," essay from www.janeyolen.com, 2000.

_____. *Here There Be Dragons*, New York: Harcourt Brace & Company, 1993.

_____. *A Sending of Dragons*, New York: Delacorte Press, 1987.

_____. *Touch Magic*, expanded edition, Little Rock: August House, 2000.

Zhao, Qiguang. *A Study of Dragons, East and West*, New York: Peter Lang, 1992.

Index

INDEX

To learn more about the author, inlcuding publications and events, please visit her on the Web at: www.annepetty.com.

TOLKIEN IN THE LAND OF HEROES:
Discovering the Human Spirit
by Anne C. Petty
ISBN 1-892975-99-8
$16.95
336 pages

"Solid scholarly content in a readable, thought-provoking format. Not just another 'Tolkien' bandwagon effort, this is another fine book from Petty."
— Ted Carlson, amazon.com review

"... a great tapestry of informative and enlightening lore..."
— Anthony Burdge, *Parma Nölé*
(The New York Tolkien Society journal)

THE TOLKIEN'S FAN MEDIEVAL READER
Selected by Turgon of TheOneRing.net
ISBN 1-59360-011-9
$14.95
400 pages

"This book is a feast of medieval narrative from all over the Northern European and British worlds, cooked up by authors known and unknown out of the plentiful ingredients of myth and legend and folktale, and beautifully served for the pleasure and enlightenment of the contemporary reader."
—From the Foreword by Verlyn Flieger, author of *Splintered Light: Language and Logos in Tolkien's World* and *A Question of Time: J.R.R. Tolkien's Road to Faërie.*

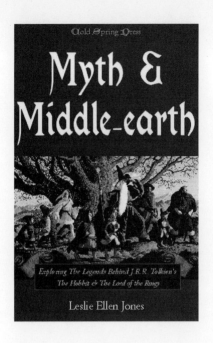

MYTH & MIDDLE-EARTH
Exploring the Legends Behind J.R.R. Tolkien's The Hobbit &
The Lord of the Rings
by Leslie Ellen Jones
ISBN 1-892975-81-5
$14.95
192 pages

"From start to finish, the author goes into considerable detail and at the same time
manages to keep the chapters rolling. The book is big enough to cover a lot of ground, and
despite this is readable enough not to feel like a sockful of sand; no mean achievement."
– Helen Armstrong, *Amon Hen* (review of The Tolkien Society)

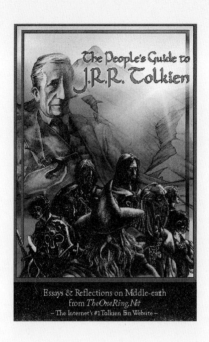

THE PEOPLE'S GUIDE TO J.R.R. TOLKIEN

Essays & Reflections on Middle-earth from TheOneRing.net

ISBN 1-892975-90-4

$16.95

384 pages

"... it is vital that a spirit of open inquiry should persist, and that is what The People's Guide provides. If you don't agree with any of it, that's fine. TheOneRing.net stands open for disagreements as for further contributions. May they long continue from what must now be a third or a fourth generation of readers."

— From the Foreword by Tom Shippey, author of
The Road to Middle-earth and *J.R.R. Tolkien: Author of the Century*

About The Author

Anne Petty received her Ph.D. in English Literature/Humanities from Florida State University. Her dissertation on the mythology of J.R.R. Tolkien was published as *One Ring to Bind Them All: Tolkien's Mythology*. It has been reprinted twice and incorporates a new introduction and expanded bibliography for its 2002 second edition. Her book on Tolkien's major themes, *Tolkien in the Land of Heroes: Discovering the Human Spirit*, was published in September 2003 and was named #1 of the "Top 10 Books on Tolkien Mythology" by reviewer Esther Lombardi of about.com.

Like Tolkien, Anne has loved dragons all her life, and finally got to write about them in *Dragons of Fantasy*, her third book of commentary on popular literature. She focused this time on dragons and the writers who create them. Her most recent article appears in the premiere issue of *Tolkien Studies*, 2004. A series of fantasy fiction novels is also in the works.

In addition to her book-writing career, Anne has taught English Literature, Creative Writing, and Journalism at both the secondary and university level, and has published in the fields of literary criticism, technical writing and editing, poetry and the arts, and multimedia development.